Like a Moth

A Life of Seeking and Software

(Black & White Edition)

Jeff Pepper

IMAGIN8
PRESS

Like a Moth

Published in the United States by Imagin8 Press LLC, Verona, Pennsylvania. For information, contact us via email at info@imagin8press.com, or visit www.imagin8press.com.

Our books may be purchased directly in quantity at a reduced price, visit our website www.imagin8press.com for details.

Imagin8 Press, the Imagin8 logo and the sail image are all trademarks of Imagin8 Press LLC.

Written and designed by Jeff Pepper
Cover art by Next Mars Media, Luoyang, China

ISBN: 978-1959043355 (Black & White Edition)
Version 1.2

Jeff Pepper

Sun and shower,
Wind and rain
In and out the window
Like a moth before a flame

        -    *From "Box of Rain" by the Grateful Dead*

Like a Moth

Acknowledgements

First of all, thanks to my daughter Katelyn. On my 70th birthday she gave me the idea for doing this project and a gift of 52 weekly memory-jogging prompts. I admit that I've mostly ignored the specifics of the prompts, but the weekly emails have helped keep me focused on completing this project.

Thanks to my distant cousin Max Rosenberg who did a lot of the original research into the Pfeffer family tree and created the Geni site that I have expanded. Thanks to the friends and family members who have answered my questions and reviewed early drafts for accuracy: Kathryn Pepper, Barbara Dannenfelser, Michael Cavallo, Ted Teele, Mark Blitzer, and Judith Rosenberg. And thanks to Yu Jin and the team at NextMars Media for the terrific cover artwork.

Online Resources

All the illustrations in this book, plus a few more, can be found in a Google Drive folder. Click this link if you're reading the ebook version, or scan this QR code if you're holding a paperback book:

Contents

Introduction

During one of my business trips to Japan I was treated to a big dinner event at a fancy Tokyo restaurant. A dozen executives from Sumitomo were there. At some point, after several rounds of drinks, someone asked me to tell a joke. I had no idea what would go over well to an audience of Japanese businessmen, so I told a dirty joke that I won't repeat here. Everyone laughed, but due to cultural differences I couldn't tell the difference between polite laughter and real laughter.

Feeling a bit awkward and trying to move things along, I asked the senior Sumitomo executive if he could also tell a joke. The room grew quiet. The executive stood up, whiskey glass in hand, and said, "In my youth I had time and health but I had no money. In my middle age I had health and money but I had no time. Now I am old, I have money and time but I have no health."

Not a particularly funny joke, in fact I wouldn't even call it a joke, more of an aphorism. But regardless, it has stuck with me. And so I've decided to organize this memoir into the three parts that the Japanese executive cited in that long-ago dinner.

In the first part of my life, from birth to age 25, I had time and health but no money; this was a time for learning the ways of the world, searching for truth, and having as much fun as possible. In the second part, from age 25 to 65, I had health and money but no time; I entered the working world as a serial entrepreneur, worked crazy hours and became reasonably successful. And now I'm in the third part where I have money and time, and good enough health to do most of the things that I want to do.

Some people, the ones who have tend to have biographies written about them, have life stories that appear to be carefully planned and executed. These lives, at least in retrospect, follow a straight line with only an occasional detour, proceeding from cradle to Nobel Prize or whatever. These people know what they want to accomplish in life and they pursue it with single-minded purpose.

But most peoples' lives aren't like that. For the rest of us, we meander through our years, going this way and that as the mood strikes us, or as financial needs or external forces compel us. If there's a pattern to what we do, we usually don't see it at the time.

Even now, it's hard for me to see a well organized pattern in the events of my life. Looking back at all that's happened so far, it feels more like a collection of short stories than a well plotted novel, a series of skits instead of a three act play. So although this book is organized into three parts, you should not assume that the story of my life can be told as a nice, clean, straightforward narrative.

As you'll see, compared to the rest of humanity I was born into a comfortable life. I grew up in a middle class Jewish family in the suburbs of New York with good health, an excellent education, and enough good luck or good karma to survive my adventures in the 1960's and 70's with only minimal damage.

I've also been fortunate enough to be born with a quick mind, which made it possible for me to get a good education, start and build a couple of successful companies, and earn enough to be comfortable in this, my later years. I have an extremely high tolerance for risk, which has served me well in my career as a serial tech entrepreneur. And I have a short attention span and an eagerness to try new things, which has resulted in a life full of fairly short episodes and few long term themes.

If there's a poetic metaphor for my life, the best fit is probably the moth in "Box of Rain," a song written by lyricist Robert Hunter and bassist Phil Lesh of the Grateful Dead. The moth is mentioned briefly in the song, flying in and out the window, attracted to and repelled by a flame. This image captures perfectly how I see my life's journey – compelled by desire to begin something, immersing myself in it for a while, departing, then being compelled by yet more unfulfilled desires to flit back through the window for another trip around the flame.

This is a good metaphor for the episodes in a single life, but it's also a good fit for a succession of lifetimes. I don't know for certain whether the notions of the soul and reincarnation are true, but the ideas feel right. And if they are true, then I've flown through a window into this life because it's the life I desired, the life I needed, and the life I chose. Have I done all the things that I planned to do? Hard to say. To quote the Grateful Dead again, I'll know "when the secrets all are told and the petals all unfold."

What you won't find here is a well constructed story arc. As already mentioned, I've organized things into three main sections, but beyond that it's just a collection of anecdotes, with a bit of philosophy thrown in from time to time. I've tried to tell the stories as simply and straightforward as possible, and to make them entertaining without making stuff up. Everything here is as accurate as I can remember it or look it up online.

The stories are told more or less in the order in which they happened. The only major exceptions are in the two long sections that describe my business adventures at ServiceWare and Touchtown. In those two sections I've told the business story all the way through with only occasional short digressions, and then gone back afterwards to fill in some of the other things that happened at the same time.

Also, in order to keep things interesting, I've pushed the details of my ancestors and relatives into an appendix at the end. This is not because they're unimportant, it's because if I put it all in the beginning of the book I don't think anyone would get past it to get to the more interesting stuff.

Shakespeare said that life is a tale told by an idiot. Well, here's the tale of my life. Let's get to it.

Like a Moth

Part One:
Time and Health

Family, Childhood, School, Spiritual Inquiries, Counterculture Adventures

Two Families

I really don't want to start this off with lots of details about my ancestors. So that's all in Appendix 2. Read it if you like, or not. It won't affect the rest of this story, I promise.

The only thing you really need to know about my parents' backgrounds is that they were totally different.

My dad, Edward (no middle name, he said the family couldn't afford one) Pepper, grew up in a poor working class Jewish neighborhood in the Bronx, New York. His dad, Harry Pfeffer, was a plumber and later a chauffeur. They lived in what could be described as a tenement apartment. Dad's family consisted of his parents, his older brother Ralph, and himself.

Harry enjoyed raising and racing pigeons. He was nearly illiterate, "barely able to add two and two" according to my dad's recollection. They were part of New York's Jewish underclass. From what I've heard, the family was close and relatively happy, though financially poor.

Young Dad with a dog.

Dad with his mother.

Dad dropped out of school in the ninth grade to go to work and help support the family. He was working at Sears Roebuck when the Japanese attacked Pearl Harbor, and he enlisted in the Army eight days later, on December 15, 1941.

He legally changed his last name from Pfeffer to Pepper on April 20, 1942 while he was serving in the Army.

One rainy day in January 1943, Harry was working on the roof, either tending to his pigeons or installing a TV antenna, depending on which version is being told. He slipped and fell onto the spikes of a wrought iron fence where he was impaled. He was still alive and was brought to a nearby private hospital, but was turned away because the family was unable to pay for his care. They then took him to a city hospital but he died on the way.

Dad received a compassionate discharge from the Army on February 1, 1943. He went home to care for his mother. But a few months later, on July 5, he re-enlisted in the Coast Guard where he served as a quartermaster's assistant in the Pacific on a rickety old supply boat. He told me that the hull on the boat was so thin that they could have been sunk by a Japanese soldier with a machine gun. He was discharged at the end of the war, on November 8, 1945.

There are lots of pigeon stories and Coast Guard stories in the Appendix.

On the other side of the family, my mom, Edith Marjorie Levy, grew up in a prosperous but seriously dysfunctional Jewish family in the Upper West Side of Manhattan. Her father was Abraham Nathan Levy, a prominent physician in New York who had a home in the posh West End Avenue section of Manhattan and an office near Greenwich Village. They were part of New York's Jewish elite. They were not tremendously wealthy, but Nathan was highly respected and the family was financially quite comfortable.

Mom.

Nathan's first wife was Anna Grace (Kurasch) Levy. They had two children: my mom Edith and her sister Floie. The trouble in the family began when Anna died of tuberculosis at age 34. Nathan, who was 39 at the time, remarried a few months later to a 22 year old socialite and trophy wife named Doris Tenzer.

Two years after marrying, Nathan and Doris had their only child together, Neicee. Doris strongly favored her own child over her two stepchildren. Mom was completely silent about the details of their home life, but from what little she said, it appeared to be pretty awful. From what I could gather, Doris ignored and abused her two stepchildren, sending them away to school to be, in Mom's words, "rid of them."

Mom graduated from Brooklyn College and volunteered as a nurse during World War II.

I don't know how they met, but it was probably before Dad shipped out to the Pacific. They were married in 1947. Dad was a handsome war veteran, Mom was an attractive young woman from a well-to-do family. They were both Jewish but neither of them "looked Jewish," and in fact my dad had already changed his name from Pfeffer to Pepper to further blend in with the non-Jewish world.

Mom and Dad, with Mom's sister Floie on left and Dad's mother on right.

The troubled Levy family dynamics are visible in this fascinating wedding picture from 1947. Note the arrangement and body language. Neicee is between her parents at left. Doris is holding on to her daughter Neicee and has turned her back on Dad, his mother, and the two stepdaughters Edith and Floie. However, Mom and her dad are exchanging a warm look.

18

From left: Mom's father Nathan, Mom's half-sister Neicee, Mom's stepmother Doris, Dad's mother Lena, Dad and Mom, Mom's sister Floie, Dad's sister-in-law Sylvia and Dad's brother Ralph.

Dad must have known something about the tension between Mom and her stepmother, because he disliked Doris intensely. He once said to me that she was "a pimple on the ass of society," probably referring to the fact that she never worked for a living. Doris lived well, spending her time playing cards with her friends, going to the theater, and not doing much else from what I could see.

After getting married, Dad went back to his job at Sears Roebuck as a buyer for ladies' clothing. Sears at that time was not friendly to Jews, which is probably why he had anglicized his name from Pfeffer to Pepper. But somehow he because caught up in some kind of trouble anyway and was, as he told the story, made the fall guy. He left Sears, vowing never to work for anyone ever again.

He started his own company, working as an independent buyer/consultant in the garment industry. In the 1950 census he's listed as a "clothing buyer, mail order retail" but it's not clear if that was at Sears or his own company. I never heard anything about this, and the only reason I know it even happened was that I found some old letterhead and envelopes from this startup tucked away in a cabinet in the house.

The consulting apparently did not go well, so he bought a hardware store in Huntington and renamed it Village Hardware. Dad told me that he'd always loved wandering around in hardware stores in the Bronx neighborhood where he grew up. This store had an excellent location right in the middle of all three supermarkets in Huntington Village. The store did well for many years, providing the family with a good income. He had up to a dozen people working during busy times. The store had a wide selection of hardware and housewares, fireplace equipment, barbeques, and gardening supplies. It also had a full basement that had all sorts of interesting nooks and crannies that I liked to explore. Mom did the bookkeeping and designed the store window displays.

Dad had no problem co-mingling business finances with personal ones. If he was short of cash he'd just dip into the cash register when he thought nobody was watching, and put a few $20 bills in his pocket. And whenever we needed something for the house, he would just pluck it off a store shelf and bring it home.

More later about my time at Village Hardware.

By this time they'd left New York City and moved to the suburbs, which for them was Levittown. Their house was at 60 Shetter Lane in Hempstead, New York.

Dad and Mom, probably in Levittown.

Levittown was a planned community, one of the first large-scale suburban housing developments in the country. There were several Levittown developments around the country, but the one on Long Island was the first, built between 1947 and 1951. The houses were made on an assembly line and could be built in a single day by a crew of 36 men. The first homes in Levittown went on sale in March 1947, and 1,400 homes were sold in the first three hours.

Levittown was a planned community in more ways than one. William Levitt refused to sell homes to Jews or people of color. There was actually a clause in the deed called a racial covenant that forbade any nonwhites from buying a house in Levittown. However, since Dad had anglicized his name and neither he nor Mom looked Jewish, nobody stopped them from buying their house.

My sister Barbara was born in Huntington Hospital on June 9, 1948, three weeks after the establishment of the State of Israel and the start of the Arab-Israeli War.

At some point they sold the house in Levittown (presumably to a white Protestant family though I have no way of knowing), and bought a nicer house, a new one, at 38 Whitson Road in Huntington Station.

My first home, 38 Whitson Road, Huntington, New York.

My First Few Years

I was born at Huntington Hospital and lived at Whitson Road until age 7. My earliest memory there is of playing with grooved wooden blocks of wood that a small wooden train could run on. The blocks snapped together like jigsaw pieces. Using a pencil I wrote "J" (my initial) and "5" (my age) on each block, and laid them out all through the house, using them as lane dividers so that people had to walk on one side of them or the other.

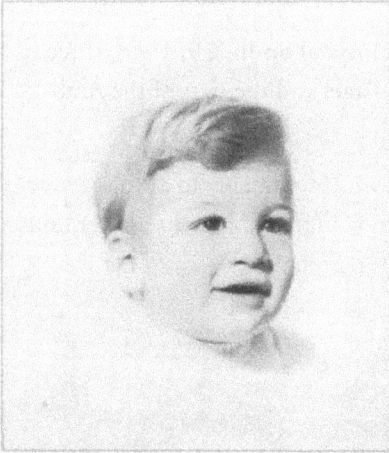

Clockwise from top left: my studio baby picture; Barbara and me in the back yard of the Whitson Road house; Barbara age 4; me with Mom and Barbara.

With Mom, in front yard of the Whitson Road house.

Dad built some raised gardens in the back yard where Mom raised flowers. He also built a brick barbeque in the back; this is memorable because of the time we found a black widow spider lurking in the cracks between the bricks.

We had two big dogs – a German shepherd named Cindy whose favorite toy was a ten foot long wooden rail from a split rail fence, and later, a shaggy collie named Bonnie. Mom trained them both in obedience and took them to dog shows, sometimes with Barbara and me. She tried to interest Barbara in training and showing the dogs, but my sister wasn't interested. Mom was devoted to the dogs, leading Dad to comment at one point that if there was such a thing a reincarnation, he wanted to come back as one of Mom's dogs.

From top left: Mom, Cindy and me; Cindy with dumbbell; Cindy with me and Barbara dressed up for some unknown reason.

One of the neighborhood kids developed chicken pox. In order to immunize me against the disease, Mom and some of the other neighborhood moms sent their kids over to play with her for several hours, something that's called a "pox party." Sure enough, I caught the virus soon after and developed lifetime immunity.

We had a large piece of furniture that had a built-in TV. It was analog, with a cathode ray picture tube for the display and a bunch of vacuum tubes and wires in the back. The TV antenna only picked up a few channels: 2 (WCBS), 4 (WNBC) 5 (a local station), 7 (WABC), 9 and 11 (two more local stations), and 13 (the public television station). Sometimes the picture would "flip," meaning that it would roll up off the top of the screen and reappear at the bottom. When this happened, we'd have to carefully adjust a screw in the back of the set to slow down and stop the flipping. If that didn't work, we'd call the TV repairman to come to the house.

Business was good at the store. Dad told us he was buying a new station wagon for the business, so we made a posterboard sign saying "Out with the old, in with the new" and greeted him as he drove up to the house in the shiny new wagon, with "Village Hardware" magnetic stickers already attached to both front doors.

Dad really liked being on the water. We couldn't afford an expensive cabin cruiser but we did have a small open boat, a runabout with an Evinrude outboard motor. In the warm weather we'd all pile into the boat and putter out to Sand City. This is an uninhabited spit of sand and gravel in Northport that juts out from Eaton's Neck into Huntington Harbor. Fishing was good there, and Dad would fish while we ate lunch on the beach and swam in the protected waters of Long Island Sound.

Mom's father Nathan Levy, who we called Poppop, died suddenly at the age of 68. I was four years old. He and Doris had come out to Huntington to celebrate Barbara's ninth birthday. While driving back to the city he had a massive heart attack. The car swerved off the road onto the shoulder. With Nathan slumped over the steering wheel, Doris jumped out of the car and ran into several nearby stores to ask someone to help. For some reason, nobody would help her. He was pronounced dead at 10:30 pm on June 9, 1957, in his car near the intersection of Queens Boulevard and 68th Road. The cause of death was listed as "coronary sclerosis."

After Nathan's death, Doris lived alone in her apartment on the ninth floor of 411 East 57th Street in Manhattan. Despite the years of mistreatment at the hands of her stepmother, Mom bottled it all up and played the role of the dutiful daughter, bringing the family (Dad, Barbara and me) over to visit Doris, who we called Nana. At the time, neither Barbara or I were aware of the tension and hostility between Mom and her stepmother.

The visits were generally uneventful, except for one time when I decided to take a walk around the neighborhood. I was maybe 13 or 14 at the time. A couple of blocks away a 30-something guy was sitting on a stoop, playing guitar for tips. I stopped and listened for a bit. He chatted me up, and suggested that we head back to his place. I asked him why. He told me, "oh, it will be really good. It will be beautiful." Something about it sounded a bit off, though, so fortunately I didn't go with him to find out.

Elementary School

Since things were good at the store and the Whitson Road house was feeling a bit cramped, Mom and Dad decided it was time to move up to an upper middle class lifestyle. They bought a house at 67 Windmill Drive, Huntington, located in a new and expensive housing development. It was a large house on a full acre of property, in a cul de sac. The streets were wide, with street trees

Two pics in the front yard at Windmill Drive.

planted on both sides of the street. They planted a dozen or so dogwood trees in the front yard near the street, and put up a small estate sign reading, "The Dog's Woods."

Dad had a basement workshop that was well stocked with all the power tools, hand tools and gadgets that he brought home from the store. For a workbench he had a large hardwood conference table that he'd somehow picked up from his time at Sears Roebuck. The workshop also had a complete HO-scale model train setup with tiny trees and other landscaping, mounted on saw horses and a sheet of plywood.

The workshop had hundreds of different sizes of nuts, bolts, screws and other assorted items, each kept in a small glass baby food jar whose lid was screwed to a rotating central spindle. When Dad wanted a fastener he'd rotate the spindle so the desired jar was right side up, then unscrew the jar.

Using this state-of-the-art workshop, I made lots of things. My most ambitious project was an apartment house for martins, a type of bird that preferred to live in multi-family structures. I attached it to a sixteen foot long 4"x4", and with Dad's help we raised it, re-enacting the famous scene of raising the flag at Iwo Jima.

My martin house.

Interestingly, the 2023 Google Maps picture shows the house almost exactly unchanged from when we lived there in the 1960's, even down to the bricks lining the long driveway and the low stone wall that Dad built to divide the front lawn. Dad also built a large redwood deck in the backyard, which of course is not visible in the photo.

67 Windmill Drive, in 2023.

I was seven years old when we moved there in 1960, and seventeen when I graduated high school and went away to Clark University in Worcester.

My best friend when I was young was Betsy Heller who lived a few doors down from us. We played together a lot. Once we decided to put on a puppet show for the neighborhood kids. Someone called the local newspaper, and we were briefly famous as a result of the photo and article that ran in the paper. This was the first time I appeared in the newspaper. We wanted to raise money for charity, and Mom arranged for us to donate to the Heart Fund. This probably had something to do with her father's death from a heart attack several years earlier.

Elementary school really wasn't much fun. This was mainly as a result of me skipping a grade. I really don't remember much about elementary school, in fact I don't even remember the name of the school itself, except that it was in the Harborfields school district.

I started school with a big head start. First of all, I was bright. This probably came from my mom, who once told me she had an IQ of 140. In addition, I got lots of preschool instruction from Barbara who was three and a half years

Jeff Pepper

The puppet show, 1964, starring. Betsy Heller and me, posing with two ladies from the Huntington Town Heart Fund.

The bottom picture with the four kids is from some other newspaper story unrelated to our puppet show.

CRAFTY LITTLE YOUNGSTERS --- We always figure kids use their hands to knock things over, grab cookies and generally cause commotion but it appears little hands are also good for craft projects. Witness the case of (picture at top) Betsy Heller, of 62 Windmill Dr. and Jeffrey Pepper, 11, of 67 Woodms who put on a puppet show for their neighborhood friends onated proceeds to the Heart Fund. They are showing their puppets to Mrs. George Maynard (left) and Mrs. Herbert ruch of the Huntington Town Heart Unit.

older than me. Her idea of playing house was to teach me how to read. This was fun. Soon I was reading all of her school books, and at some point, probably before I started school, I began reading the entire World Book encyclopedia collection – this consisted of 20 or so green hardcover volumes that Mom had bought, one per month, at the local supermarket. Eventually I read the entire set from beginning to end, but of course not by the time I started school. Still, I started school reading at a 4th or 5th grade level when the other kids were still learning their ABC's.

One day, probably in first grade, the teacher gave everyone a chance to read a simple story out loud to the class. One of the girls in the class was struggling to read her story, and she kept pausing to figure out the next word. I started "helping" her by calling out the next word. In itself that was not unusual (but certainly annoying). However, what made it unusual is that I didn't even have the text in front of me and had never heard it before. I got almost every word correct though.

After a while it became obvious that I was not learning anything in class, and was becoming a distraction. I was bored and disruptive. So the administrators suggested to my parents that I should be "skipped ahead" a grade. At that time, grade-skipping was considered a good option for kids like me, especially since the school didn't have any other option for keeping me interested academically. Many years later, grade-skipping was discredited and replaced by other forms of academic enrichment.

Anyway, my parents didn't object, and I didn't know enough to object either. So after a long battery of psychological and academic tests, which apparently I must have passed, they moved me from 2nd to 3rd grade over Thanksgiving break.

I was now one of the smallest kids in the class and by far the youngest. And also one of the brightest. This of course was not a good formula for achieving social success in primary school. It also didn't help that whenever we had a test, I always finished before everyone else, walking up to the front of the classroom to proudly hand in my finished test while everyone else was still working.

Here's one other incident, which came later, maybe in 4th or 5th grade. We had a math test which was easy. There was an extra credit question at the end:

what's the sum total of all the whole numbers from 1 to 100? I thought about it for a minute. Clearly it would take forever to add up each number. Then I had an insight into how to solve it quickly. I wrote the answer, 5,050, and handed in the completed test. Much later I found out that I had independently discovered a theorem that was first discovered by the famous mathematician Carl Friedrich Gauss in 1787, when he was ten years old. I'm not saying that I was the only kid who had ever independently figured out the method for quickly summing a series of numbers, but it did impress my teacher.

Here's a story I wrote in 4th grade, when I had just turned 9. I'm sure that Mom typed it up for me. The writing isn't bad, though I got the science completely wrong.

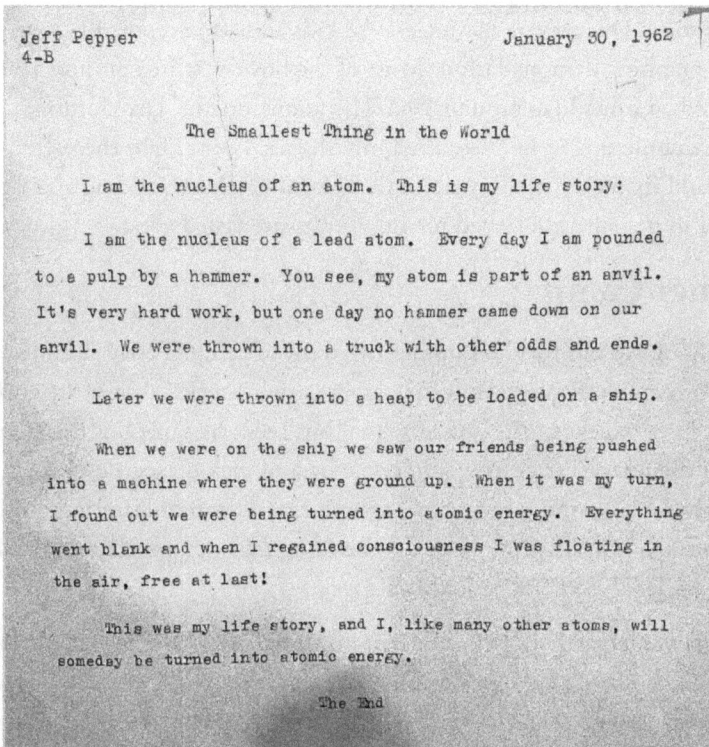

Jeff Pepper   January 30, 1962
4-B

                    The Smallest Thing in the World

        I am the nucleus of an atom. This is my life story:

        I am the nucleus of a lead atom. Every day I am pounded
    to a pulp by a hammer. You see, my atom is part of an anvil.
    It's very hard work, but one day no hammer came down on our
    anvil. We were thrown into a truck with other odds and ends.

        Later we were thrown into a heap to be loaded on a ship.

        When we were on the ship we saw our friends being pushed
    into a machine where they were ground up. When it was my turn,
    I found out we were being turned into atomic energy. Everything
    went blank and when I regained consciousness I was floating in
    the air, free at last!

        This was my life story, and I, like many other atoms, will
    someday be turned into atomic energy.

                            The End

The social effects of skipping that grade lasted all the way until high school. I was always the youngest, one of the smallest, and one of the smartest. So to survive (and to avoid boredom) I became a clown, disrupting class in various ways. I was banished to sitting in the corner quite a few times. In junior high I once annoyed my science teacher so much that one of them actually threw a battery at me, hitting me on the head. And a science teacher was demonstrating a static electricity device where you spun up a flywheel to create a static charge. He was also annoyed at me, something that happened frequently. So he actually forced me to put one hand on the positive pole and the other on the negative pole, giving me a strong electric shock. This was in the 1960's, of course, and nobody ever thought of this sort of science-based corporal punishment as being unacceptable. I'm sure my parents knew about both of these incidents, but nothing ever came of it. They probably thought it was good for me.

In addition to being small, I was very skinny. Partly this was genetic, and partly because I didn't play any sports other than running around with the kids in the neighborhood. During one math class the kids all had to report their weight as part of a graphing demonstration. Most of the boys weighted around 130 to 150 pounds, I came in at around 100. The family doctor, Dr. Gordon, thought I needed to bulk up. So he prescribed milkshakes. Every night thereafter, my mom would fix me a big chocolate milkshake after dinner, adding a raw egg for protein. I'm not sure it fattened me up, but it sure tasted good.

Summer Camp

When school was out for the summer, we went to camp. Today summer camps are one- or two-week events, but for us it was eight weeks, almost the entire summer. Every weekday the yellow school bus (yes, the same bus that took us to school the rest of the year) would come by and pick up several of the neighborhood kids, and take us to Shepherd Day Camp in Huntington. Here's an ad from the May 18 1967 issue of *The Long Islander*, proclaiming "THIS IS THE AGE OF THE SPECIALIST."

The camp was located on a 13 acre campus. It had everything we could want: ballfields, a go-kart track, outdoor ping pong tables, a pool, and some woods for exploring and getting into trouble. They served lunch, and there was a freezer in the kitchen where the staff kept the frozen desserts. I learned how to sneak into the kitchen and swipe a handful of desserts, earning me the nickname "Fudgsicle Hocker."

I played a lot of ping pong outdoors. I also loved the go-kart track, especially after we learned how to disable the speed governors on the karts by turning a little hex nut on the throttle.

There was a kid at camp who was older and bigger than me – not surprising, as most kids were bigger than me. He was a bully and had already pushed me around a few times. One day I was with a group of kids walking somewhere, accompanied by an older teenaged counselor. The

kid pushed me, hard. Without thinking, I jumped up and attacked him, fists flying. Before I knew what was happening I had him on the ground and was pummeling him. All I could think of was, "Why isn't the counselor breaking this up?" The counselor was just standing there, enjoying it. After a while the other kid realized he was, in fact, bigger than me, and he began to fight back. At that point the counselor stopped the fight. But the kid never bothered me again.

Heading off to boy scout camp.

Another day at camp I was upset about something and wanted some revenge. So I went out into the woods with a friend and dropped a lit match in a pile of dry leaves. We left the leaves burning and went back to join the others. A while later I started to have second thoughts about this, so I went back into the woods. Fortunately for everyone, the fire had been spreading slowly and was only a circle of low flames around six feet in diameter. Quickly I stamped it out. Nobody ever found out as far as I know.

I was also in Boy Scouts. They ran Camp Baiting Hollow on the north shore of eastern Long Island. It was a one week sleepover camp, where we'd sleep 2 to a tent. During the day we'd do various scouting related things like tying knots, cooking over an open fire, and seeing who could drink the most "bug juice" (something like Kool Aid) at dinner time.

Camp Baiting Hollow. The camp's Native American name was Thayendanegea, after the head chief of the Iroquois Confederation in the late 1700's.

Once my parents came out to see me. Mom looked around and asked, "Where do you brush your teeth?" I answered truthfully, "At home."

The final year that I went to Baiting Hollow, Dad had agreed to serve as a volunteer staffer for the week. I think he stuck around for the first day or two, using his Coast Guard skills to show us how to tie various kinds of knots. Then, running out of things to teach us, he disappeared for the rest of the week and played golf.

Junior High School

Nope, no stories about junior high.

Bar Mitzvah

Our family belonged to Temple Beth El in Huntington. This was a reformed Jewish synagogue, meaning it was the least strictly religions of the three main branches of Judaism (reformed, conservative and orthodox).

Our family was culturally Jewish but not religious at all. Mom told me once that after the World War II Holocaust she could not believe in a god, especially one that was supposed to protect his chosen people, the Jews. This belief was widespread among the members of the temple from what I could see, and so the temple was more of a place for social identity rather than actual worship. The temple was sparsely attended throughout the year but was jammed on the High Holy Days of Passover and Rosh Hashanah, so the building's architects had cleverly designed the temple so that the main room where services were held could be tripled in size by sliding back a couple of floor-to-ceiling folding walls.

Despite my parents' lack of religious belief, they did want me to be Bar Mitzvah'd on or about my 13th birthday. I was in seventh grade.

For several months leading up to the big day, I went to the temple on Monday evenings to study Hebrew with Rabbi Schatz, with the goal of being able to read a few paragraphs of Hebrew text from the Torah at a Friday night service. I didn't mind this, as long as I could get out of there quick enough to catch "The Man From U.N.C.L.E." on TV at 8:00 pm every Monday night.

Temple Beth-El in 2022.

The Bar Mitzvah ceremony went off well, and I think I only stumbled a couple of times while reading the Torah in front of a few dozen people.

Afterwards everyone went to the Vernon Valley Inn for a reception. The bill of sale listed the menu as something called a "supreme of fresh fruit," celery stuffed olives, onion soup, cheese, rolls and butter, half broiled chicken, peas and carrots, cake with filling to be determined, coffee, tea, a bottle of J&B scotch, a bottle of 4 Roses rye, and rainbow parfait. I don't know how two bottles of liquor were enough for forty guests. There were also 4 centerpieces, one for each large table. A note on the receipt stated, "Cold canapes left over to be wrapped to take home." Total cost for the event for 40 people was $240.

*The Bar Mitzvah
reception.*

Be Your Own Boss

Running any business is a constant challenge, and anyone who says it's easy has
probably either forgotten the hard parts or just plain lying. Dad's hardware
store was no exception. Overall, the store was prosperous enough to enable us
to live in a nice house in a nice neighborhood and take the occasional vacation.
But there were always difficulties, and Dad would often talk about them at the
dinner table. In order to put a positive spin on things, he'd usually say at some
point in the conversation, "You're always better off being your own boss."
Hearing this dozens of times as I grew up, I suppose I came to accept it as a
fact, and this certainly affected my own career path as I got older.

Divorce

My parents' marriage was rocky, with plenty of fights. Their personalities were very different – Dad was impulsive, unlike Mom who was tightly controlled. And coming from a working class background and only having finished the 9th grade in school, he felt (with some justification) that Mom looked down on him as an uneducated brute. He wasn't a brute, of course, but it may have seemed that way to Mom. And Dad perceived Mom as remote, cold, and judgmental, which was mostly true.

The fights were strictly verbal, I don't think anyone ever hit anyone. But once at dinner, Dad threw a small pitcher of milk over Mom's head. The milk splashed on the ceiling, and the marks stayed there for years. Another time, there must have been some argument that we kids didn't hear, and shortly afterwards, Mom went into the bedroom and swept everything that was on Dad's dresser onto the floor.

Things continued to deteriorate, with lots of yelling in the house. Then one day in the summer of 1966 Dad moved out. I was 13, a few months after having my Bar Mitzvah that marked my crossing of the threshold into manhood in Jewish tradition. I suspect that Dad had been waiting for that before making his move. He was 53. He left work, headed home (Mom was out, probably at work), gathered up his things, and moved to an apartment he'd previously rented. Then he came to see me at summer camp, told me what was happening, and reassured me that he loved me. I don't know where Barbara was at the time. After he left I just sat in the woods for a while, wondering what my life would be like now that I was from a broken home.

Later that day Mom of course found out, and she came and picked me up from camp.

That was the end of the arguments and tension at home, but just the start of an acrimonious divorce process that lasted for a long time. Both parents were vying for our loyalty, Dad by taking us out and giving us money, and Mom by telling us all the terrible things she could think of about Dad. Eventually the divorce was finalized, with Mom getting custody of us, the right to stay in the house, monthly alimony, and some child support, I think $25/month each for Barbara and me. That plus whatever she made from her bookkeeping jobs wasn't enough for her to afford to stay in the Windmill Drive house, but she managed to stay there for four more years until I finished high school, then she sold the house (splitting the proceeds with Dad, per the divorce agreement) and moved to a much smaller house at 130 East 24th Street in Huntington Station.

At first, Dad lived in a dark and depressing basement apartment, but later he moved to a nicer place. He'd always carried a flame for a woman named Rae Sals, who he'd known before his marriage to Mom. I think the two of them might have even been engaged at some point. As soon as he and Mom split up, he started dating Rae, who had also split up from her husband. They were together (or at least dating) for less than a year.

Rae had a daughter about my age named Joanie, and four sons. The winter of 1966 the four of us (Dad, Rae, Joanie and me) went on a ski trip to New England. We got caught in a huge snowstorm on the interstate heading north. Traffic stopped, the snow kept falling, and we ended up having to spend the night in the car. Dad and Rae were in the front, Joanie and I were in the back. There were blankets in the car, so fortunately we did not freeze to death. Dad started the car every couple of hours to get some heat. The next day the road was cleared and we got to the ski lodge where we stayed for the weekend.

That night at the lodge Joanie and I, who were just friends, were hanging around somewhere in the lodge, talking. Dad found out that we were not in our (separate) rooms, and he angrily went to find us, thinking we were shacking up somewhere in the lodge. It was funny to Joanie and me to think that Dad was so angry at the thought that we were doing exactly what he and Rae were obviously doing in their room.

After Dad and Rae broke up, he met and married Wilma Fielding, who was much younger. That marriage lasted a couple of years, but from what I'd heard, Wilma had misgivings about being married to someone as old as Dad, who might have been in his early 60's by that time. Also, things were not going well at the store, so Dad was not as prosperous as he had been. So not wanting to end up being a nursemaid to an old man with limited funds, she divorced him.

High School

As I got older and entered high school, things improved quite a bit, especially in my junior and senior year.

There were several reasons why these two years were, really, the first time I could honestly say that I liked school. First of all, early in senior year I was accepted to Clark University, so all academic pressure disappeared. This was actually a big deal, because my grades were mediocre, generally in the B+ range. I was definitely not performing up to my potential, since my standardized test scores placed me well up in the 99th percentile. I'd scored a 777 out of 800 in English and 780 out of 800 in Math, high enough to win a small scholarship from my mom's employer and make it a slam dunk to get into Clark.

My two best friends in high school were Scott Marcus, a tall and confident kid who lived on Buttercup Lane, and Burton Webster, a serious kid who came from a fundamentalist Christian family at the other end of Windmill Drive. Scott and Burt were both nearly a year older than me. The three of us did lots of things together. Ping pong was a major afterschool activity. Scott had a table in his basement, and the three of us played there, a lot. One time Scott and Burt played a game for a dollar. Burt lost. He challenged Scott to a double or nothing match, and Scott won. He did it again, and Scott won. And again. And again. And again. Finally Burt owed Scott $64, and Scott said that was enough. Burt got a summer job and eventually paid him back.

This was 1968, '69 and '70, an intensive period of social upheaval. My friends and I were deeply involved in this, spending hours discussing politics and philosophy, and playing and listening to music. There was a profound different in worldview between our parents and us. Our parents grew up in the Depression, lived through World War II, and were just happy to be alive and safe from overt threats to their lives. But we grew up in comfort. Our world, the "counterculture," was shaped by the new wave of youth-written rock and folk music, protests against the Vietnam War and racial injustice, the philosophy of Eastern-influenced writers like Alan Watts, and antiwar films like *Easy Rider* and *Billy Jack*. I read books on eastern philosophy and smoked a lot of marijuana, which we could buy easily. The going rate was $15 for a one-ounce bag of dried leaves, seeds and stems. We would stay out late, usually

Scott Marcus, 1970 yearbook photo.

Burton Webster, 1970 yearbook photo.

My 1970 high school yearbook photo.

hanging around outside in parks or graveyards. I became interested in girls but didn't have a serious girlfriend.

The summer after junior year of high school, Scott and Burt and I drove down to Florida in Scott's old car. I was 16, they were 17. We headed south, driving through New Jersey, Virginia, the Carolinas, and into the South. We avoided the interstate, taking old US routes and other secondary roads. We camped wherever we found a quiet spot off the road. At some point in the Carolinas we picked up two guys hitchhiking. They were big guys with short haircuts, but friendly enough. After a while they told us that they'd both broken out of prison and were heading south to meet up with family. No problem, the three New York teenagers and the two escaped convicts from the Deep South got along just fine. We let them off somewhere in Georgia. The next day we reached south Florida. Someone told us that Coconut Grove was the place for people like us, so we drive there and hung out in Peacock Park, the meeting place for hippies and freaks. Music and marijuana smoke were in the air.

We got invited to a party at someone's house and headed there after dark. More weed, some of which must have been laced with something stronger. Scott and I were fine, but Burt must have smoked more than us, or smoked something stronger, or just been more susceptible. He became upset and paranoid. Scott and I stayed with him all night, helping him through the episode. But it must have had some kind of lasting effect on him. He returned to New York with us, but at some point later he left, saying he was going to join the circus. I never heard from him again.

The first Earth Day was April 22, 1970, early in my senior year. Our high school had an outdoor event planned. My physics teacher asked me if I wanted to give a speech at the event. I'd never done anything like that before, but I said yes. I remember standing in the school parking lot, bullhorn in my hand, giving my short speech to several hundred students and faculty, shouting, "We have the power!" That was surprisingly fun, and also my first real public speaking opportunity.

That was also the "summer of love" with the Woodstock music festival in mid-August 1969 on Max Yasgur's farm in upstate New York. Mom would not let me go, but Scott went. I heard afterwards that he had a great time.

Barbara and Randy

My sister Barbara was (and still is) three and a half years older than me, so she was in junior college at Nassau Community College when I was still in high school. She was on the dance committee, and one of the rock bands that played there had a guitarist named Randy Dannenfelser. Barbara and Randy started dating and soon got married. Randy was a big fan of the Who, so their two children, Peter and Keith, were named after band members Peter Townsend and Keith Moon .

Randy and Barbara, 1968.

Me, Mom, Barbara and Randy, in our living room on their wedding day.

Me, Barbara and Randy on the steps of Mom's house in Huntington Station.

Baby Katelyn with Keith and Randy Dannenfelser, circa 1987.

First Jobs

I had a few brief summer and part time jobs before senior year. The first, not counting helping out at Dad's store, was at the Huntington Library when I was about 15. My job was to put returned books back on the shelves and "read the shelves" to make sure all the books were in the correct location.

The next job was a brief stint as a camp counselor at Shepherd Day Camp, where I and another kid were both fired after two days for being disruptive.

Next, I sold Amway. This company makes soap and other household basics and sells them through a multi-level marketing (MLM) system of independent sellers. I came in at the lowest rung, going door to door in my neighborhood and demonstrating the amazing cleaning power of the premier Amway product, Liquid Organic Cleaner or LOC. I bought the stuff at wholesale and sold it at retail, making about a 40% profit margin. Another 20% went to the people higher up in the pyramid who collected a commission on my sales. Once a month or so I'd attend meetings where these higher-level people told us stories of how they'd worked their way up, building their network of sellers and achieving the American Dream through hard work and determination.

My first real job was at Shearson Hamill, the brokerage office where Mom worked. I worked there over the summer of 1969 and continued part time for a while afterwards. This was a traditional office where the men worked as stockbrokers and the women worked in the back office. The men spent most of their time trying to "churn" their customers; that is, enticing them to sell their existing stocks and buy different ones to generate sales commissions. When they got an order to buy or sell stock, they'd write it on a slip of paper and drop it in a little conveyor belt that ran past all their cubicles. The slip of paper would zip down the belt and through a gap in the wall where it entered the back office. There, Mom and the other women would process the trade.

I was the office gofer. One of my jobs was to update a big thick reference book of publicly traded companies that was used by the stockbrokers if they needed to look up some stats for a customer. Every company had a page of detailed information – financials, stock price history, and so on. The Shearson main office sent us thick envelopes full of new pages several times a week, and my job was to insert each page in its proper location in the big thick book.

That was the year of the Miracle Mets, when the awful New York Mets baseball team, which had never finished higher than ninth in the 10-team National League, somehow won their newly created 5-team division, finishing with 100 wins and 62 losses. Then they went on to beat the Atlanta Braves in the playoffs and the Baltimore Orioles in the World Series. I listened to every minute of every game on the radio at the office, along with most of the men. I'm not sure what the women were listening to in the back office.

Academics

As I said, I wasn't a particularly good student. In fact I was lazy. I was in advanced placement classes in most subjects, but I did my homework at the last minute, didn't work hard, and managed to graduate with a B+ average. As a result, I didn't develop good study habits, trusting that I could always write the paper or study for the big test the night before and still do all right.

I had one memorable teacher though. My junior year math teacher was Mr. Marceau, and he was the first math teacher I met who actually loved math. He used to tell us how a particular equation was "beautiful," and I learned to see mathematics through his eyes. This inspired me.

Being in a well-to-do suburban school district, our high school actually had a computer lab. This was before personal computers were available and the state of the art was a mainframe computer that could support multiple users on dumb terminals. Our school had a small timesharing computer in the basement which was connected to a couple of dozen teletype-style terminals in a classroom. I never actually saw the computer, but I think it was a PDP series machine from Digital Equipment Corporation.

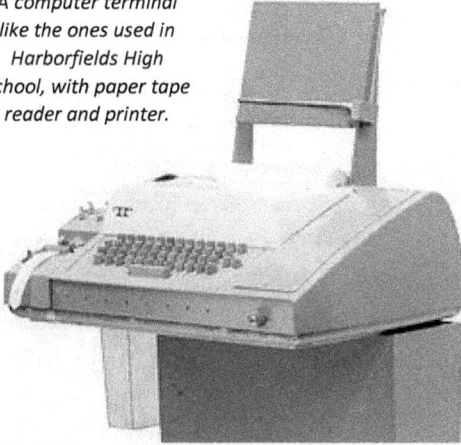

A computer terminal like the ones used in Harborfields High School, with paper tape reader and printer.

These terminals did not have screens. Instead, they had a teletype keyboard with cylindrical keys, a built-in printer, and a paper tape reader/writer on the left side. We wrote programs in the BASIC programming language by typing the code and storing it temporarily in memory so it could run. If we wanted to save the program we mounted a roll of paper tape in the reader/writer, typed a SAVE command, and the device would write the program one byte at a time by punching holes in the paper tape. We'd then fold up the paper tape and take it home. The next day, we'd give the READ command and insert the paper tape into the reader. The terminal read the holes in the paper tape to load the program back into memory.

This was my first experience with computers. I wrote some simple game programs like tic-tac-toe and moon lander. I also wrote a program that calculated and printed out pricing grids for the nuts and bolts that my dad sold in bulk in his store.

The Summer After the Summer of Love

I graduated high school in June 1970 at the age of 17. For a graduation present Mom gave me her old Plymouth Fury which had high mileage but was very fast. Scott and I decided this was a good enough reason to take another road trip, this time out west. We had two stops planned: visit my friend Betsy Heller who had moved to St. Louis with her family a few years earlier, and visit my future college roommate Stevenson "don't call me Steve" Palfi in Chicago. I contacted Betsy to tell her we were coming, but did not bother to contact Stevenson.

We headed out west, hitting 100 miles per hour on the open interstates in the Midwest. After a couple of days we reached St. Louis and found Betsy's house. She and I didn't have any sort of romantic relationship, so we just hung out together. However, Betsy had a friend, and she and Scott became quite friendly.

After a couple of days visiting in St. Louis, we headed up to Chicago. We found Stevenson's house, parked the car, and knocked on the door. An older man opened the door. I told him who I was, and that we were looking for Stevenson. "Ah," he said, "that's my son. Sorry you missed him, he's out of town for a few weeks." This was disappointing. But Mr. Palfi was nice. He invited us in for dinner, and we stayed overnight. The next day we headed back, driving through Canada and down through New York State back to Long Island. By the time we got back, the Fury was shaking from worn out ball joints and was barely drivable.

That summer, another major rock festival was planned, the Powder Ridge Rock Festival from July 31 through August 2, 1970, in Middlefield, Connecticut. This year I was old enough not to be deterred by Mom, so I went with Scott. There was supposed to be a terrific lineup of musicians including Sly and the Family Stone, the Allman Brothers, Janis Joplin, Richie Havens, and dozens more.

When we got there, we discovered that the event was cancelled due to some legal hassles that kept nearly all the musicians from coming. However, 30,000 kids showed up anyway, most of whom had already bought tickets. So, the event turned into tens of thousands of kids, lots of drugs including large barrels of "electric water" laced with LSD, inadequate plumbing, and no music. Facing huge financial losses, the promoters simply abandoned the festival, leaving things to the kids, the volunteers, and the local police. According to one writer, "Powder Ridge was an accident waiting to happen, and it happened."

I remember seeing a middle aged guy dancing trance-like by himself, listening to some nearby boom box music. He was very, very stoned. As he danced he took off nearly all of his clothing, one item at a time, and tossed the items into the crowd.

The folk singer Melanie Safka was the only musician on the ticket who actually did show up, and she gave a free show on an improvised stage powered by some Mr. Softee ice cream trucks. Her music was wonderful. Apparently a few local bands also managed to get into the festival grounds and perform for appreciative (and stoned) audiences.

Scott and I managed to avoid the more serious drugs, and we both volunteered in the kitchen. I worked in a kitchen tent helping to make big vats of spaghetti. One of the event organizers showed up at one point, taking down names and

Folk singer Melanie Safka performing for free at Powder Ridge, 1970.

addresses of the volunteers, and a few weeks later I received a small check in payment for my services.

Clark University

In September 1970 I began my freshman year at Clark University, a better-than-average liberal arts college in Worcester MA. I'd visited a few liberal arts colleges and one or two large universities, but decided on Clark. Luckily Clark also decided on me, accepting me through their early admissions program in the first few months of my senior year of high school.

The Vietnam War was at its peak at the time, and as Bob Dylan said, "revolution was in the air." In Worcester there were demonstrations against the war, some of them organized by the local Students for a Democratic Society, a socialist group that kept trying to recruit me. I didn't join, but I did participate in some of their marches and protests. Clark was so liberal that when the U.S. expanded the war and started dropping bombs on Cambodia in December 1970, we students didn't even have a chance to go on strike like at other schools, because the university administration shut down the entire school in protest before we had a chance to do it for them.

Because the Vietnam War required so many soldiers, the U.S. Selective Service instituted an annual draft lottery, starting in 1970 and continuing through 1976. Every year they randomly assigned a number between 1 and 365 to each birthday. The lower the number for your birthday, the higher the likelihood that you'd be drafted. For me and other men born in 1953, the lottery drawing was held on February 2, 1972, late in my freshman year at Clark. I was relieved to learn that the number assigned for my birthday was 298, a safe number. That year, men with numbers up to 95 were drafted.

I lived in a nice dorm on campus called Sanford Hall. My roommate was Stevenson Palfi, who I'd attempted to meet the previous summer in Chicago. His parents had named him after Adlai Stevenson, a prominent Democrat and presidential candidate in the 1950's. He was bright, a year or so older than me (of course), and more experienced, and we got along well.

I lost track of him after college, but learned much later of the path that his life had taken. He'd become a filmmaker and lived in New Orleans where he was known as "the Big Easy's big encyclopedia of music." He had amassed a huge collection of files, photographs and film at his home. It was all destroyed in Hurricane Katrina's floodwaters. Afterwards he became severely depressed, and died from a self-inflicted gunshot wound in 2005 at the age of 53.

Stevenson Palfi, undated photo.

Living on campus was also my first experience with people who were nonwhite. Clark had a small but vocal and radicalized group of black students. Many of them were openly hostile to white students. They even had their own wing in one of the dormitories, with an informal but strictly enforced "no whites allowed" policy. I remember being friends with a black girl and walking with her back to her dorm, only to be turned away when we reached the forbidden zone. I suppose they were just reacting, or overreacting, to the racial discrimination that they'd experienced all their lives, and that was the first time I'd ever been discriminated against because of the color of my skin. A teaching moment, I suppose.

In between the political protests, the racial confrontations and the social stresses of being away from home for the first time, I did manage to squeeze in some academic work, but not much. Clark had, not surprisingly, a liberal attitude towards classwork. There were few or no required classes, and classes could be taken on a "pass / no record" basis, meaning that if you did well you got a "pass" and if you didn't do well, it didn't even show up on your transcript. I took lots of introductory classes in a variety of subjects. Some (Introduction to Non-Western Music) were enjoyable, others (Economics 101) not so much. Overall, though, nothing really captured my interest.

My friend Scott was at Wesleyan University in nearby Middletown, Connecticut. I visited there a few times. During winter break I stayed in his group house at Wesleyan for a week or so. I learned to play in a Javanese gamelan orchestra of bells, and hung out with Scott and his musician friends.

49

Like a Moth

Scott had become interested in the jew's harp, built up a large collection of different harps, and within a fairly short time had become a leading authority on the instrument.

I also saw Mahavishnu John McLaughlin in concert. This was a powerful experience. He was one of the world's great guitarists. I remember him coming out onto the stage, waiting for the audience to quiet down, saying "I'd like to bring you a few minutes of peace," and then launching into the most riveting guitar solo I'd ever heard.

I did make one small contribution to Clark University, other than Mom's tuition payments. In chemistry class one day, I was absentmindedly looking at the periodic table of the elements. I started putting the abbreviations together, wondering if they would spell out any English words. To my amazement, the three consecutive elements 17 (Cl for chlorine), 18 (Ar for Argon) and 19 (K for potassium) spelled out "CLARK"! I jumped up in the middle of the lecture and told everyone. Stunned silence. No applause, unfortunately. But I think that sometime later, the chem department had some t-shirts made that spelled out Cl-Ar-K.

At the end of my freshman year I headed home for the summer. I worked in Dad's store and went to the beach a lot. I became reacquainted with a girl named Valerie Hoffman, who I'd known in high school. She was one year junior to me and had just graduated at the top of her class. She became my first serious girlfriend.

Don Vangel, undated photo.

Second year at Clark was much the same as the first. I moved to a different dorm. My roommate was Don Vangel. We got along well, though Don was a bit more emotional than my previous roommate. He also lifted weights and was so heavily muscled that he could not even fully straighten out his arms. One time we had some kind of minor argument, and after I turned and walked away he put his fist right through a wall. Fortunately the wall was sheetrock and not brick. Later Don went into banking and consulting, ending up as a principal at Ernst & Young.

Another friend, Chris Liese, had the same risk tolerance that I had, which is to say, extremely high. We decided that we could get free phone service by going down to the basement of the dorm and splicing a phone wire directly into the main phone line. This was of course a really stupid idea which had no chance of working. To make it worse, we didn't know which wires were data and which were power. Chris borrowed my pocketknife and cut into one of the wires. Alas, it was a power line. There was a huge explosion of sparks and Chris flew across the room, unhurt but shaken up. We looked at the knife. The blade was melted three quarters of the way through.

I kept in touch with Valerie, my girlfriend from the previous summer. She was at University of Pennsylvania in Philadelphia. She wasn't happy, writing to me at one point that "all the guys want to do is drink and lay." In late fall I hitchhiked from Worcester down to Philadelphia to visit her. The visit was okay, not particularly memorable, but the hitchhiking was interesting. On the way south I got picked up by a friendly and well dressed black family. It turned out that they were relatives of James Earl Chaney, one of the three civil rights workers who were murdered in Mississippi in 1964.

On the return trip, I got some rides northbound, the last one leaving me on the New York State Thruway at the point where the Massachusetts Turnpike split off to the east. I stuck out my thumb and got a short ride that left me just over the state line in Massachusetts. A state highway patrolman stopped and picked me up. He told me in an unfriendly way that he needed to get me off the highway before I became a splatter on the road that he would have to clean up. He dropped me off at an exit ramp and told me to never, ever get back on his highway. It was getting dark. I walked into the nearest town, a typical small New England town. I asked around to find out where I could sleep, and someone said that the local church was always open. So I spent the night on the wooden floor of the church. The next day I went out onto a local road and got a series of rides back to Worcester.

There was one more hitchhiking story worth mentioning. I was trying to become friendly with some girl, and so I suggested that we go for a day hike at Mt. Monadnock, a state park around 30 miles northeast of Worcester. She

51

agreed. Neither of us had a car, so we walked out on to the road in front of campus and stuck out our thumbs. We got one or two rides in the right general direction. Then we got picked up by a guy. We got into the car and sat in the back seat. As soon as we sat down I noticed that the door handles were missing on both sides of the back seat. Odd. The guy also seemed a little bit agitated. At some point he turned off the main road and started driving around a rundown residential neighborhood. Just looking for his friend, he said. Not finding his friend (fortunately), he got back on the main road. I was starting to get a bit worried, and was fingering the small pocketknife in my pocket and wondering if I'd need to use it. My traveling companion said she was getting really hungry and asked if he'd take us to a diner to get something to eat. He agreed, drove to a local place and opened the door to let us out. We took off, ran a few blocks, then hitchhiked back to school.

By the spring of 1976, the end of my second year at Clark, I began to feel that I needed to leave school. I'd taken classes in something like ten different departments and hadn't found anything that I wanted to major in. And Clark was expensive. I knew that Mom had been saving money to put me through college and it didn't seem right to use up all those funds without really knowing what I wanted to focus on. So I decided to take a break at the end of my sophomore year, until I could figure out what to do with the rest of my life.

Leaving Clark was the end of the first chapter of my life. It was the time that I stepped off the path that had been laid out for me by my family, and the beginning of my own explorations into life, the universe, and everything.

A Brush With Death

It was the summer of 1972. The Watergate scandal was just starting, the Vietnam war was winding down, and the Grateful Dead has just released their Europe '72 double album. I was a college dropout living in my mom's house, with no idea what I wanted to do next. My friends were all still in college. I bought an old Ford Econoline van, spray painted it green, and stuck a peace symbol on the back. Econoline vans were cheap and easy to drive, but extremely dangerous because the engine was located between the two front seats, and there was nothing but a bit of sheet metal between the passengers and whatever was in front of the van.

The Grateful Dead were playing in Roosevelt Stadium in New Jersey on September 19, so my friend Carol Warsager and I went to see them. We drove across New

York City, then got on the Garden State Parkway heading west towards Jersey City. We were smoking dope, talking, and listening to music on the van's cassette player. I wasn't paying much attention to the road.

At that point the Garden State Parkway had five lanes in each direction – three express lanes and two local lanes, with a low concrete divider about the height of a curb separating the two sets of lanes. I was driving in the leftmost local lane. We were going around 50 mph and I was talking with Carol. Suddenly I looked at the road. Traffic was stopped up ahead, way too close for me to stop in time. I looked to my right – wall to wall trucks, no way to change lanes to the right. I hit the brakes but I knew we could never stop before slamming into the car in front. And of course there nothing but sheet metal between us and those stopped cars. "Oh Christ," I muttered, then shouted to Carol, "Hang on!" and I cut the wheel hard to the left. The van jumped the divider going around 40, teetered but did not flip over, and we ended up in the rightmost express lane, where, thankfully, there was no traffic. Shaken but not deterred, we continued on to the Grateful Dead concert and had a great time.

Eagle, Colorado

Somehow this did not convince Carol to avoid me, and later that summer we drove out west together. Carol had friends in a small town in Colorado called Eagle, so the plan was that I would drop her off there, then continue on to California. We took a few days to get to Colorado, camping along the way. Carol was not interested in sleeping with me, which was unfortunate since I had gone to the trouble of building a small bed in the back of the van. But we coexisted cheerfully enough, and we arrived in Eagle where I met her friends. John Cornwall was a bright and well educated guy who was interested in spiritual topics, especially the American "sleeping prophet" Edgar Cayce. And Ron Ryan was a bearded hippie originally from New Jersey, also interested in spiritual topics and working at Mountain Laundry. We all became good friends.

John had received a prophesy from someone telling him that he would partner with a Jewish person and make a fortune. So when he met me he felt it was preordained that we would go into business together. We started a company, Peppercorn (since Cornpepper didn't sound nearly as good) Products. The idea was that we'd make and sell "mummy" which was a food made from figs and dates that, according to Edgar Cayce, was a staple food eaten by the priests and priestesses of ancient Egypt and Atlantis. We needed some figs and dates for our cooking experiments. So we drove the van over Loveland Pass and the Continental Divide (this was before they built the tunnel bypass) and down to Denver. There we bought about fifty pounds of figs and dates in the wholesale district, then headed back to John's trailer to experiment with the stuff.

We made, and we forced our friends to eat, a variety of mummy-inspired food including mummy pie, mummy cookies, and my favorite, peanut butter and mummy sandwiches. Neither of us knew much about starting a food company, and we had no money to start production, so before long the company disbanded and John did not make his preordained fortune with me.

As a result of meeting John and Ron and getting involved in their lives there, I abandoned my vague plan to head to California and just stayed in Colorado. I got a job working outdoors at a local sawmill called Kaibab Lumber. My job was to pull freshly sawn boards off a conveyor belt and stack them in pallets, then cinch up the pallets with tight metal bands so they could be loaded onto trucks for delivery. The difficulty of the work varied from day to day depending on the kinds of boards being sawn. An easy day was when lightweight 1x4s came off the conveyor belt. A rough day was when they were cutting 2x12's, because the wet boards could be up to 16 feet long and incredibly heavy. My first day on the job we were loading 2x8's, which were heavy enough. I was struggling. A young guy with scraggly blond hair under his hardhat came up to me and said, "Hey dude, the only way to do this job is stoned." In retrospect, working in a sawmill while smoking dope was probably a really bad idea, but since I wasn't personally working near any sharp spinning objects I tried it. It did seem to make the days go by faster. Sometimes we'd eat lunch at my house, smoke a joint, then go back to the sawmill. My stoner friend, whose name was Jim, operated a forklift, high more often than not. I was more careful than he was, though once on a dare I drove my van (yes, the same Econoline van) up a steep hill on the sawmill property. With everyone watching we made it about halfway before the wheels started to spin. I turned the van around, which was quite tricky on a steep hill. Jim jumped out of the van. I barely avoiding having the van flip and roll, with me in it, all the way down.

Over time I began to understand the social structure in Eagle. There were three main factions: the cowboys (traditional short-haired Colorado guys who drank, hunted, wore big hats and drove pickup trucks), the freaks (hippies and other like-minded souls who took drugs and read philosophy), and the Mexicans. There were also a few Native Americans, including a tall and powerful man called Eskimo Jim, no relation to my stoner friend Jim. Eskimo Jim was well respected around town, and he had a teenaged daughter. We all got along reasonably well, and there was some cultural intermingling between the cowboys and the freaks, mainly involving poker games. The Mexicans tended to stay to themselves.

One day there was a breakdown at the sawmill, and the company had to idle the mill for a few days while they waited for replacement parts. Rather than laying us off, they decided it was a good time to install insulation in the big warehouse where the freshly sawn lumber was stored to dry. Installing insulation was easy at the lower levels of the walls, but above around ten feet it was dangerous, and the Mexicans and cowboys refused to do it. My friend Jim also refused, probably a good idea considering how stoned he always was. So I volunteered, and spent a couple of days climbing around on steel girders way off the ground, stapling sheets of insulation to the walls without a safety rope.

I did make one mistake, though, which fortunately only cost me a better job and not my life. I'd called in sick and was just hanging out and reading in John's trailer where I was living temporarily. My friend Stoner Jim was running the forklift, but he had apparently screwed up at work and the foreman decided to replace him. The foreman called me at home and offered me the job. This would have been a lot of fun and a major step up from hauling heavy wooden planks off the conveyor belt. But I wasn't feeling good at the time, so I told the foreman I couldn't do it. Later I realized that I should have just ignored the mild cold and said "yes" to the opportunity.

Living in Eagle was the beginning of the spiritual awakening phase of my life. John, Ron and I were interested in everything metaphysical, philosophical and spiritual. We read everything we could get our hands on, and often talked into the night. On Saturdays we'd pile into someone's car and drive three hours through Glenwood Canyon to Aspen, where we'd visit a little metaphysical bookstore there. I'd buy books and borrow other books from John and Ron, devouring everything I could get my hands on. I also became friends with Eskimo Jim's daughter, but was careful not to go past the "just friends" stage, especially after Jim came up to me in the local bar, towered over me, and said softly, "Just remember, son, that there is my daughter."

I'd been interested in trying LSD, especially after reading *The Doors of Perception* by Aldous Huxley, *The Electric Kool Aid Acid Test* by Tom Wolfe, and listening to rock and psychedelic music. But I was also wary of taking acid that had been cut with other chemicals, as there were stories of people taking something they thought was pure LSD but was actually cut with speed, rat poison, or whatever. Somehow I managed to get my hands on about twenty hits of pure windowpane acid, which was LSD infused in a tiny quarter-inch square of translucent gelatin. It was alleged to be 100% pure.

So one Saturday I dropped a tab of the stuff, and sat back to see what would happen. I waited for an hour or so and nothing seemed to be happening. So having nothing else to do, I walked out to Interstate 70 which ran past my house and stuck out my thumb. It was a beautiful day, and I stood there just enjoying the fresh air and the Colorado scenery. Soon a gigantic moving van approached and pulled off by the side of the road. I walked over to the cab, opened the door, and climbed up and in. The truck was being driven by a large insect. No, I realized, he's not an insect, he's just a thin guy with really big teardrop sunglasses. The insect man explained that he was delivering a truckload of furniture to a minister's house in Colorado Springs. If I helped unload, he'd pay me $40 and give me a ride back to Eagle afterwards. What a great deal, I thought, and agreed.

We had a nice drive to Colorado Springs, though I neglected to tell him that he'd just hired a helper who was tripping on LSD. Fortunately for me and my new employer, the dose was relatively mild so I wasn't actually hallucinating (well, not much anyway). But everything I saw and heard seemed to be really interesting and intense.

We got to the minister's house and unloaded the truck. At one point the minister cornered me in a room, sat me down, and attempted to convince me to accept Jesus as my lord and savior. That led to an interesting conversation about the nature of God and the universe, but I declined his offer. We finished up the job, the insect man and I went out and had a really good steak dinner, and, true to his word, he paid me and dropped me off in Eagle late that evening.

That was my first LSD trip, and I really liked it. I took it a couple of more times – once on my own in my house, where I spent the day writing feverishly about the nature of the universe, and a second time when a bunch of us went to a dance at a nearby town. That wasn't as much fun, and I realized that for me, LSD was not really a social drug or a source of entertainment, but was a tool for exploring one's inner realms.

William Blake could have been talking about LSD when he said, "If the doors of perception were cleansed, everything would appear to man as it is, infinite. For man has closed himself up, till he sees all things thro' narrow chinks of his cavern." The value of LSD was that it stripped away the mental filters that separate us from the infinite world. During an acid trip, everything is more real, more intense, and more immediate.

In fact, I had one very interesting realization while sitting in my house in Eagle while on LSD. I looked inward at my own state of consciousness to find out where the "I" was. And to my utter amazement, I found that there was no "I"! What I'd thought was my inner identity, the little guy inside my head, was really just an array of interacting processes. It was as if my mind was nothing more than a blackboard where various mental processes wrote things. There was no little guy inside my head, there were just thoughts appearing on the blackboard.

Eckankar

John Cornwall went to Denver one day, and came back with a brochure about something called Eckankar that someone had given him on a street corner. The brochure had to do with out-of-body travel. John knew I was interested in this so he gave me the brochure. I read it and was excited, because it appeared that Eckankar was exactly what I was looking for: a pure exploration of the nonphysical worlds, without all the religious baggage. Following that, I picked up a copy of *The Tiger's Fang* by Eckankar's founder Paul Twitchell, where he describes his Soul Travel adventures through all the planes of existence, from the lowest to the highest planes, in the company of his spiritual guide Rebazar Tarzs. It wasn't just that the book was well written, it was that every word seemed to be infused with some kind of powerful force. It was almost like I recognized the words and the ideas in the book. A few years later Bob Dylan wrote *Tangled Up in Blue* and wrote this, which perfectly captures the feeling I had reading that book:

> Then she opened up a book of poems
> And handed it to me
> Written by an Italian poet
> From the thirteenth century
> And every one of them words rang true
> And glowed like burnin' coal
> Pourin' off of every page
> Like it was written in my soul from me to you
> Tangled up in blue

By this time winter was well underway and it was getting really cold at the sawmill. I didn't relish the idea of working outdoors in below-zero weather, and I started to feel that my time in Colorado had come to an end. So I quit my job, parked my van behind Ron's trailer, left my guitar with Stoner Jim, and caught a flight back to Long Island.

Out of Body Experiences

Back on Long Island I went to work for my dad while living in a back bedroom at my mom's house. I'd brought a little baggie full of marijuana back with me. Mom saw it and asked me about it. I admitted that I liked to smoke the stuff.

She liked to garden, so she suggested that the two of us could grow some marijuana plants in the back yard. This was a delightful idea. How could I refuse? I extracted a few seeks from my stash, planted them, and by summertime we had three six-foot high plants which I harvested and dried. None of the neighbors ever noticed.

I continued to read Eckankar books. But I also branched out and read books on other spiritual paths. One of the most interesting was *Journeys Out of the Body* by Robert Monroe, written in 1971 and covering a couple of decades of his experiences. Monroe, a middle-aged electrical engineer, started to find himself involuntarily separating from his physical body and having fully conscious experiences in other planes of existence, mainly what would be called the Astral Plane in Eckankar and other eastern teachings. He could fly, he met other

Me in 1973, age 20.

beings, and had experiences that were incredible but sounded like they actually happened. Because Monroe was not a "true believer" and not a particularly religious person, the book had an authentic feel that appealed to me. I felt that Monroe was just an ordinary guy who found himself outside his body and was trying to figure out what was happening. His story was fascinating, and I read the book several times.

Towards the end of the book he offered some simple techniques that he found to be successful in helping people voluntarily initiate out-of-body experiences (OOBEs) at the Monroe Center that he founded in the Blue Ridge Mountains. The simplest technique involved lying comfortably, closing the eyes, and focusing on a point a few feet away, then "bending" the lines of sight ninety degrees upward, so the focus shifts to a point a few feet above one's head. This sounds odd, but if you try it, you'll get the idea.

I started doing this exercise every night before going to sleep, but didn't have any positive results. Then one night I read the book, worked on the exercise for a while, then went to sleep. I woke up a short time later feeling a strong pulsating electrical current running through my body. It started at my head, moved down to my feet, then back again. It felt like I had been plugged into an electrical outlet. I recognized this from Monroe's book where he described this vibration as a common first step in having an OOBE. He'd talked about how one takes control of this current or vibration and voluntarily moves it up and down. So I tried that. I was able to move the vibration up and down along my body a few times. After a while, though, the vibration faded and I thought the experience was over. But no. Even though the vibration had subsided, something strange was still happening. I felt light and a bit "buzzy" from the lingering vibration in my body. My hands and arms were under the bedcovers, and I tried lifting my right arm. It lifted right through the blanket! This seriously scared me, even though I had been working to achieve this for weeks and I was glad to be having some success finally. So I did not attempt to do anything else, like trying to move my entire self out of my body. Eventually I went to sleep, and that was it.

This was a really important experience for me. I was a bit disappointed that I didn't completely leave my body and fly around as Monroe had described. But it was a clear demonstration that the things Monroe talked about were valid and not just some con game he'd devised to sell books. Moreover, if Monroe's experiences were valid, that made it much more likely that the spiritual experiences described by Paul Twitchell and others also had some basis in fact and were not simply delusions or scams.

In short, this proved to me that yes, there's really something to all this spiritual and metaphysical stuff. It was enough to convince me to move forward and start studying Eckankar.

(Incidentally, I learned much later that Robert Monroe had created The Monroe Institute in the Blue Ridge Mountains of Virginia, where one could go and learn how to travel out of the body using techniques that Monroe developed. The primary method was called "hemi-synch," where a pair of headphones plays a different frequency in each ear, synchronizing the two brain hemispheres and inducing an out-of-body experience. I spent a week at the Institute in the 1990's, enjoyed it quite a bit, met some really interesting people, but did not experience an OOBE.)

Leaving For Las Vegas

As a result of my brief but convincing OOBE, I decided to join Eckankar. I wrote to Paul Twitchell and told him that I wanted to study with him. Shortly afterwards I received an envelope from the Eckankar office in Las Vegas containing a press clipping which described how Paul had died in September 1971 and had been succeeded by someone named Darwin Gross, who'd taken on Paul's role as the Living Eck Master and head of the movement. There were also some brochures that seemed to indicate that one could study Eckankar by signing up for monthly mailings called "discourses" and studying them in a local study group called a "satsang."

This didn't appeal to me at all. I was looking to immerse myself in this, not take a correspondence course. So I decided to head out to Las Vegas and live on the Eckankar campus, or ashram, or whatever they had out there. Unfortunately I had no car, having left my van parked behind Ron's trailer in Colorado, and little money. I had already done a lot of hitchhiking over the previous few years, but it was a really long way to Las Vegas. So I decided to try hitching a ride on a plane.

I packed my backpack (light brown canvas, Boy Scout vintage, with the words "Eckankar" and "Freedom" written in black magic marker on the back) and got a ride from my mom to the private aviation terminal at La Guardia airport in New York City. I walked into the waiting room, backpack and all, and looked around. There were a handful of people sitting in the room, mostly in ones and twos, talking quietly while waiting for their private planes to be ready. I walked up to the nearest one, a man sitting alone. "Hi," I said, "I'm trying to get to Las Vegas, would you give me a ride?" He was nice but said he couldn't, because the plane was too small to take an additional passenger. I moved on to the next person, and the next. I finally got a positive response from a businessman who said he was heading to Dallas and I was welcome to tag along. I thought about this for a bit – it was in the right direction, to be sure, but I didn't like the idea of being stuck in the airport in a strange city (especially in what I considered to be the Deep South), so I thanked him but declined.

By the end of the day I'd met lots of nice people, but alas, no ride to Las Vegas. I didn't want to give up, though, so I decided to stay the night in the terminal.

I found an unlocked storage closet, unrolled my sleeping bag and went to sleep on the floor. I was awakened early the next morning by a terrified cleaning lady who was sure she'd uncovered a dead body in her closet. I reassured her that I was alive, thanked her for waking me up, and I got dressed and out of there.

It's important to note here that yes, this really was a major U.S. airport, and yes, I really was hanging around the airport, soliciting rides from strangers, and had absolutely no trouble from any security personnel. It was a different time in America.

The second day was no more productive than the first, so I called my mom and got a ride back to her house.

My next thought was to register with a driveaway service, where people like me with lots of time and not much money were matched up with people who wanted their cars driven somewhere while they flew overhead. No luck there, apparently nobody wanted their car driven to Las Vegas. I then ran an ad in the local Pennysaver and got a call from a woman who wanted a driving companion to help her drive her Thunderbird to California, but when husband found out that she'd be riding for several days with a twenty year old guy, he nixed that idea.

So, running out of options, I decided to hitchhike the regular way, on land. I started off in Huntington, Long Island, got a series of rides cross country, was dropped off by a trucker in Barstow, California, then got a final ride from another trucker who let me off in a deserted parking lot on the outskirts of Las Vegas.

I stood in the parking lot for a while, pondering my next move. It was getting dark when a young guy walked up to me and asked, "Hey dude, you looking for a place to crash?" Sure, I said. So he took me to a fleabag hotel where he was sharing a room with a buddy. I found a place on the floor for my sleeping bag, and that was home for the next week or so.

The next morning I got cleaned up, relatively speaking, and headed out to find Eckankar headquarters. According to my map it was in an industrial district, which I thought was an odd location for a spiritual center. The building was a nondescript one-story structure with a sign reading "ECKANKAR, The Ancient Science of Soul Travel." I walked in. A nice, rosy cheeked, middle-aged and conservatively dressed woman greeted me. She looked like someone selling cookies at a church bake sale. I told her I had hitchhiked from New York and was there to join Eckankar. She cheerfully explained that this was the international office for the Eckankar organization, not an ashram or spiritual center, but I was welcome to become a member and start studying in a local satsang class. This was disappointing, but I agreed and signed up for classes.

The next task was to find a job. I walked through the industrial area and into a commercial district, stopping at every building to see if they were hiring. The creepiest part of this process was when I stopped in a jewelry store, and the clerk who was on duty, a guy in his thirties, walked up to me while talking about the possibility of me working there, and actually brushed his hand across my crotch. This didn't seem like a good recruiting method, at least for me, so I left in a hurry. I stopped in a few more stores, and eventually got a job working in the lawn and garden department of a locally owned department store.

That job wasn't particularly memorable, just loading bags of dirt and fertilizer into customers' cars. But one day I was having a conversation with some of my co-workers about something to do with politics. One of them, a Hispanic guy maybe 25 years old, said in a fake pompous voice, "The more liberal I was in my youth, the more conservative I am in my old age." At the time this sort of annoyed me, but now, several decades later, I can see some truth in it. I am still a reliable Democrat when it comes to voting, but I've also come to appreciate some of the values associated with conservatives, such as the virtue of hard work and self reliance. I've also developed a distaste for the kind of artificial language used by some progressives. I doubt if I'll ever vote Republican because of their ignorant positions on the environment, their disdain for the rights of minorities, and their disinterest in helping the disadvantaged. But these days when I look at an issue, I'm often surprised to find myself having more sympathy for the conservative point of view than the liberal one. So I guess I've become a moderate.

Anyway, getting back to life in Las Vegas. I needed a set of wheels, so I found a small used 90cc motorbike that someone was advertising in the Pennysaver. I'd never driven a motorbike before, but the seller showed me the basics, and after riding up the block and back, I bought it. I drove the bike for a month or so, until a close call with a careless motorist convinced me that riding a motorbike was stupid and dangerous (as opposed to, say, hitchhiking across the country and sleeping in a motel room with strangers). My van was still in Eagle, so I took some time off from work and started hitchhiking from Las Vegas to retrieve the van.

This was a long way through desolate country. Between Las Vegas and western Colorado lies Utah, and there's a point in the high desert where I-15 running north from Las Vegas to Salt Lake City splits, and I-70 begins, heading east to Denver. My first ride was heading up to Salt Lake City, so I had to get out at the I-15/I-70 junction. It was in the middle of absolute nowhere, without a person or building for miles. I stood by the side of the road for what seemed like forever until the first car drove past, then waited a long time for the next car. Nobody stopped. It was getting dark and cold, and the wind was picking up. A large car came into view, towing a camper. Abandoning the usual hitchhiker coolness, I jumped up and down and waved my arms. The car stopped. Inside were a young couple with a little girl. I told them I was heading to Eagle and was afraid of being stuck there overnight, and could they please give me a ride. They said sure, they were heading to Denver and would be going right past Eagle, and they invited me to hop into the camper. They drove for a few more hours, then stopped at a motel. They went into the motel room, and they let me sleep in the camper. They even gave me some of their food. The next day they dropped me off in Eagle, where I picked up my van. I also discovered that my so-called friend Jim had skipped town and taken my guitar with him. I drove the van back to Las Vegas.

Now that I had wheels I moved out of the motel room, which was crowded and smelly. It also seemed less attractive after I discovered that my two buddies made a living by shoplifting and petty theft. I got a room of my own at a different motel, but was looking for something a bit nicer. Checking the classified ads in the local paper, I saw an ad for a room for rent in a private home located at the edge of town, where a middle-aged couple and their daughter lived. I soon learned that the room they were renting out to me had been the bedroom of the couple's son who had died within the last year. The husband's response to this tragedy was to drink heavily and constantly, while the wife's response was to go out and attempt (with a surprising degree of success) to sleep with every young man in Las Vegas, including, it turned out, the teenaged son of my Eckankar satsang teacher. Of course it didn't take long for her to hit on me too, but I wasn't interested.

So I began my life in Las Vegas. I went to work every day in the garden lot store, and studied the books and writings of Eckankar every evening. I didn't have much of a social life, being too young to gamble or even enter the casinos. I did have a little bit of pure windowpane LSD left over from my time in Colorado, but it was just some crumbly flakes of gelatin wrapped in paper, so I decided to convert the drug into a better form. I bought a 12-pack of chewing gum, warmed up a little bit of water in a saucepan in the kitchen, dissolved the LSD in the warm water, then used an eyedropper to carefully put a few drops of water in each stick of gum. Then I rewrapped the gum and hid it in a secret compartment in my van. My landlady got a big kick out of this, as it was the first and only time I'd ever used her kitchen for cooking anything.

Since Eckankar had a strict no-alcohol and no-drugs policy, I didn't smoke marijuana or drink. But I couldn't resist using the LSD, especially after performing the chewing gum transformation. So I decided to do one more trip. I popped a stick of gum in my mouth, filled a canteen with water, and headed out into the desert for the day. It was a wonderful day, and every growing thing in the desert seemed absolutely perfect. This was by far the best of my half-dozen LSD experiences.

Return to the Store

Even though my parents were both supportive of my various adventures, my dad seemed to have reached his limit. So he contacted me and told me that he really needed me to help him at the store. He was in his mid-60's by then and had been running the hardware store for about twenty five years. In retrospect, though, I think he was worried about my footloose lifestyle. I suspect that he'd also talked with my mom and that together they'd cooked up this plan for pulling me back to Long Island.

Since there wasn't really much keeping me in Las Vegas other than my weekly Eckankar satsang class, I agreed to move back to Long Island. I packed my few belongings in the van, moved back to my mom's house, and started working at my dad's store. By this time I'd become used to a certain amount of independence and didn't want to stay in the back bedroom at her house, so I built a room in her basement and lived there for six months or so, before moving out – first, briefly, to a couple of rooming houses, and then to a nicer second floor apartment on Carver Street, close to the hardware store.

My dad's store was, at that time, called Village Hardware and Fireplace. It was located on Gerard Street in Huntington Village. His original store had been much larger, almost a department store instead of a hardware store. That original store had a terrific location, surrounded by three supermarkets.

Village Hardware with Dad's original signage, circa 1960.

The Hamburger Choo Choo, circa 1960.

A couple of blocks away was the Hamburger Choo Choo, a little luncheonette with a cool feature: a Lionel train that ran on a track in a loop all around the lunch counter. The train cars were flatbeds to which they had attached lunch plates. If you ordered something from the grill (preferably, a hamburger), the cooks would put it on a plate, reach over the grill and put the plate on one of the flatbed train cars, then press a button that would send the train around to stop in front of you. Then you'd take your plate off the flatbed rail car and eat your lunch. Their burgers were good, and they had the town's best milkshakes.

Business was good at Dad's store but he didn't own the building, and when his lease expired the landlord evicted him and sold the property to a bank. This forced Dad to relocate the store to a much smaller building on Gerard Street. I was working for him at the time, and I remember pushing the store's heavy safe on its little wheels several blocks to the new store.

The hardware business dwindled, so he started focusing more on fireplace accessories, as well as barbeque equipment in the warmer months. Eventually he got rid of the hardware store items and sold only fireplace accessories and barbeques.

Me, the budding capitalist, with a handful of bills taken from the cash register.

As the store's revenue shrank, its financial troubles grew. Dad was kiting checks, meaning that he wrote checks to vendors on the assumption that by the time the check was cashed, there'd be enough money in the store's bank account to cover it. This rarely happened. Most of the time the store's checking account was overdrawn. The bank always covered the check but they charged a $10 overdraft fee each time. Over the course of the month these fees added up to several hundred dollars. So one of my jobs was to go down to the bank every month, bringing the most recent statement, and ask our banking rep to waive the overdraft charges. This was a humiliating experience, and I vowed never to get into that situation myself.

A "Merchant of the Week" clipping from the Long Islander newspaper. Jerry Mortenson (stock boy), Annette Benedict (saleslady) and Dad wearing plaid pants.

Why do so many homeowners visit Village Hardware at 40 Gerard Avenue in Huntington Village? Perhaps it's because they've been in business for 24 years; perhaps it's the full line of housewares, plumbing and electric supplies; perhaps it's because new homeowners have found they can depend on Village Hardware to stock those necessary mailboxes, barbecue and fireplace equipment and other sundry household items. Ed Pepper, proprietor, stands with salespeople Annette Benedict and Jerry Mortensen amid surroundings that Huntington people depend on. Members of the Huntington Village Businessmen's Association; open six days a week, 9 a.m. to 6 p.m., Fridays until 8 p.m.

Another more enjoyable part of my job was going to customers' homes and measure their fireplaces for custom-made fireplace screens and enclosures. If it was a simple hanging firescreen the task was simple, just some measurements and checking off some boxes on the order form. But for custom enclosures I had to use a large sheet of cardboard that overlapped the fireplace opening, then cut out a hole in the middle, reach in and trace the borders of the fireplace opening on the inside of the cardboard sheet. Then I'd work with the customer to decide on the details of what they wanted, and take the order. Finally I would go back to the store and convert this to a paper stencil and send the order in to one of the fireplace enclosure companies that we worked with. During the time I spent at my dad's store, I stuck my head into hundreds of fireplace enclosures in expensive homes all over Long Island. And maybe ten percent of the time, the customer had a fire already going in the fireplace, which greatly increased the difficulty of sticking my head inside it.

Incidentally, Dad's store is still in business. It's still called Village Fireplace and Barbeque. In 1999 the current owner, Kevin Tagariello, bought out his partner for "a song and a dance" and moved the store to 1979 New York Avenue in Huntington Station.

Today's Village Fireplace store.

My Brain

While working at the store I noticed that I had a lot of trouble remembering the names of customers, even the ones who came in regularly. This was a bit annoying to some of the regulars, since they expected to be recognized and greeted by name when they came in. This was hard for me. Later I discovered that this is actually a disorder with a name, nominal aphasia, which is just a Latin term for "can't speak names." Of course giving something a Latin name doesn't really add any deeper understanding to it, but it's nice to have a name for it anyway.

I don't think I had this problem when I was younger (say, as a child or teenager), probably because in those years I came in contact with fewer people and didn't have to remember as many names. As I got older and became involved with business, I came in contact with hundreds of people every year. The problem persisted. I worked around it by writing down names and memorizing them later. Now that I'm much older, the problem seems to be getting a bit worse year by year, as the memory loss that comes with aging, the dreaded "senior moments," combines with the aphasia to make it really hard to remember some names.

Oddly, I also have trouble with binary things, like remembering which way to turn an unlabeled faucet handle to make the water hotter or colder, or whether a gate opens inward or outward. One of my university professors, the head of the behavioral neuroscience department, told the class that he had this problem,

69

and that's the first and only time I heard of anyone else having it. If it has a Latin name, I haven't been able to find it.

So, these are two odd deficiencies in my brain. On the other hand, I'm really, really good at tasks that require processing instead of remembering, such as doing complex mental math, solving problems, seeing patterns in noisy data, and analyzing business challenges. When I was young and my brain was more nimble I was able to multiply two three-digit numbers in my head. I also have a really good intuitive time sense, and can estimate accurately the duration of some event or how long ago it occurred, without having to calculate it. For what it's worth, my guess is that for some reason, possibly genetic or possibly environmental, some parts of my brain have been reallocated from one function to another. So perhaps the part of my brain that's supposed to remember names can't do it because it's been tasked with doing math instead.

Donna

Soon after moving to the Carver Street apartment, my high school friend Diane Crimi introduced me at a party to a friend of hers, Donna Williams, her friend and classmate from nursing school. Donna and I went to the beach together, I drove her back to Huntington in my van. She stayed over with me on Carver Street, and she was my girlfriend after that. Donna was very experienced, at least compared with me. We had lots of fun together. She'd stay over at my place in Huntington, or I'd go in and stay with her at her apartment in Manhattan.

Donna, on a camping trip

We also had some memorable trips together. Once we drove up to New England and stayed over at a bed-and-breakfast somewhere in Vermont. I woke up in the middle of the night and saw the room lit up with a strange glow, with all the edges of the walls and ceiling glowing brightly. Another time, we were camping in Florida and we both woke up in the middle of the night, enveloped in some kind of spiritual energy.

Donna's parents were poor and lived in a tiny ramshackle house in Lewis, New York, in the Adirondack mountains near the Canadian border. I really liked the Williams family. Her dad was a construction worker, her mom was a homemaker. The first winter we were together, we headed north to visit her folks. It was snowing and really cold, and somewhere around Albany the heater failed in my van. We rigged up a plastic sheet behind the front seats to try and keep some warmth in the front of the van, but soon it became too cold to drive. So we called her dad, who came down and picked us up.

Donna lived in New York City, working in a hospital as a psychiatric nurse. A few times we went to the hospital together to visit the kids in the cancer ward; I played guitar and we both sang songs like Peter Paul & Mary's "Puff the Magic Dragon," Paul Simon's "Duncan," John Denver's "Country Road," and Cat Steven's "Moon Shadow." I also played guitar as the hired entertainment at a dinner party somewhere on Long Island, and Donna came with me.

Donna, New York City

Eventually she met a guy, a New York stockbroker, who decided that he wanted to marry her. He made a strong play for her, offering her money, success and stability. This was really attractive to Donna, who was coming up from poverty and desperately wanted to be successful. She felt that I had a lot of potential, but at the time I was still a college dropout working at my dad's hardware store, so there was little evidence that I would be a good provider. For a while I competed with the guy for Donna's affection, and the battle went back and forth. Donna's family liked me a lot and distrusted this well-dressed city slicker. The guy had given her an engagement ring, and during of our visits to Lewis her big beefy cousin told her to "throw that damn ring in the river." Donna had strong feelings for me, and we continued to see each other even though she was technically engaged to him. Eventually, though, she made her choice, broke up with me, and married the stockbroker.

India

Being dumped was painful. So I felt that I needed to do something radically different with my life, yet again. My best friend from high school, Scott Marcus, had gone to India to study music several years earlier, so I wrote him and suggested I come visit. He wrote back and said that was a terrific idea. He'd been in India for a long time, having gone there for his junior year abroad studying ethnomusicology at Wesleyan University. He'd stayed on to study Indian classical music at Benares Hindu University and was practicing sitar for five or six hours every day. But his teacher had recently died, and Scott was now ready to come back to America after several years in India. He was worried about the difficulty in re-entering American life after being gone so long (keep in mind that this was the 1970's, and things were changing culturally really fast). So Scott offered to be my host for the summer in India, and in return, he wanted me to help him return to America.

I arrived in New Delhi in May of 1975, age 22. Scott met me at the airport, along with Chedi Lal, the chowkidar (houseboy) who, along with his wife, worked for Scott for $10 per month plus food and lodging. We took a taxi to a modest hotel in Delhi. I remember walking out in the street and being completely overwhelmed by the street scene – crowds of people, cattle and rickshaws, so many sounds and smells, so completely confusing. I felt that if I walked even a half block down the road I would have become lost.

Street market in New Delhi.

Me on the road to Kulu. Scott and Chedi. Three real people in Delhi in front of three idealized poster people.

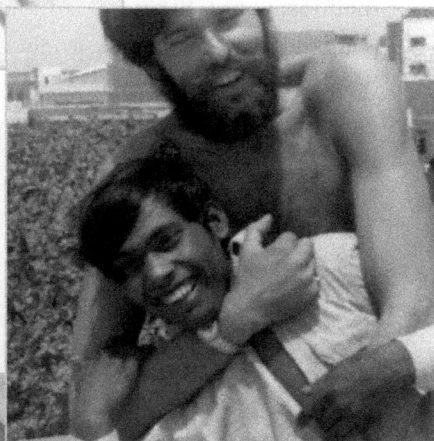

Like a Moth

We headed back to Benares but made a few touristy stops along the way. We visited the Red Fort in Delhi, then took a train to Agra, home of the Taj Mahal and a hub of the Indian gemstone industry. The Taj was beautiful, of course, but coming from an entrepreneurial family I thought this would be a good opportunity for me to buy some gems and set up an import business. So I wandered into the marketplace, sat down with a gem merchant, and over cups of tea I purchased $100 or so worth of lapis lazuli and other semiprecious stones. I also stopped at a brass merchant and bought some brassware which I had shipped back to Dad's store. When I returned to the U.S. I sold the lapis at a good profit, but when I reordered, the gem merchant took several months to fill my order and I felt I couldn't build an import business around that. The brassware sold, very slowly, at my dad's store, and I think I still have a couple of items somewhere.

From Agra we traveled by train to the holy city of Benares where Scott and Chedi lived. The city had recently been renamed Varanasi as part of India's effort to replace garbled British versions of place names with more accurate traditional ones. Benares was an incredible place. At first glance it just looked poor and dirty, but that was only when viewed through Western eyes. In fact, the city was full of people carrying out their daily lives just like in New York or Paris, but with much less material wealth. People slept on the sidewalk and roof tops, but not because they were homeless but because it was cooler outside than inside. About a month after arriving, I was sitting in a marketplace just enjoying the day, when a gaggle of Western tourists came bustling through, led by a tour guide. I could tell by looking at their gaping faces that they really weren't seeing the place in the same way that I was able to, even after just a month, and I imagined them going home and telling their friends how crowded, dirty and poor India was.

Scott and a bottle of Kingfisher

74

The Ganges River (called Gangaji by people in India) flowed through the city, and is sacred to Hindus. A dip in the river is believed to wash away all sins, and when a loved one dies, the family brings the ashes of the deceased person to the river. Every day there were funeral processions where a body, covered with

Maureen Skelly with my Ovation guitar.

flowers, was carried by relatives on a stretcher down to the burning ghats. Priests would then burn the body and place the ashes in the river. The ghats operated around the clock, with priests chanting and singing all day and all night. It was eerie and beautiful.

Scott's house was in one of the nicer parts of town, not far from the river. It was also at the upriver end of Benares, where the water was cleaner than further downriver.

Scott shared the house with his girlfriend, Chedi and his wife, and Maureen Skelly, who was also a student of Indian music and was the daughter of noted composer Marga Richter. The house was stucco, with windows that opened without glass or screens. Insect control was handled by a bunch of geckos, small lizards that walked on the walls and ceilings looking for tasty bugs. There was no air conditioning of course, but on hot days we used an evaporator machine that simply sprayed water which cooled the room a bit as it evaporated. We slept on simple beds called charpoi, just tight-woven hammocks on four posts.

I stayed in Benares for six weeks. I took Hindi lessons from a local tutor, went swimming in the Ganges, wandered around the city, and listened to lots of Indian classical music. Scott practiced sitar all day, and in the evenings we'd often go to free outdoor concerts. Chedi and his wife cooked our meals, which mostly consisted of sabzi (greens), roti (flat bread) and dal (lentils), with chai tea. Breakfast was eggs, toast and chai tea. We got raw buffalo milk from a local vendor who obtained it fresh every day from his family's water buffalo and delivered to us, unfiltered and still warm, in a stainless steel container. When we were out walking around, we could stop at a street vendor and buy a chai in a clay cup. After drinking the chai, we just threw the clay cup on the ground, where it degraded almost instantly into ordinary dirt.

My Hindi teacher arriving for a lesson.

One day Scott discovered that some of his textbooks were missing. He confronted Chedi with this, and learned that Chedi had stolen the books in order to sell them, not for the value of the book itself, but to a paper merchant who destroyed the books in order to re-use the paper inside. This precipitated a crisis that involved the entire neighborhood. Scott felt that this theft was a serious breach of trust and required a major show of anger, so he publicly and loudly berated Chedi in the courtyard, in Hindi, so that all the neighbors could see and hear. Chedi's mother arrived and pleaded on her knees with Scott to show mercy to her son. This was almost entirely play-acting by both Scott and the mother, and so the public show was interrupted from time to time by Scott going inside and sitting with us and talking through the whole situation, wondering what right he, a wealthy American, had to punish a man who worked for practically nothing. Eventually Scott went outside and publicly announced that Chedi was pardoned and could resume his job in the household. Chedi's mother made a dramatic show of gratitude, and the neighbors went back to whatever else they were doing.

As May turned into June and then July, Benares became intolerably hot, and we headed up to the beautiful and much cooler hill stations of Kulu and Manali. These were towns in the Himalayan foothills where prosperous Indians spent the summer. At one train station I made the mistake of buying a goat meat sandwich from a vendor, and an hour later I got violently sick. Fortunately the train had a toilet consisting of a small room with a hole in the floor, and I spent much of the train trip there. We arrived in Kulu and moved into a small rented cottage, not much more than a hut on a hillside. It was beautiful "Sound of Music" country, much like western Colorado or

At our cabin in Kulu.

Switzerland, with lush rolling hills and rocky mountains. But unlike Colorado, if you were to hike up one of the mountains you were more than likely to find a village at the top, speaking some obscure language that neither Scott nor Chedi could understand. In one village we encountered a religious festival where hundreds of villagers were carrying a religious statue in a procession from one place to another. Scott jumped right in, taking pictures and somehow getting permission to walk alongside the statue as the villagers installed it in its proper place in the village's temple.

Kulu was only a five-hour bus ride from Dharamsala, the town where the Dalai Lama lived after escaping from China in 1959. I left my friends in Kulu, boarded a bus for Dharamsala, and spent a few days there. The town was different from other Indian towns, dominated more by Buddhists than by Hindus. Buddhist monks tended to be cleanshaven, well fed and wore clean robes, whereas Indian holy men, *sadhus*, were mostly ascetics with long beards, long hair and filthy clothes.

A Buddhist monk and a Hindu sadhu in Dharamsala. Who would you rather sit next to on the bus?

78

Tibetan refugee artisans trimming a carpet in Dharamsala.

I wanted to visit the Dalai Lama, but was told that he was on a meditation retreat and could not be disturbed, so I contented myself with long hikes in the mountains around the Dalai Lama's compound. Down in the village I stopped into a carpet weaving business called the Tibetan Handicrafts Production Cum Sale Industrial Society Limited. In the building were dozens of Tibetans, men and women, weaving traditional Tibetan carpets. I thought the carpets were beautiful, and bought one, a 4' x 6' carpet featuring two snow leopards. They rolled it up, wrapped it in burlap, and I carried that carpet around India for the final two weeks of my stay there. This became another business venture. When I got back to New York I put together a brochure about custom made Tibetan carpets, stuffed them in hundreds of mailboxes around Huntington, and also hung one up behind the cash register in my dad's store. All told, I think I sold a dozen or so carpets.

Mind Over Matter

Finally it was time to go home, but there was one more adventure awaiting me. For reasons that I cannot remember, I took a different flight than Scott did. The plane departed from Delhi, and was scheduled to make a stop in Bombay and then head out across the Indian Ocean, refueling in Kuwait and ending in London. I sat down and found that I was sitting next to an incredibly attractive Indian girl, maybe 25 years old, slim, well dressed, with light brown skin and the deepest and most expressive eyes I'd ever seen. Her name was Pia. She told me she was returning to London after spending a couple of years in India as the companion of Conrad Rooks, a famous film director who'd been in India filming the movie Siddhartha, and they'd just broken up. We got to talking, then we got to snuggling a bit, then we put a blanket over ourselves and snuggled a lot more. I'd never met anyone as exotic and magnetic as this girl. I was completely captivated, and found myself wishing really, really hard that something would happen so that I could spend more time with her, in private.

We stayed on the plane during our scheduled stopover in Bombay, then the plane headed out over the ocean. More serious snuggling, and even more fervent wishes on my part. Suddenly the plane banked hard to the left, stayed tilted for a while, then leveled out. A moment later the pilot came on the intercom. Normally pilots have that super calm intercom voice, which must be something they teach in flight school. But this pilot must have skipped that class, because he announced in an unsettlingly nervous voice, "Ladies and gentlemen, we have… umm… some trouble." Pause. "We have to go back." The plane returned safely to Bombay, and to my delight, we were told that the airline would be putting all passengers up in a hotel in Bombay that night, and we'd depart the following morning. We chose double occupancy, of course. Prayers answered!

I saw Pia once more. She stopped by to visit me in Huntington when she came to the U.S. the following year. Acting as a local tour guide, I showed her around the shops of Huntington Village. There was one clothing shop that was owned by an Indian family. We walked in, and it turned out that Pia knew the young woman working there!

I wondered for a long time afterwards, though, how much my wishes had to do with the plane having engine trouble. Things like this have happened to me many times, where outer events have synced up with my inner imaginations.

A blurry pic of Pia, visiting me in Huntington.

80

Most of the time, it appears as precognition: a person will pop into my thoughts, and a few seconds later the phone will ring with that person on the line or I'll get a text message or email from that person. Or while playing a competitive match in table tennis, I'll get a flash of insight into what serve my opponent will use, just before he uses that exact serve. But sometimes it's more than that, and my thoughts appear to have actually caused physical effects. This is less common, but it's happened a few times. Once I was sitting with some friends at a restaurant during an Eckankar seminar and I wanted to get the waitress's attention. I sent her an urgent "turn around!" thought, and she stopped, whirled around, and looked right at me with a "what did you do?" look on her face. Another time I was in a rush to reach a ferry before it was scheduled to depart, but was stuck behind a slow-moving car. Both cars came to a T junction, and the car signaled that it was about to turn left, the same way I was going. "Get out of the way!" I shouted inwardly, and the driver of the car ahead immediately switched his blinker to the right, and turned out of the way. And once I was riding my motorcycle home from New York Tech to my apartment in Huntington, and I had to pull off the road because a missing hex nut was causing something important to come loose on the bike. I really, really needed to fix this so I could get home, and I imagined how great it would be if I could find a replacement hex nut. I looked around on the ground, and there, a couple of feet further up the road, was a dirty but perfectly serviceable hex nut, exactly the right size for what I needed.

A skeptic would say these are just coincidences, and maybe a couple of them are, but not all of them. My understanding of this has evolved over the years, as I've tried to reconcile the rational scientific worldview with the experiences I've had. I now believe that the way that we see things is inaccurate. It's shaped by our physical senses which, in turn, have evolved to protect us and enable us to survive and reproduce in the physical world. But though we spend our days and nights immersed in this sea of sensory information, and though our brains are evolved to work with the data coming in from our senses, I believe that there is another reality that's not perceived by our senses, and in that reality there is no separation at all between individuals. Rather, all of us co-exist somehow in the same place. So things that seem to be ESP or mysterious linkages between people and events really don't entail connections over a distance at all, because there is no distance separating us. *We are all here, together, right now.* So because we're all in the same place, my thoughts can affect you, and vice versa. The stronger the emotion, the stronger the effect. And so if my mind is quiet and receptive, I can detect these effects and act on them, and possibly I can even cause things to happen in the world that affect others.

To be honest, I have absolutely no idea where this other plane of reality is. People with religious or spiritual points of view seem to be comfortable talking about these nonphysical realities, whether it's Christians talking about heaven or Eckists talking about the many planes of existence. But scientists, who have some powerful tools, have never detected these. So it's a puzzle. Where exactly are these other planes, and how can they be so faint that science can't detect them, but so powerful that they can cause a plane to have engine trouble – and not bad enough trouble to crash the plane, but just enough trouble to put me in a hotel room in Bombay with my new friend? I don't know. There's an awful lot of nonphysical stuff that's unaccounted for, somewhere. Maybe this is the "missing mass" in the universe that has caused physicists to posit the existence of dark matter and dark energy, but that's just a half-baked idea. But I'm sure that all this stuff – all the heavens and hells, the astral planes, the nirvanas and Valhallas and all the rest – all exist somewhere, and eventually science will detect this and open up a huge and incredibly important new area of rational inquiry.

Back in the USA

I'd been in India for ten weeks, and that was more than enough time for me to adjust to life in a world with far fewer material goods than I'd been used to. When I returned to the U.S., I was overwhelmed for a while by all the stuff that everyone had. Even my mom's house, which was modest by American standards, seemed to be bursting at the seams with furniture. There were cars everywhere instead of bicycles and rickshaws, and there was so much food!

Eventually, of course, I readjusted. I went back to work at my dad's store, hanging the Tibetan carpet on the wall and putting the brassware up for sale on a countertop. I looked up Maureen's mother, the composer Marga Richter, who lived just up the road from Huntington Village. Her husband, Alan Skelly, was a philosophy professor at a nearby university. Marga offered to teach me to play the piano, and we became good friends. Once she offered me a taste of some yogurt she'd made, and it was very good. I asked her where she got her culture. "Julliard, of course!" she shot back.

Marga encouraged me to write music, and I wrote a couple of Eckankar-inspired piano pieces which, in retrospect, weren't all that bad. Since I was also studying computer science at New York Tech, I also wrote a primitive

computer program that created melodies using a random number generator and some basic musical rules, and we experimented with playing these melodies on the piano. Marga's composing was on a completely different scale than mine, of course, and I listened to her most famous composition, *Landscapes of the Mind*, many times, attempting to understand it and, as a consequence of that effort, expanding my understanding of what music could be.

Alan Skelly, Marga Richter, Maureen Skelly, and Maureen's new husband from India.

As my Eckankar studies progressed, I became eligible for my Second Initiation which normally comes after about two years of study. There isn't really a First Initiation, since that is said to occur when the student first commits to the Eckankar teaching, so the Second is really the first physical initiation. Just before I was scheduled to have the initiation, I had a dream. I was walking along a beach, and came upon a thick cable of some sort that was lying on the beach. My companion told me that I could touch it if I wanted. I did, and felt a strong electrical current pour through my body. This, I realized after I woke up, was the inner version of the initiation I was about to take. I received my outer Second Initiation shortly afterwards, from a higher initiate named Katie King in New York City. At that initiation I was given a secret word, a mantra, that I was instructed to use as part of my spiritual exercises.

Carver Street

I moved out of my mom's house and rented a room in a house on Jericho Turnpike in Huntington. On my second evening as a tenant there, there was a knock on the door, and we heard someone say in a deep voice, "Police, open up!" Someone opened the door. A half-dozen teens and young adults rushed in, brandishing knives and at least one gun. They took everyone's wallets, then searched the house for drugs. Not finding any, they left. Later it turned out that one of the tenants in the house actually knew these guys, and their notion that there were drugs in the house was not unfounded.

This seemed like a poor choice of housing, so I moved out the following day. My next stop was a rooming house in Huntington Village, where I lived for a couple of months. Finally I got an apartment on Carver Street, a few blocks from my dad's store. I needed a roommate, so at a local Eckankar function I asked Michael Cavallo, another Eckist about my age, if he wanted to share the apartment with me. He moved in, and we became close friends and have remained close for fifty years. At the time, Michael was exploring his identity as a gay man, and he brought a series of friends and lovers to the apartment, giving me a good second-hand insight into the gay social world.

Michael with bird.

I went with him to a local gay bar once, just for fun, and it was an eye-opening experience to be the object of other men's attention and desire. As a straight guy, I'd grown accustomed to the role of being the one to take the initiative in new social encounters with women, and so this role reversal, having guys come up to me, making small talk but obviously interested in something else, was new and actually kind of nice. However, I had no interest in sex with men, so a bit of arms-length flirting was about the extent of it.

Well, ok, there was one experience that went beyond flirting. I went to an Eckankar seminar in Connecticut where I met a guy, a physics major as I recall. We got along ok, and he surprised me by writing me a letter asking if he could come visit me for a few days. Sure, why not, I replied. So he came to visit, and we spent the day hanging around Huntington Village. That

Michael looking into my van.

night we returned to my rented room (this was when I was living in the rooming house before moving to Carver Street). We talked for a while, but when it got late I brushed my teeth and got into bed, expecting him to go to sleep in his sleeping bag on the floor. Instead, he just stood over my bed for a while, not saying anything, just staring at me with a look of indecision on his face. This was odd, I thought, but I had no idea what was going on in his mind, so I just said good night and went to sleep. Nothing else happened, and the next day he drove back to Connecticut. A few days later he wrote me another letter, professing his love and affection for me. Unfortunately (for him, anyway) I had neither love nor affection for him, and so I had to gently discourage him from having any more contact with me.

Living with Michael I became completely comfortable with him and his gay friends. Michael was going through all sorts of personal growth challenges – moving from his Catholic upbringing to becoming an Eckist, coming out of the closet as a gay man, and getting his life in gear by changing from a quality control worker at a manufacturing facility to studying to be a chiropractor. Since I was going through personal transformations of my own, we got along great.

The Drag Race

One night Michael and I were sitting in a diner in Hicksville, about a 20 minute drive (at normal speed) from the Carver Street apartment. We'd arrived by separate cars. Somehow the conversation turned to road racing. One of us, I forget who, said half joking, "Race you back to the apartment!" Immediately we both got up, threw some money on the table, ran out of the diner, jumped into our cars, and screeched out of the parking lot and onto the road. This was late, but not very late, in the evening in a crowded suburban area. Normally there would have been lots of cars on the road. But the universe smiled on us this night, and there was not a single other car, police or otherwise, anywhere on the ten mile route from the diner to the apartment. We raced at top speed down Woodbury Road, Michael in front and me close on his tail. We got to a traffic light on Jericho Turnpike but it was green as we sped through the intersection. We were both going at top speed, skidding around curves and flooring it on the straightaways. Finally we got to Huntington Village. As we came down the final block before getting to New York Avenue, I roared around into the left lane and passed him as we finally stopped at the traffic light. We pulled up at the apartment, tires smoking.

Obviously this was insane, and probably the most dangerously stupid thing I've ever done. But we survived, and I've never had any desire since then to race.

My not-really-a-drag racing car, buried in the blizzard of 1978.

Moving Floie

Mom's older sister Floie was tall and awkward, both physically and socially. She never married. Apparently she had a boyfriend/suitor early on, but from what I heard, the family liked him but Florence decided not to marry him. Mom recalled that around age 30, at the same time that Mom and Dad were married, Floie was living in St. Louis and was having "a nervous breakdown." She was hospitalized with what was probably schizophrenia. She seemed to have recovered from this, thought I don't know if she was on medication or therapy or just grew out of it somehow.

Floie devoted most of her life to earning a Ph.D. in psychology, which we all believed was an effort to live up to the memory of her father, the successful doctor. It took her an extremely long time. Her final thesis, "The Stimulus Barrier: An Experimental Study" was submitted to her dissertation committee at the New School for Social Research in January 1973, when she was 55 years old. I have a copy of the dissertation. It's 126 typewritten pages and is actually quite good. She was awarded her Ph.D., but having spent so much of her life working on her degree, she never achieved much professional success. She worked in the field of psychological

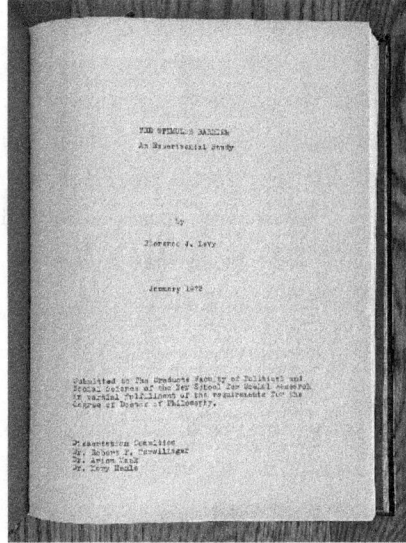

Title page of Floie's unpublished doctoral dissertation, January 1973.

testing and lived alone in a small apartment in New Rochelle, just north of New York City. Eventually she moved to a publicly funded and dilapidated nursing home where she lived her final years.

I liked Floie. Sometime around 1976 she moved to a different apartment. I offered to help her move and asked Mike Cavallo to help out. We rented a U-Haul truck and drove it from where we lived in Huntington to her place in the city. Unfortunately I ended up driving on Northern State Parkway, which was restricted to passenger cars only and had a number of bridges with low clearance that were designed specifically to prevent trucks like ours from driving on it.

We drove for a few miles without incident. But somewhere in Nassau County we came to a bridge that was too low for us to pass underneath. I stopped the truck in the middle of the highway. We got out and looked at the clearance, or lack thereof, and saw that it would not have helped to deflate the tires to pass underneath. So we got back in the truck and having no other option, I began to back the truck up, flashing the lights and honking the horn and hoping that nobody would crash into us. After backing up a couple of hundred yards without a collision, I looked to the right and saw some homes in a residential neighborhood near the highway. Well, I thought, we have to get off this highway before something really bad happens. So I drove the truck up onto the grassy strip on the side of the highway and straight through a wooded area, crashing through trees and leaving some serious scrapes on the truck body. We kept going and finally passed between two houses and lurched onto a side street. Somehow we managed to find our way onto the truck-friendly Long Island Expressway and continued on our way to meet up with Floie.

When Floie became frail and had to move to a nursing home, we moved her furniture and other personal things into a storage unit somewhere. She died on August 22, 1994, a few months after her stepmother Doris. Mom and I went to the storage unit to decide what to do with everything. I expected that Mom would want to keep some mementos of her sister, who was the only member of her family that she was close to. But for some reason Mom became frustrated and angry, and decided that she didn't want anything at all. We ended up giving away or throwing away absolutely everything that was in the storage unit.

Like a Molecule

One of my best friends at the time was Beth Quenneville, a fellow Eckist. We spent a lot of time together, just as friends. One day we were riding on my motorcycle, a Suzuki 380cc. It was a cold day and I mentioned how chilly it was. "I'm not cold at all," Beth responded. "How can you not be cold?" I asked. She said, "It's easy. Just be a molecule."

This made perfect sense to me, even though it's impossible for me to explain exactly why. It has something to do with removing

My molecular friend Beth Quenneville.

the barrier between self and non-self. The self might experience being cold, but the rest of the world (the non-self) is just fine. So be like a molecule, remove the boundary between you and the rest of the world, and instantly you're warm and comfy!

Leadership in Eckankar

Once I got my second initiation in Eckankar, I was permitted to lead satsang classes. I volunteered to lead a Satsang I class, which was the introductory class for new members, and started it in the Carver Street apartment. Two new people showed up, both with same first name: Michelle Readinger and Michelle Focardi. The class met twice a month for a year. Michelle Readinger finished up the class but did not continue. But Michelle Focardi and I became close friends, starting a stormy and complicated relationship that lasted for many years. She was a friend, my on-and-off (mostly off) girlfriend, my roommate at Carver Street, and my partner in running various Eckankar events on Long Island.

In addition to leading classes, I also started the first Eckankar newsletter on Long Island, called the *Soul Travel Press*. (This is one of the few things I have in common with Walt Whitman, who also lived in Huntington and started a small local paper, the *Long Islander*, in 1838). I was the editor, lead writer, and layout guy. Once a month I pasted together the 8 pages of the newsletter using scissors and scotch tape, then ran it off on a copier. Then I hand-collated and stapled them and mailed them off to local ECKists.

I also wrote a couple of articles for Eckankar's national monthly publication, ECK World News. The first was *UFO's: The New Mythology*, which ran as the lead story in the March 1975 issue. The second, *The New Scientists*, ran as the lead story in the June 1978 issue.

Shortly after the UFO story appeared in ECK World News, I was sitting in the living room of the apartment with Michael and Michelle, watching the *I Claudius* mini-series on Channel 13, the local public television station. The phone rang. Michelle picked it up. She turned to look at me with her eyes wide, and said, "It's Helen Frye. For you." Helen Frye was a legend in the international Eckankar community. She was a high initiate in Eckankar, a major financial donor, and had generously given her Wings of the Wind ranch

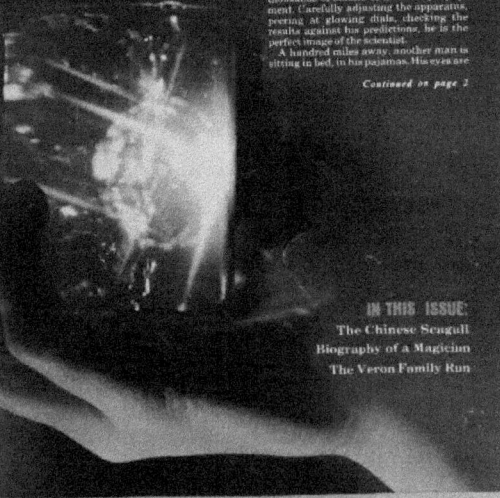

My two cover stories for the ECK World News, March 1975 and June 1978.

in Sedona, Arizona to the Eckankar organization to use as a retreat center. Helen was calling me to chat about my article on UFO's. We had a nice talk, though I can't remember any of the details.

Around this time I was thinking seriously about going to Israel. This was not the sort of Zionist pilgrimage that Jewish people often do, I just thought it would be interesting to visit for a while and see the Holy Land. I made some tentative plans to visit a kibbutz called Kiryat Anavim in the Judean Hills, and was working on travel plans. But Elsie Dettman, one of the local Eckankar leaders, pulled me aside at a class. She told me, a bit reluctantly, that the previous night she'd had a dream in which someone had told her in no uncertain terms, "Tell Jeff not to go to Israel." I knew Elsie well enough to know that she was not making this up. So I took her advice and cancelled my travel plans. But I never learned anything about why I shouldn't have gone.

Retreat at Cormaria

One memorable experience was a two day retreat that the local Eckankar leaders put on at Cormaria, a retreat house and mansion in Sag Harbor on the North Fork of Long Island. This was in 1974, when I was 21 years old. The guest of honor at the retreat was Tom Flamma, a well-known and controversial Eckist. Tom was a balding, bespectacled and overweight man in his late 50's or early 60's. He'd had a long and colorful life as a metaphysical writer and speaker, before finding and joining Eckankar in his later

The Cormaria retreat center on Long Island

years. Since Eckankar wanted to avoid being lumped in with metaphysical groups like the Rosicrucians, Tom was often perceived as a nuisance and "off message" by the Eckankar organization. But he was certainly a magnetic and compelling person. He could sit and tell stories for hours. He seemed to always have one foot in the physical world and the other in the inner worlds.

Like a Moth

At one Eckankar major seminar Tom was scheduled to give a talk, but the room that was reserved for his talk was unavailable. Everyone milled around the hallway, unsure what to do next. Tom stood stock still, eyes half-closed, then suddenly opened them, pointed down the hallway, and shouted "That way!" leading the crowd to larger available room.

The Cormaria retreat consisted of a couple of dozen local ECKists and Tom. There clearly was a lot that Tom wanted to say, so he planted himself in a big overstuffed chair in the main living room of the retreat center, with all of us seated around him like kids around a campfire. He'd laid down a ground rule in the beginning that we were not allowed to tape-record him, but Bill and Elsie Dettman, the honorary grandfather and grandmother of all Eckists on Long Island, brought a small tape recorder with them and tried to hide it as they recorded Tom's talks. Tom certainly saw it, but didn't say anything about it.

Tom talked practically nonstop for the entire two and a half days, only pausing briefly to eat and take short breaks. He talked about the prophesied return of Jesus – "Last time *I* talked to Jesus, he said let 'em wait." He told stories about the many lifetimes he'd lived, and noted how often he'd died at a young age and how unusual it was for him to be as old as he was in this current lifetime. He said he'd been a soldier many times and often died in battle, most recently as a German soldier in World War II. (This was interesting, as I'd had a vivid dream once of being a young man running across urban rooftops and being captured and killed by German soldiers, probably also in World War II.)

A week after the retreat ended, we got word that Tom Flamma had died, or in Eckankar terminology, translated. For the next issue of the *Soul Travel Press* I wrote a story about Tom and the retreat, and ran it on the front page accompanied by a beautiful pen-and-ink sketch of Tom created by local artist and Eckist Kevin McMahon

Sketch of Tom Flamma, by Kevin McMahon.

during the retreat. It was by far the best rendering of Tom that I'd ever seen. Later, I heard that Eckankar was going to run an article in *ECK World News* about Tom's passing and I thought it would be a good idea to send them the sketch. I searched all over my apartment but could not locate it anywhere. A few years later it appeared on the floor in my bedroom.

Ten years after Cormaria, I wrote up a story about the weekend called "Tommy and the Gimmes" and submitted it to Eckankar, but they didn't run it.

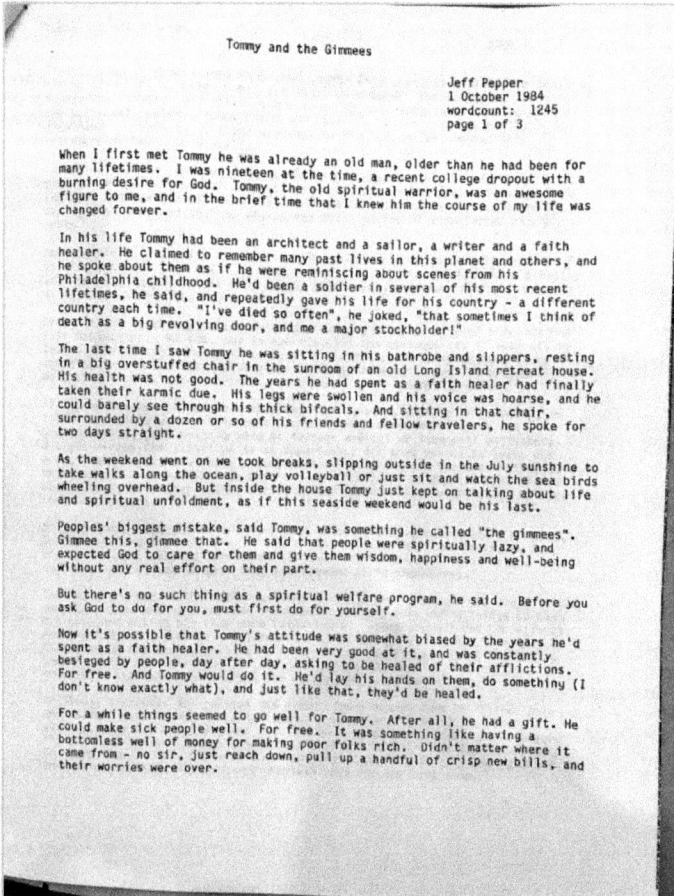

Tommy and the Gimmees

Jeff Pepper
1 October 1984
wordcount: 1245
page 1 of 3

When I first met Tommy he was already an old man, older than he had been for many lifetimes. I was nineteen at the time, a recent college dropout with a burning desire for God. Tommy, the old spiritual warrior, was an awesome figure to me, and in the brief time that I knew him the course of my life was changed forever.

In his life Tommy had been an architect and a sailor, a writer and a faith healer. He claimed to remember many past lives in this planet and others, and he spoke about them as if he were reminiscing about scenes from his Philadelphia childhood. He'd been a soldier in several of his most recent lifetimes, he said, and repeatedly gave his life for his country - a different country each time. "I've died so often", he joked, "that sometimes I think of death as a big revolving door, and me a major stockholder!"

The last time I saw Tommy he was sitting in his bathrobe and slippers, resting in a big overstuffed chair in the sunroom of an old Long Island retreat house. His health was not good. The years he had spent as a faith healer had finally taken their karmic due. His legs were swollen and his voice was hoarse, and he could barely see through his thick bifocals. And sitting in that chair, surrounded by a dozen or so of his friends and fellow travelers, he spoke for two days straight.

As the weekend went on we took breaks, slipping outside in the July sunshine to take walks along the ocean, play volleyball or just sit and watch the sea birds wheeling overhead. But inside the house Tommy just kept on talking about life and spiritual unfoldment, as if this seaside weekend would be his last.

Peoples' biggest mistake, said Tommy, was something he called "the gimmees". Gimmee this, gimmee that. He said that people were spiritually lazy, and expected God to care for them and give them wisdom, happiness and well-being without any real effort on their part.

But there's no such thing as a spiritual welfare program, he said. Before you ask God to do for you, must first do for yourself.

Now it's possible that Tommy's attitude was somewhat biased by the years he'd spent as a faith healer. He had been very good at it, and was constantly besieged by people, day after day, asking to be healed of their afflictions. For free. And Tommy would do it. He'd lay his hands on them, do something (I don't know exactly what), and just like that, they'd be healed.

For a while things seemed to go well for Tommy. After all, he had a gift. He could make sick people well. For free. It was something like having a bottomless well of money for making poor folks rich. Didn't matter where it came from - no sir, just reach down, pull up a handful of crisp new bills, and their worries were over.

I became fully committed to my life as an Eckist. In addition to running satsang classes and publishing the *Soul Travel Press*, I also traveled to three major Eckankar seminars every year (the Spring Seminar in the spring, the

Youth Conference in the summer, and the largest, the Worldwide, in the fall). I went door to door in commercial areas, asking merchants permission to put up posters advertising local Eckankar events.

At one seminar, I went to a restaurant with some friends. It was a self-serve style restaurant where the food was displayed in a glass case. Customers went up to a counter, pointed to what they wanted, and got it. One of the items on display was a piece of meat on a dish. I looked at it. Something in my mind said, "This is not food." That was it. I became a vegetarian on the spot. Actually to be completely accurate, I became a pescatarian, since I generally eat some seafood once a week or so. But I haven't deliberately eaten any meat since then, other than on business trips to Japan where turning down food would have been a serious faux pas.

Death Threat

Taking more of a leadership role, I organized a "Day of Eck" at a local VFW hall, which was memorable for being the only time in my life I'd received a credible death threat. The hall was in Halesite, a little town where Revolutionary War soldier Nathan Hale supposedly said, "I regret that I have but one life to give for my country" just before he was hanged by the British.

A young woman had been attending one of my Eckankar classes. Apparently her family were fundamentalist Christian and were convinced that Eckankar was a satanic cult, that her soul was in mortal danger, and that I was doing the devil's work. The woman arrived at the Day of Eck and told me that members of her family were coming to kill me that day. This was upsetting news! I went into the men's room and pondered this for a while. I finally concluded that running away or changing my plans for the day would be cowardly, and my only option was to continue on with my original plan, trusting in Spirit for the rest. The Day of Eck went off without a hitch, or a gunshot. One member of the woman's family did show up, thankfully unarmed, and we had an intense but ultimately futile conversation where he failed to convince me to accept Jesus and I failed to convince him that Eckankar wasn't a cult. At the end of an exhilarating but exhausting day, I plunked myself down in a folding chair in the back of the room, just to catch my breath and soak it all in. Michelle came up and, without a word, just sat next to me and kept me company for a while.

So many stories I could tell from my time as an Eckist. Once I went to a major seminar in Tulsa Oklahoma, and I arrived a couple of days early so I could volunteer to help set up. The crew was putting together the stage, and they needed a certain kind of chair for Sri Darwin Gross. It had to be a tall metal chair that could rotate so Darwin could move it around and face different parts of the audience. So they sent me out to find one. I walked around downtown Tulsa for a while, then wandered into a large office building. There, in the middle of the office, was exactly the chair that I was looking for. Not knowing any better, I asked someone in the office if I could borrow the chair for a few days, explaining its intended use. Sure, they said, no problem, just bring it back when you're finished. So I taped a note on the back of the chair saying where it should be returned, and brought it back to the seminar. Since I left as soon as the event was over, I never found out if they returned the chair or not.

An important element in Eckankar is the "darshan," the gaze of the Master. I had never met Paul Twitchell of course, since he'd died before I joined the organization. And although I'd seen Darwin up close several times (back then, he would walk through the crowd shaking hands at the end of his keynote talk at the major seminars), I'd never actually met him. Then, at one major seminar, I was sitting in a chair in a hotel lobby. There, a dozen paces away, Darwin was sitting with a couple of his assistants. Nobody was talking to him and he seemed somehow available. Time seemed to stand still. Without even thinking about it, I got up, walked over to him and stopped a foot or two away. He looked up at me, not saying a word, and just took my hand. The experience was incredibly powerful. It was like meeting Aslan the lion in the *Chronicles of Narnia* stories by C. S. Lewis. Darwin didn't say anything, but when he looked at me, his gaze left me feeling both lightheaded and energized.

The Ouija Board

Michael and I were sitting around at his parents' house in Hicksville Long Island. Somehow we found a Ouija (pronounced "weejie") board that must have belonged to one of his many brothers. The Ouija board had a laminated board like the kind used in Monopoly, and it's covered with some ornate artwork, two arcs of letters A through M and N through Z, plus a row of numbers 0 through 9, and the words YES and NO near the top. There is also a slider gizmo that you could move around on the board with your hand and point to the numbers, letters and other items on the board. The idea is that two people (players?) would each put their hands on the pointer, someone would ask a question, and the pointer would move in some mysterious way to answer the questions by pointing to things on the board. Supposedly the Ouija board is a tool used to communicate with spirits beyond the physical world, but both Michael and I believed it was a crock.

Nevertheless, it was a quiet day, so we sat down and started asking questions. We started with the easy obvious ones, like "Is anyone out there?" Nothing happened at first. Then the pointer started to move. Just like in a B horror movie, I looked at Michael and asked, "Are you moving this thing?"

"No," he replied, "you must be doing it." The pointer was definitely moving across the board, seemingly under its own power, and it ended up pointing to the "YES" box. Somewhat unnerved, we kept asked more yes/no questions. From the answers we gathered that we were talking to someone, or something, who knew Michael. And apparently liked him. A lot.

"What's your name?" we asked, and the pointer quickly spelled out a girl's name.

At this point we were too deeply involved to take our hands off the pointer. Suddenly, without either of us saying or asking anything, the pointer slid quickly to the letter "T," then up and left to "I," then right to "M." Sensing that something complicated was coming, I kept my left hand on the pointer and used my right hand to jot down the letters that came quickly, with no spaces in between. It was coming too quickly for me to understand, so I just wrote without thinking. Finally the pointer stopped moving. I looked down at what I'd written:

TIMEHASNOPLACEINYOURFACEILOVEYOU

Yike. We'd been fooling around with this thing, but it was getting serious quickly. And no, there was no way that the two of us could have consciously coordinated our hands to spell this out. Just a few more questions, we decided. "Are you alive?" we asked. The pointer jumped to YES. "Can we call you?" The pointer wiggled then returned to YES. Then without us prompting it, the pointer jumped to the row of numbers and spelled out a seven digit phone number. Whatever the person or spirit was, it was nearby. No area code.

There was a phone on the wall, so we called. An older man answered. "Is _____ home?" we asked. "Who's calling?" he demanded, angry and suspicious. "Umm... a friend." "Don't call here again," he snapped, and hung up.

That was it. We put the board away and never touched it again.

(Oddly, I showed this story to Michael, and he has absolutely no memory of it ever happening. But I'm sure it did!)

What was interesting about this experience is that it was, to me, clear evidence of the existence of the non-physical. I'd had a couple of experiences in this category before, most notably the out-of-body experience at my mom's house after reading *Journeys Out of The Body*. Each one of these, though rare, reinforced my commitment to explore the nature of the universe through my work in Eckankar.

Trouble in Eckankar

As time went on, I received more initiations in Eckankar, rising from a second initiate (permitted to lead Satsang classes) to third, fourth, fifth (a so-called "higher initiate" permitted to give initiations to others), and later the sixth and seventh initiations. Each one consisted of an inner initiation that generally happened in a dream, as well as an outer initiation given by an Eckist who was at a higher level that the one receiving the initiation. In the first few initiations the initiator gives the initiate their mantra or secret word, but for the higher initiations, one receives one's own mantra in a contemplation exercise during the initiation ceremony. Once I became a fifth initiate, I was authorized to give initiations to others, and I performed a couple of second initiations at a major Eckankar seminar.

During this time there were signs of trouble within the Eckankar organization. Darwin Gross had taken on the leadership of the organization upon the death of Paul Twitchell, and had immediately married Paul's widow Gail Twitchell. This of course led to speculation but it was accepted by most Eckists with little difficulty; one of my friends said, "Well, after you're married to one Living Eck Master, it only makes sense to marry another one." But Darwin's leadership style was unlike Paul's. He didn't communicate well, he wrote almost nothing, and his management of the organization was erratic. One time he sent out a mass mailing to every member of Eckankar, printed on brightly colored paper, denying that he was having an affair with one of the women who worked in the Eckankar main office and basically telling everyone to just mind their own business.

One night I had a dream. I was in a large cavern with many rooms and alcoves. I saw Darwin there, but he appeared to be in distress. An older and wiser individual came over to me, gestured to Darwin, and simply said, "No music." This had a double meaning, because not only was Darwin a jazz musician, but the Eck itself was often compared to a stream of music or spiritual energy. I pondered the meaning of this dream quite a bit.

There was also an odd thing that happened one evening, when I went with Michael, our friend Joanne, Phil Dunn, and some other Eckist friends to see the film version of *Jonathan Livingston Seagull*, based on the bestseller by Richard Bach and with music by Neil Diamond. Even though the movie was panned by critics, I loved it and so did

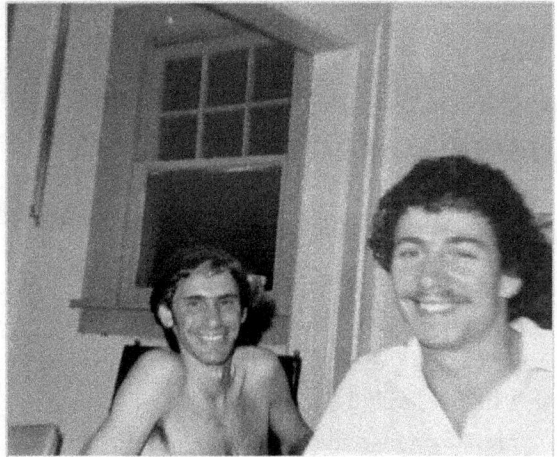

Phil Dunn and Michael Cavallo.

my friends. But while we were waiting for the film to start, the movie theater played some soft jazz over the speakers. One song came on, and I recognized it as one of Darwin's songs from his jazz album *It Just Is*. But it wasn't Darwin's

98

song; it was a song by another artist with almost identical melody and song structure to Darwin's song. I turned to one of my (non-musical) friends and said, "Hey, that sounds like one of Darwin's songs!" He listened for a bit and said that he couldn't hear the similarity. I jumped up and ran into the theater lobby to ask the popcorn seller what song was playing on the speakers. He looked at me oddly and said he had no idea. I let it go at the time, but later, I wondered if Darwin had in fact "borrowed" some of that song in his own. Of course, it's also possible that Darwin wrote the tune first and someone else borrowed it.

 Later, after I'd moved to Pittsburgh, things came to a head. Two things happened within a few days of each other. The first was that I received a letter from the Eckankar international office, inviting me to take the fifth initiation (making me a higher initiate) and also offering me the position of Area Representative for the greater Pittsburgh region. This position was both administrative and spiritual, and I would be replacing three other (and much older) higher initiates who jointly held the position: Betty Rapin, Terry Eles, and Margaret Philippi.

The second event was the online publication of David Lane's exposé of Eckankar.

David Lane was a young divinity student who had a strong personal interest in Eastern religion and spiritual cults. He became interested in Eckankar and did a substantial amount of research on the organization's origins and practices. The result was a short self-published book, *The Making of a Spiritual Movement: The Untold Story of Paul Twitchell and Eckankar.* Written in 1977, Amazon sums up the book nicely:

> "One of the first critical studies ever done on the hidden history of Paul Twitchell and Eckankar. It was first completed as a term paper when David Lane was only 20 years old as an undergraduate student at CSUN. Later it evolved into a controversial book which caused a worldwide stir in the Eckankar organization. Contains extensive documentation on how Paul Twitchell created a fictional mythology about himself while denying his association with certain spiritual teachers. Also contains extensive correlations of Twitchell's extensive plagiarism."

Lane's book was just a term paper, but it was picked up by a Christian anti-cult group called the Spiritual Counterfeiters Project, which was founded in 1973 and describes itself as "a frontline ministry confronting the occult, the cults, and the New Age movement." SCP was (and apparently still is) committed to stamping out any religion or spiritual practice that is inconsistent with their own fundamentalist Christian beliefs. They published their own book, *Eckankar, a Hard Look at a New Religion*, based on Lane's research, in an effort to discredit and destroy Eckankar. They nearly succeeded.

Much of the information that Lane unearthed was extremely damaging to Eckankar's credibility. The most serious was a compilation of over 400 side-by-side comparisons of writings of Paul Twitchell and other authors, demonstrating beyond doubt that Twitchell plagiarized many of his ideas and writings from others. Most of these other writings were from the Radhasoami branch of Hinduism that Twitchell had studied in his time in India, and especially *The Path of the Masters* written by Julian P. Johnson and published by the Radhasoami organization. Lane, who had also studied Radhasoami for five years and was initiated into it, made a convincing case that Paul Twitchell was not, in fact, the 971st in an unbroken line of Eck Masters going back millions of years, but rather, was a skilled popularizer of ancient wisdom, adapting this particular branch of mystical Hinduism for a modern American audience.

Lane's facts were hard to dispute, but the interpretation of the facts is where things got interesting. The fundamental Christians behind SCP were delighted to use Lane's research to discredit Eckankar, to brand it a destructive cult, and to try and convince Eckists to abandon the teaching and come back to Christianity. Lane himself made no such claims; he never said that the teachings of Eckankar were not valid, he simply said that the individual who brought these teachings to the Western world had misrepresented their origins.

Eckankar's reaction was swift. They sent out a notice to all Eckists saying that anti-Eckankar propaganda was being spread by SCP, and that members of Eckankar should not read Lane's book. My first reaction, of course, was to read the book, which was readily available online.

The material in the book was compelling – it was well researched, well written, and backed up with references and direct quotations from the books Paul

Twitchell had apparently plagiarized. (There was also some nastiness and general bad-mouthing of Eckankar in particular and non-Christian paths in general that was layered on top of Lane's book by the SCP people, but I just ignored that.) After reading the book, I was left with the obvious question: now that it was clear that the founder of Eckankar plagiarized much of his writings and fabricated most of the spiritual path's backstory, was Eckankar still of value to me, and could I serve as a leader in the organization?

I wasn't sure about the first, but I was sure about the second. I wrote back to the Eckankar office and said that I respectfully declined their invitation to take on the Area Rep position. I explained that after reading Lane's work, I didn't feel that I could present the Eckankar teachings in their current form to the public. The office wrote back, accepting my decision but still offering me the fifth initiation. They also sent some pre-written materials which attempted to explain away Lane's work, saying that he simply didn't understand the depth of the Eckankar teachings.

On December 26, 1986, I received a personal handwritten letter from Sri Harold Klemp, who had replaced Darwin as Living Eck Master in 1981. In the letter Harold did not try to actually dissuade me from leaving Eckankar, nor did he argue with the facts that I'd presented. Instead, he suggested a spiritual exercise that might help me to determine whether or not the Eckankar teachings were valid. I was honestly impressed that Sri Harold would take the time to write to me.

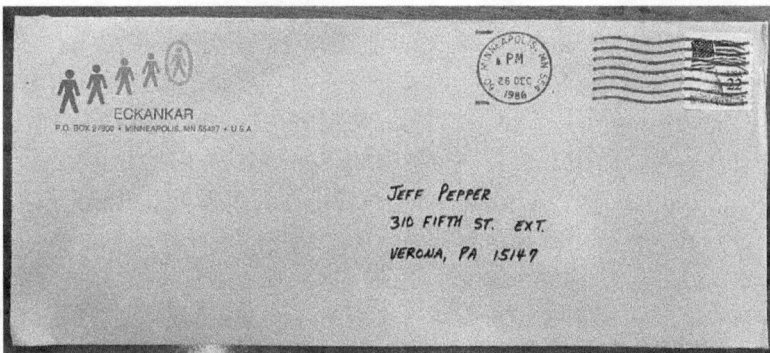

Handwritten letter from Sri Harold Klemp, 1986.

So I took the fifth initiation (and later, the sixth and seventh) and remained in the organization for several more years. I think a lot of my reluctance to leave was derived from Eckankar's claims that someone who leaves the teaching essentially gives up all the spiritual progress they've made up to that point and will be doomed to reincarnate again and again until, at some future point, they finally accept the Living Eck Master and get back on the path.

Notably, this threat of punishment did not end with the passing of Paul Twitchell, but continued through the times of his successors, Darwin Gross and Harold Klemp. In one of his spiritual discourses written for third-year Eckankar students, Sri Harold stated:

> The wrath of the ECK crashes down upon anybody who is still a slave to the ego and deserts the Master. Not once will he see the connection between his betrayal of the ECK and the horrendous troubles that strike him like a plague on every hand. And thus, he goes downward on the spiral of awareness until he leaves this body in hopeless despair, still wondering why the fates have treated him so.

> -- Harold Klemp, Satsang III, #8

Having invested almost two decades in the path, I was reluctant to throw away all my apparent progress in escaping the great wheel of reincarnation. Only later did I come to realize that this was a trick, a transparent attempt by the Eckankar organization to keep followers from leaving. It's an old trick: the Catholic Church threatens eternal damnation, Islam threatens punishment in the next world for apostasy, and so on. Once I recognized this threat for what it was, I was able to make a final break from Eckankar.

And I have to say, since leaving Eckankar I have certainly had ups and downs in my life, but I have not had "horrendous troubles that strike like a plague on every hand." I have not gone on a "downward spiral of awareness" and I currently have no plans to leave my physical body in "hopeless despair," although I suppose that still could happen. But overall I actually feel good about my life, my state of consciousness, and the prospect of leaving the physical body when the time comes. I am grateful for the time I spent with Eckankar, the things I learned, the experiences I had, and the good friends I met and who have stayed friends throughout my life.

I can honestly say that, after living for seven decades, reading untold numbers of books on spirituality and having studied a spiritual path for 25 years, right now I have no idea whatsoever about what happens after death. On one hand, I've read and heard literally thousands of stories of people passing beyond the gates of death, experiencing things and returning to share what they've seen. I've read many stories of past life recall, and I've had personal experiences that lead me to believe that reincarnation is possible. But on the other hand, the rational and scientific part of my mind says that these are illusions, byproducts of a brain under severe stress or suffering from delusions.

Whether or not there is actually life after death, my *desire* to believe in it is a byproduct of the design of the human mind, which has evolved with only one goal: protect and preserve the physical self and pass on its genes to the next generation. Minds that do this successfully are able to pass on their design to their descendants; minds that don't just disappear from the gene pool. So like it or not, we are the proud owners (or inhabitants, or prisoners) of minds that are designed for individual survival. And for that reason, stories about surviving after death are appealing.

Here's a quick mental exercise to demonstrate this. Suppose someone offers you the opportunity to download your brain into an android, reproducing every nerve and synapse in computer hardware. And suppose they guarantee that the computer-based copy would think, feel and act exactly the same as you did, with the added benefit that the "new you" would be able to live for centuries. The only catch is that your current brain would have to be destroyed in the process. Looking at it objectively, this would be a big win for you because you'd lose nothing and essentially become immortal. But I'm guessing that you would not like this idea at all, because that hardwired compulsion for self-preservation would be telling you that you would die, and we are programmed to see that as unacceptable.

And so, regardless of what *actually* happens after death, we all want to believe that we survive.

So what do I believe about life after death? If I had to be pinned down, I'd probably say this: the true nature of the universe is infinitely greater than what we can ever hope to perceive or understand with our evolution-optimized senses and brains. So when we die, we discard all that. What happens next is unknowable, but is probably not simply the end of things. We probably continue, in some fashion, into something else. It's unlikely to be a straightforward case of the individual ego continuing with all its memories, emotions and personality left intact. It's probably something else. But trying to understand it is futile. Better to focus on where we are now, and let the future take care of itself. As Kabir said, "The musk is in the deer. The deer need not search for it, she merely looks for grass to eat."

The Laundromat

Let's back up a bit to when I was living on Long Island. I'd been working in my dad's hardware store for about four years. He had recently promoted me to Vice President, but the title didn't mean much in a company consisting of him, me, Annette the clerk, a surly and racist stockboy named Jerry, a part time bookkeeper, and Annette's cousin who installed the fireplace screens. The job wasn't bad, but it was repetitive and didn't offer much in the way of mental stimulation. Every day was much the same: wait on customers, restock shelves, sweep up, and count cash at the end of the day. From my dad's point of view I was in the role of apprentice, learning the ropes, but after a while it was clear to me that there were no more ropes to learn. The store ran itself, and we were just keep it going on the same track it had been running on for years. For a kid who'd been near the top of his class in school I was feeling that whatever abilities I had were going to waste. Still, I had no idea what else I wanted to do, and I did feel an obligation to help my dad out.

I was living in the Carver Street apartment with Michael. We didn't have a washing machine, so one day I took my laundry to the local laundromat. I was folding my clothes when a guy came over and we started talking. What struck me immediately was that this guy was not the usual hardware store customer. He was thoughtful and intelligent, clearly a professional or teacher of some kind. I can't remember exactly what we were talking about, something to do with chemistry, possibly related to the chemistry of washing clothes. I asked him at one point if he was a teacher. "No," he replied, "I'm a chemist."

This was, believe it or not, a major turning point in my life. It hit me that it was possible to do something complex and intellectually challenging with your life. I really, really enjoyed talking with this guy, and it was not the kind of conversation I'd ever had, or was ever likely to have, in the hardware store. That day, I decided to do something different with my life.

But what?

I went home and considered all the career directions that I could imagine, trying to decide which ones interested me. I was good in math and I liked new things, so computer science ended up at the top of the list. This was 1976 and computer science was a new and exciting field. It was years before the PC and decades before the internet, and computer science was closely tied to electrical engineering. It mainly had to do with doing binary math, designing circuits, writing assembly code, and using so-called high level languages like FORTRAN and COBOL to program large mainframe and timesharing computers.

I had done a little bit of programming in high school, simple programs written in the BASIC programming language. I was good at it, and it was fun. So I went to Huntington Library, picked out four books on computers and computer science, took them home, and read them all from cover to cover. By the end of the fourth book I was still interested. Taking that as an encouraging sign, I signed up for night school classes at New York Institute of Technology, and started my career in the tech industry.

The Bogus Equation

New York Institute of Technology was a small school with an impressive name that seemed to put it on a par with Caltech or MIT. But despite the world-class name it was just a community college with a relaxed admissions policy ("If you've got the money, we've got the classes") and a focus more on short term career training rather than on the research and advanced studies taking place at similar sounding institutions. But for me, restarting my education after four years of pushing a broom in a hardware store, it was perfect.

I started off with a couple of night school classes in math, which I aced with no trouble. Then I moved on to more career-specific courses. One of them was an electrical engineering course in low level computer programming, focusing on things like binary arithmetic ($10 + 10 = 100$), predicate calculus (if P and P -> Q, then Q), and the math behind simple electronic circuits. I loved all of it, and got straight A's for the first time in my life.

At one point we learned something called the Quine-McCluskey algorithm for minimizing a set of Boolean functions. It was developed in the 1950's and was used mainly to analyze and simplify a truth table – a useful skill at the time, because the simpler the truth table, the simpler and cheaper the electronic circuit that was needed to implement it in hardware.

For homework we were given a few pages of truth tables and told to simplify them using this method. After a couple of hours of doing this, it occurred to me that the method was tedious and inefficient, and could be improved by replacing several steps with a couple of shorter ones.

I showed my improved method to my professor, who encouraged me to write it up for possible publication in an academic journal. This was a completely new idea for me. I had no idea how to write a journal article, but I figured that at the very least the paper should be written in a learned style so it would appeal to the academics who would review it for publication.

So in search of academic trappings I went to see a math professor who I'd had for a previous course. I showed him my idea and asked him if he could help me put it into a more rigorous mathematical style instead of the simple step-by-step recipe that I'd developed. This in itself was not a mistake, but what followed was.

A few days later he handed me a long and completely incomprehensible equation, which he told me was the thing I'd asked for. The equation had lots of variables in it that made no sense to me and seemed to have no relation to the problem I was solving, but I figured he was the math professor so it must be ok. I thanked him and inserted the equation into my paper, along with a sentence or two of introduction, something along the lines of "Here's the math." That was the mistake.

I sent the paper around for review, but unsurprisingly, nobody was interested in publishing it, probably because of the math gibberish it contained. If I'd had the courage to say "no thanks" to the math professor's gift, who knows, maybe the paper would have been accepted for publication, and subsequent generations of electrical engineers would have shaved countless seconds off their circuit optimization by using the Quine-McCluskey-Pepper method.

Teaching Marta

One day, halfway through my final computer programming class at New York Tech, my instructor came up to talk with me during class. She said that one of the students in her class was having trouble and could use a bit of extra help, and would I be willing to tutor her? Of course I agreed. She introduced me to the student, who I already knew from the class: Marta Amieva, a middle aged Cuban woman with a big smile and a quick wit. I had no idea why she was in the class, and figured she was an empty nester interested in going back into the workforce with some new skills. We agreed that I would come over to her house once a week and help her with her programming assignments.

When I got to her house I was surprised by how big the place was. Marta told me that the house once belonged to Alice Coltrane, the famous jazz pianist and composer. OK, I thought, Marta is prosperous, no big deal, maybe her husband is in construction or something.

I worked with Marta for the rest of the semester. She was a quick study and did well. But she floored me when at the end of our tutoring sessions she offered me a summer job. Turns out that she wasn't just a housewife looking to make a few extra bucks. She was Vice President of International Systems and Data Communications for Republic National Bank in New York City. She'd been taking the computer science course in order to stay current with her technical skills so she could better manage the teams of programmers who worked for her. And she invited me to work as a summer intern at the bank.

That was the start of my first job in the tech industry. I didn't see Marta much after that, since she was in a big office a couple of floors up from where I worked with the other programmers. But she did come by and say hi from time to time.

There's an odd coda to this story. Several years later I received a phone call from someone who said that he worked for Republic National Bank. He said that there were some "grave concerns" about Marta, and he wanted to know if there was anything bad that I could say about her. Reading between the words, I gathered that some kind of power struggle was going on within the bank, and the forces that were opposing Marta were looking for reasons to get her demoted or fired. I told him that Marta was one of the nicest and most decent people I'd ever met, that she gave me my first programming job, and that there was nothing else I could (or wanted to) tell him. That was the end of that phone call.

The Bank Job

Republic National Bank was an odd bank. It had no branch locations, just a single building in midtown Manhattan. Their marketing seemed haphazard, consisting mainly of ads for free gifts in return for large deposits: "Buy a $3000 certificate of deposit and get a free 19 inch TV!" There were stories about the guy who ran this program. They said that he was so good at his job that the senior managers could tell him how much new deposit money they wanted to attract, and he could hit the target by tweaking the value of the free gift. So if the bank wanted more deposits, he'd just offer a bigger TV.

So, how did this odd little bank manage to afford its classy midtown office building? I found out one day. Since I was low man on the programming totem pole, most of my work focused on reports. Not creating new reports (at least not in the beginning), but tweaking existing reports. For example, one of the bank managers wanted his depositor report subtotaled by country of origin. I would get the assignment, and crawl through the BASIC code that generated the report and make it do what the manager wanted.

Of course, this required running reports against actual bank data. That's when I saw the names of some of the bank's customers, and how much they'd deposited. Many of the names were leaders of foreign governments, or departments within those governments, like (just to make one up) the Uzbekistan National Guard Reserve Account. That's when I realized that Republic's main business wasn't trading TV sets for four-figure deposits. It was managing the wealth of some of the world's richest clients and most secretive organizations.

Most of the time I worked on a backed up copy of the bank's database. But once I was part of a team that had to make a change to the bank's live database. That was probably the most excitement we had in the office all summer. After the changes were coded and reviewed, they had to be installed in the live database. One mistake and the bank's computer systems would at the very least be unavailable, and in the worst case be corrupted or deleted. So the head of the department sat down at a computer terminal, with all of us standing around behind him. For each line of instructions, he would first type the instructions but would not hit the Enter key. Then he would read the instructions out loud to the group, and wait for the senior team members to say it was ok (or, presumably, for one of the junior programmers to yell "WAIT!"). Only then would he hit the Enter key and send the instructions to the mainframe.

This was the summer of 1978. One of the bank's products was a 20 year note, which meant that the notes they were selling that summer were scheduled to mature in summer 1998. Since computer storage space was expensive back then, all of the bank's databases used a 2-digit shorthand for the year, so 1998 was stored as just "98". In another year or so the bank would start selling 20-year notes that would mature in the year 2000, which would be stored as "00". The bank's computer systems would try to do arithmetic calculations involving this zero date, and bad things would happen. So in my first summer job, I became one of the first wave of computer programmers working to solve the so-called Y2K (year 2000) problem. Obviously I was not the last. A couple of decades later I met a guy from Republic National Bank at a technology conference, and as a way of making small talk I mentioned that I was a summer intern there in 1978 and worked on solving the Y2K problem. "Oh yes," he replied with a smile, "we're still working on that."

Like a Moth

Part Two:
Health and Money

Move to Pittsburgh,
Early Entrepreneurial Attempts,
ServiceWare and Touchtown

Heading to Pittsburgh

New York Tech was an easy school academically, and I cruised through my coursework maintaining a 4.0 GPA. Things were going well and I was learning things, but it also became clear that I was not being challenged by the coursework. I also saw that the school's mission was to train workers for entry level jobs in business and industry, not to change the world. New York Tech was not going to help me reach the upper echelons of business or computer science. For that I'd need to find a much better school.

The field of artificial intelligence was in its infancy at the time and seemed to be poised to accomplish great things. So I decided to focus on that and find the best school that would take me. The three top AI programs in the United States at the time were Stanford University in California, MIT in Boston, and Carnegie Mellon University in Pittsburgh.

First I flew to California and visited Stanford. Pretty place, certainly not bad, although the people (at least, the few people who I met) were a bit stand-offish. Then I visited MIT which was impressive but also extremely geeky, totally focused on technology. For example, the school had a longstanding tradition of referring to buildings by their numbers rather than their names, so you might hear someone say "I'm heading over to 24, but I'll meet you in front of 20 at 5:00." I thought this was an ominous cultural sign.

That left CMU, which had a reputation for maintaining a healthy balance between the hard sciences (what's now called STEM) and the arts. I decided to try an unusual approach. Instead of writing to the admissions office I wrote directly to Dr. John McDermott, the head of the computer science department, sketching out a bit of my personal history and asking if he'd meet with me. He wrote back and agreed to meet with me. He also gave me a pre-meeting homework assignment: to read Dr. Daniel Dennett's book, *Content and Consciousness*. This was probably the most difficult book I'd ever read, but I thought it was cool that a computer science professor would want me to read a philosopher's book on the relationship between mind and body. He also gave the admission's office the heads-up that I was interested in applying.

The drive from Long Island across the state of Pennsylvania to Pittsburgh was beautiful, and the school had cleverly provided directions that routed me through some attractive residential streets on my way to the campus. I got there in late afternoon, walked around a bit, then decided it was time to look for a place to stay. I asked a bearded student for a hotel recommendation. "Best place to stay is the Edison Hotel downtown," he told me. "Just take Fifth Avenue all the way downtown, you can't miss it." I checked in, and found the place to be run-down, dirty and dangerous. In the morning I heard on the local news that someone had been murdered at the hotel the previous day. I switched to a different hotel for my second night.

Returning to campus, I met briefly with the admissions people, then headed over for my meeting with Dr. McDermott. He was one of the smartest and most incisive people I'd ever met, and I had so much trouble keeping up with him, especially when he grilled me on aspects of Dennett's book, that I felt sure I was never going to get in. But at the end of the meeting, he said that I was exactly the sort of person that he wanted in his department. Looking back, I don't think he was overwhelmed with my intellectual horsepower which was so inferior to his. I think he just liked my personal story and thought I'd be an interesting addition to his department.

He handed me off to a grad student who gave me a tour of the department, including the basement where many of the larger computers were. I saw another bearded grad student sitting at a green-screen computer terminal in the basement, running a space invaders game that the students had written. A Klingon had just appeared on the screen, cackling and saying, "Have a Coke!" before blasting the player to atoms.

Later that day, I met with the financial aid people. They told me that the decision of whether or not to accept a student was completely separate from the student's ability to pay the tuition. CMU first decided who they wanted, regardless of the student's ability to pay, then the financial aid department did whatever was needed to make sure the student could afford to come. Since I was living on my own (having moved out of my mom's house six years earlier) and had essentially no money at all, this was incredibly good news. It was also an example of what a great institution CMU was, and how by thinking deeply and clearly about problems they often came up with unique solutions.

Needless to say, I was sold on CMU. I called Michelle and her then-girlfriend Pat to tell them the good news, and I drove nonstop to Huntington except a brief stop for gas. When I got home, Michelle and Pat had a Sara Lee cheesecake and a half gallon of chocolate ice cream waiting for me, and together we ate it all.

Carnegie Mellon

My first semester at CMU was really, really hard. Up till then I'd never had to exert myself in school. Junior high, high school, two years at Clark, and a couple of years at NYIT were all easy; I could get B's without trying at all, and A's if I worked at it a bit or if the course material interested me. In those schools the instructors covered all the material in class, so as long as I paid attention and took good notes, it wasn't hard for me to get A's on the tests. And I generally didn't have much trouble with the papers and projects that were assigned.

But at CMU that simply didn't work. I soon discovered that in my math and computer science classes, every student was at the top of his or her class in high school. They were all as smart as me, and in most cases smarter. Most of them had better work habits too, and they worked hard on their assignments. The nature of the classwork was different too. The faculty at CMU didn't teach to the book; they expected that when you showed up for class you'd already read the textbook and understood it. This allowed the instructors to use class time for deeper discussions of the material. One of my favorite professors, Nobel laureate Dr. Herbert Simon, didn't even come to class with prepared lecture notes. At the start of class he'd ask us for a handful of questions or topics for discussion, and he'd jot them on the side of the board, then lecture on these topics for the next hour and a half. If you hadn't read the assignments before class you'd be lost in no time, and if he called on you and found you were unprepared, you wouldn't last long in his class.

So midway through the first semester I was flunking two of my classes and getting C's and D's in the rest. I couldn't blame it on partying; being 26 years old the school had placed me in Mudge Hall, a graduate student dorm that was deathly quiet compared to the undergrad dorms and frat houses. And my roommate was a professional engineer at AT&T who was spending a year on campus getting a Master's degree at his company's expense, so he wasn't much of a partyer either. So other than playing a lot of ping pong, working part time as a programmer at a local firm called Aptech, and going to local Eckankar meetings, I really had no major distractions, and there were no good excuses for my lousy performance. I was just lazy and unprepared.

I realized what was happening, and somehow got myself together and started working as hard as I needed to. I wasn't pulling too many all-nighters compared to, say, the engineering Ph.D. students in my dorm, who apparently never slept at all. But I worked hard enough to bring my grades up to a mix of A's and B's by the end of the first semester. One of the teaching assistants in my computer science course looked at the improvement in my grades over the semester and remarked, "Nice second derivative, Jeff!" which was what passed for humor in the computer science department. Overall, for the two years I was at CMU, I think my GPA was 3.7, good enough for the Dean's List.

Dr. McDermott was my faculty advisor for the first year. I'd meet with him every few weeks, until eventually I realized that he wasn't really all that interested in advising me, and I stopped seeing him. (I wondered if he would contact me to find out why I wasn't making any more appointments, but he never did.) But before our meetings ended, he helped me to realize that the best use of my time at CMU was not to devote it to classwork, but to get involved in research projects outside of class. The courseload for undergrads like myself who were in the math program but with a computer science focus was light compared to other disciplines, but I found out that this was designed to give us time to get involved in projects outside class. And there was no shortage of opportunities.

My first project, which Dr. McDermott told me about, was to serve as a programmer on a "naïve physics" cognitive science project run jointly by CMU and Pitt faculty and researchers, and headed up by Dr. Simon. The goal was to write an expert system that could solve the sorts of simple physics problems you'd see in the exercises section of a high school physics textbook, such as, "A 2 kg. ball rolling at 10 cm/sec collides with a 1 kg. ball at rest. What's the velocity of the 1 kg ball after the collision?" The point of this was not simply to solve the problem, any programmer could do that. The point was to write an expert system that modeled the way humans approached this type of problem and which reasoned about the problem in the same way that a human physics student would. Being a lowly undergrad on the project, my job was to convert the questions from plain English into a set of expressions in the Lisp programming language, so that they could be fed into the expert system that Dr. Simon and the others had designed (the expert system did not have a natural language processing module at that time). The work was interesting, but more important, I got to sit in on meetings with Dr. Simon and other brilliant researchers, seeing how they thought, how they tackled problems, and how they worked together. In retrospect, these meetings were more valuable than all my classwork, because they showed me how world-class scientists went about their work.

Though I managed to catch up to the other students and improve my GPA, I did realize that I was never going to be as brilliant in computer science as many of the other students. But I had other skills and some life experiences that they didn't have. I used this to my advantage. One of the first times I realized this was when I was thrown together with three other students and we were given the task of writing a computer program on whatever topic we wanted. We had two weeks. Two of the people in the group were good programmers, one was a humanities major with good art skills but terrible at programming, and me. I took charge of the group and allocated tasks to everyone. We selected a task that was challenging but do-able, a personnel tracking system. The two programmers wrote most of the code, I wrote up the final paper, and I gave the artist the task of illustrating the final paper with lots of cute little drawings. It all came together nicely and we got an "A" for the project, much to the annoyance of other teams that had tackled more difficult technical problems but hadn't produced such a nice final product.

I got a part time job as a programmer working at Aptech Computer, a software development company that did projects for clients using the Wang BASIC language that was called, of course, the "Wanguage." It wasn't particularly interesting work, I think my main project had something to do with mailing labels. But it paid well and gave me some additional work experience. I worked there from August through December 1979.

I also got interested for a while in the idea of using computer software to win money at the racetrack. From what I knew about betting on horses, a lot of it was done more or less randomly, based on the name of the horse and such things. If I could write an expert system to predict the outcomes of horse races,

I could probably do better than human bettors and make some money. I wrote some prototype code, ran it, and the results were promising. But it required a great deal of historical data about race results, and that was only available in printed format. I contacted the publishers to see if they could supply me with the information electronically, but of course they had no interest in that, so that was the end of that project.

I was active in the local Eckankar community during this time. I led some classes including a creative writing workshop, helped put on seminars and other events, and put up lots of posters around town. I met Frenshetta Herron, a local Eckist and daughter of a conservative Baptist minister. We dated for a while. Walking around town and visiting with friends, I got to experience first-hand some of the racial discrimination and micro-aggressions that black people experience all the time. Honestly, having experienced just a little bit of that, I'm amazed that someone can grow up black in a white-dominated world, face overt and covert racism day after day, and still turn out reasonably healthy.

Frenshetta Herron.

Teaching

A second and much more ambitious project came along towards the end of my first year. The department was looking for teaching assistants to help with the Fundamentals of Programming course for non-technical majors. This was known to all as 15-112, not to be confused with 15-111 which was the much tougher version of the course intended for math and computer science majors like me. Normally the teaching assistants were grad students in the Ph.D. program, but I applied for it anyway. The department head, my ex-advisor Dr. McDermott, as usual did not show much enthusiasm for using me in this role, but he surprised me by calling me at home over the summer and leaving a terse message on my answering machine, "Tell Jeff he can teach the class."

The culture in CMU's computer science department was egalitarian and assumed that everyone was intelligent and reasonable. In fact, there was even a "reasonable person principle" that guided most interaction in the department and replaced reams of more formal rules used at other schools. So when it came to the role of the TA's, the school gave us a tremendous amount of latitude in how we taught the class. The professor would give the main lecture once a week to the entire class. Then the TA's would meet with their sections twice a week to go over everything in more detail. As TA's we could choose to cover the material any way we wanted. We created the assignments, gave tests, graded student work, detected and punished plagiarism in programming projects (which was surprisingly common and really easy to spot), and met with students one-on-one as needed. So in most respects we were more like instructors than teaching assistants.

My office mate and fellow TA for 15-112 was Ellis Cohen, a brilliant and wonderful Ph.D. candidate who later went on to teach and conduct research at Brandeis University and Boston University. Ellis and I took our TA responsibilities seriously, and we often worked together to come up with innovative ways to teach our students.

However, I wasn't impressed with the textbook that we were given to use. It seemed to be confusing, and I heard a lot of grumbling from my students. So I thought I could improve it. So I asked my students what they didn't like about the book, what they liked better about another book, and in general what they wanted to see in a textbook. Based on that feedback, I selected a topic in the textbook which we hadn't covered yet, and wrote a new chapter using the suggestions that I'd received earlier from the students. I gave half the students the chapter I'd created, and gave the other half the chapter from the regular textbook. Then I assessed the students' mastery of the subject. Happily enough, the students who used my chapter did significantly better! Encouraged by this, I wrote a paper, "Following Students' Suggestions for Rewriting a Computer Programming Textbook."

Using the "start at the top" philosophy that I'd picked up at CMU, I sent it off to the most prestigious journal in the field, the *American Educational Research Journal*. They accepted the paper and published it as the lead article in their Fall 1981 issue. The article has since been cited in 43 other scholarly works. I even got a letter from a researcher telling me that the paper was a finalist for a major contest that his institution was running. The letter was addressed to Dr.

Pepper, and I enjoyed telling him that I didn't have a Ph.D. and was, in fact, an undergrad when I wrote the paper.

American Educational Research Journal
Fall 1981, Vol. 18, No. 3, Pp. 259–269

Following Students' Suggestions for Rewriting a Computer Programming Textbook

JEFF PEPPER

Three Rivers Computer Corporation

This paper discusses the results of two experiments in technical text-book design. In the first experiment, excerpts from two existing computer programming texts were given to a group of college students. Comprehension of both texts was found to be poor, and surprisingly, the subjects overwhelmingly preferred a verbose and poorly written text over a concise and well written one. It was concluded from the students' comments that they were looking for an easy-to-read text with lots of examples. A chapter was written in this style, and it was found that the students' comprehension improved substantially, and they also liked the new "text" much better than any of the others.

INTRODUCTION

It's not unusual for college students to complain about their textbooks. An interesting question, though, is whether a particular textbook is unpopular simply because the subject matter is difficult, or whether there are problems with the design of the textbook itself—problems that the authors and instructors might be unaware of, but which are quite obvious to the students who must try to learn from the text. After listening for 2 years to students' (and instructors') complaints about the textbooks used in an introductory computer programming course, it was decided to run some experiments to see if the complaints were justified.

The experiments described in this paper were carried out in the spring of 1980, using students enrolled in Carnegie-Mellon University's "Introduction to Programming B," a freshman-level computer programming course using

Many thanks are due to John Hayes of the Psychology Department, Carnegie-Mellon University, without whose guidance and encouragement this research could not have come about.

Cheri d'Emu

It was a cold January day in Pittsburgh. I'd just returned to Mudge House after my afternoon classes. As I walked through the lobby of the dorm, I noticed a girl standing up against the cinder block wall, blond hair, interesting face, and all bundled up in a winter coat and hat. I thought I knew her, so I blurted out, "Hi!" then realized with some embarrassment that I probably didn't know her after all. Odd feeling, though. She just smiled and waved back at me. I kept going to my dorm room.

A couple of days later I saw her again, and we started talking. Her name was Cheri Vasek. She was from Riverside in Southern California, which explained why she was bundled up with so much winter clothing the first time I saw her. It turned out that she and her sister had invented their own private language that they called Farni, as in, gee, you sure talk Farni. In Farni, her name was Cheri d'Emu, and her sister was Dresdinette. Cheri was a grad student in the theater department, majoring in costume design. We clicked immediately, and within a day or two we were sitting on the floor in my dorm room sketching out the floorplan for the house we were going to build together. We became inseparable, much to the annoyance of my roommate, the guy from AT&T, who had the upper bunk bed in our dorm room. It seemed like we'd known each other forever.

As we got to know each other, I found out that Cheri had led an extremely sheltered life. I think this first became apparent when I suggested we go see a movie, and she said that the only movie she'd ever seen was *The Sound of Music*. Despite growing up in California in the 1960's and being an artist, she'd never taken any recreational drugs, and somehow had managed to miss the whole counterculture movement.

Cheri Vasek.

We made plans to spend the summer together. I had been offered another summer's work at Republic National Bank in New York City, this time as an actual programmer and not an intern anymore. Cheri's skills were much more specialized, but incredibly, she found a job designing costumes and sets for a summer camp on Long Island called the Usdan Center. (I thought USDAN was an acronym for United States something-or-other, but it turned out to be named after the founder, Morris Usdan.) So after school was finished we headed out to Long Island and rented a cheap basement apartment for the summer.

Cheri had been planning to go back to California to see her family, and of course I wanted to go with her. She was reluctant, obviously worried about something, but she agreed anyway. We arrived at her parents' house in Riverside and I finally met the family. Her dad, Dr. Frank Vasek, was a botanist at University of California Riverside – he joked that he'd became a botanist because he liked the fact that his subjects stayed in one place. He was also the Director of the UCR Botanic Gardens, and one of his claims to fame was that he'd discovered the world's oldest living plant, a 11,700 year old ring of creosote bushes in the desert that he called King Clone. Cheri's mom was an artist, talented but without much to show for her career. And her sister Dresdinette (her real name was Cindy) was terrific – very close to Cheri and an island of sanity in a household whose craziness I was about to discover.

Two Weddings

The trouble started almost immediately, when the parents learned that Cheri and I were living together without being married. To me (and everyone else I knew) this was a perfectly normal state of affairs, but the Vaseks were horrified. To make things worse, they started working on Cheri, trying to convince her that I was a terrible person and was using her, to put it politely, without making the sort of long term commitment that any honorable man would do.

After a few days I'd had enough, and I left the house to stay in a nearby motel, just to get away from their constant nagging. An unfortunate side effect of this was that it removed my point of view from the situation, and Cheri began to fall under their spell and started wondering if I was indeed such a terrible person. Soon the parents moved on to the next step, which was to insist that we get married immediately before returning to New York. Cheri seemed powerless to resist.

The thought of an forced marriage was repulsive, but I loved Cheri and decided it was the only path open to us. So I called my parents (one at a time, of course), and told them. Understandably they were both angry and upset, but Cheri and I offered to have a second wedding, a "real one," in New York later in the summer.

So a few days later, on June 4, 1979, four of us got in the car – Cheri, Dr. Vasek, Dresdinette, and me. We drove down to the local magistrate to get married. Mrs. Vasek refused to go, even though she was the one who had insisted on this in the first place. The ceremony was in the magistrate's office, short and businesslike. On the drive back to the house I think I used the term "shotgun wedding" and her dad angrily corrected me by pointing out that Cheri was not pregnant. This was interesting, as I learned later that Cheri's mom's art career was cut short by her own unplanned pregnancy with Cheri. This had apparently forced the two of them to get married, leading to a lifetime of bitterness and regret about a career lost, and misguided resentment towards Cheri for having caused it. Obviously this was not Cheri's fault, but rational thought was in surprisingly short supply in the Vasek household.

Soon after, the parents drove us to the airport. At a stop light her dad reached back and handed us a couple of $100 bills. Apparently this was their idea of a wedding present for the happy couple. I was too shocked to say or do anything, and besides, we really needed the money. But on the plane ride back to New York I thought of lots of clever and cutting remarks that I could have made while throwing the bills back at him.

Obviously, this was a lousy way to start our life together, but we tried to put it behind us and get on with things. And we decided to go ahead with a second, "real" wedding.

I was active in Eckankar at the time, and although we decided not to have an official Eckankar wedding (though that would have really annoyed Cheri's parents, which was a point in its favor), I did like the Eckankar notion of having the wedding at sunrise, with the rays of the rising sun symbolizing the start of our new life together. So we arranged to have the ceremony at my favorite beach, Robert Moses State Park on the south shore of Long Island, where I'd spent so many summers when I was growing up. Cheri's parents did not come but her sister Dresdinette was there, as were most of my family, including my elderly grandmother who'd come out from Manhattan the night before and had stayed over with my mom. Cheri and I had to get up at some ridiculous hour, maybe 3:00 am, to get ready and head down to the beach. Unfortunately we both slept through the alarm, and if it weren't for our landlady banging on the door to wake us up, we would've missed the whole thing.

We got to the beach, met the rest of our family and friends, and walked down to the water. It was dark, chilly, and raining. A few seagulls drifted quietly over the water. We waited until the scheduled arrival of the sun, and I kept hoping the clouds would part, or at least that the rain would let up, but neither happened. Eventually we all retreated to one of the beach shelters and we had the ceremony while the cold rain fell on the beach.

Overall, it was better than the civil ceremony in the magistrate's office in Riverside, but not quite what we were hoping for.

The Calendar

While staying at the Vasek house in Riverside, I created a unique calendar of the life that Cheri and I were planning to have together. This project started before the shotgun wedding was proposed, but we were planning to be together for a long time regardless. I started with a half sheet of plywood, and cut it into a circle 3 feet in diameter. A one-foot circular area in the center was reserved for artwork, and I carved something in there though I can't remember exactly what. So between the center circular area and the edge of the wood was a two foot wide ring. I drew 52 equidistant lines radiating outwards, like rays, slicing the ring into 52 small slices. Then I drew 7 concentric rings which separated the ring into 8 thinner rings, creating a cross-hatch effect. Each thin ring represented a year and was divided into 52 little boxes representing the weeks in the year. The innermost ring was the first year of our relationship and was the smallest. The boxes in each successive year's ring were the same thickness but a bit wider because they were further from the center. I then used a carving tool to emboss all the lines. Finally there were 416 little curved rectangles (8 circles of 52 boxes each), each box surrounded by grooves on all sides. The idea was that at the end of each week, Cheri and I would sit down together, review our week, pick one event or theme, reduce it down to a few words and/or pictures, and write it in the calendar. Then after 8 years I would add a second ring for the next 8 years, and so on, though that ended up being unnecessary. As I worked on the project in the garage, Dr. Vasek came in to check on progress from time to time. He seemed interested in the geometry aspect of the project.

Navigation Program

When summer ended, Cheri and I returned to Pittsburgh and rented a third floor apartment at 5512 Margaretta Street in the East Liberty neighborhood. I was finishing up my final year of my B.S. degree program, which by now had spanned nine years and three different schools. I spent the year teaching my 15-112 class, taking advanced classes in artificial intelligence and computer science from outstanding professors like Raj Reddy and Herb Simon, and started thinking about what I would do after graduation.

One fun project was for Dr. Reddy's AI class. We had been learning techniques for efficiently searching and evaluating large problem spaces (that is, lots of possible solutions to a problem). This was important for game playing and other AI applications. I was interested in using AI to rapidly find the shortest driving distance between any two points on a map. This was 1979, before Google Maps, before MapQuest, even before Garmin and GPS, back when wayfinding meant looking at a paper map and asking people for directions.

I built a database of all the streets in the South Oakland neighborhood around the CMU campus, including all the intersections, the permitted traffic directions, speed limits, stop signs and traffic lights. Then I wrote a program to find the fastest driving route between any two intersections (the database didn't have street number in it, so I had to use intersections for starting and ending points). There were many thousands of different routes and computers were relatively slow at the time, so I used an AI technique called "beam search" to limit the search to the most promising possibilities.

The program worked fine and could print out turn-by-turn directions. I showed it to Dr. Reddy. He liked it and told me that it really needed a map-like graphical user interface, which was unheard-of at the time but was, in retrospect, exactly what was needed to make the program commercially viable. But I had no skills in building a graphical user interface, and was more interested in AI than graphics anyway, so I didn't take the project any further.

A few years later, a company called MapQuest released the first wayfinding program that used a graphical user interface. It was a huge success.

Slippery Rock House

I bought a small cabin in Slippery Rock, an hour and a half north of Pittsburgh. The cabin was at 106 Graham Road, a gravel and dirt path that ran along Slippery Rock Creek near I-79. I can't recall any particular reason why I bought the place, I just thought it would be nice to have a vacation house. I owned the house for a few years but only stayed in it overnight a couple of times. Instead, I fixed it up a bit and rented it out.

It was not an ideal rental property. The house was small, run down, and had a coal furnace in the basement for heat. There was a coal chute going into the basement, and whoever lived in the house had to shovel coal into the furnace. The only nice feature of the house was that the back yard went right down to Slippery Rock Creek, making it ideal for canoeing, kayaking and fishing.

The Slippery Rock house.

Most of my tenants were good, but when the last tenant moved out unexpectedly, I discovered that he'd converted the basement to a marijuana farm, complete with grow lights. He didn't leave any of the plants behind, just the grow lights.

Realizing that the house was really just an unprofitable distraction, I sold the place right after that.

Three Rivers Computer / Perq

During the final semester of my time at CMU I interviewed with a few on-campus recruiters from big companies, but the jobs that they were offering didn't appeal to me. Then I heard about a technology spinoff called Three Rivers Computer that was just starting up on Craig Street in Oakland, not far from campus. The founders were two CMU grads: Brian Rosen, a bearded young hardware engineer who'd just returned after working on a radically new single-user computer at the Xerox Palo Alto Research Center and Paul Newbury, a mild mannered (compared to Brian) business and finance guy. Brian was convinced that the world was ready for a high performance single user workstation with a large bitmapped display, and that Xerox PARC would never bring it to market. (Turns out he was correct on both counts.) So he, to put it politely, "borrowed"

Brian Rosen with the first Perq.

a lot of ideas from Xerox PARC and started Three Rivers Computer Company with Paul. They designed a new computer called the Perq. It had a proprietary operating system that went by the unfortunate acronym "POS." It was optimized to run a single user's jobs incredibly fast on the new hardware.

I was the 9th employee, hired in May 1980 to be the company's IT manager and reporting to Paul. Starting salary was $1600/month. Part of the job was just maintaining the existing payroll and accounting systems, doing backups, and other routine stuff. Weekly backups were to magnetic tape, but daily backups were done by opening up the big disk drives and swapping out the hard drives. The disk drive machines were each about the size of a small washing machine, and the hard drive itself was a 12" wide layer-cake of dark orange disks that had to be lifted like a load of laundry out of the top of the machine. Each disk drive weighed a few pounds and

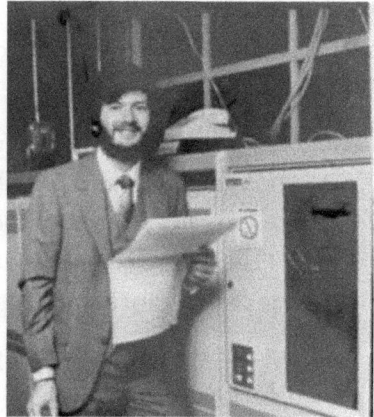

Me at Three Rivers, with a line printer printout and the tape backup

had a 10 megabyte capacity. It would take about 25,000 of them to equal the storage capacity of the iPhone in my pocket.

My first real project was to improve a system that Paul had created for tracking inventory and predicting when we needed to reorder items like circuit board components. Paul was not a professional programmer, and he'd already created

126

a truly bizarre inventory control system that ran on our PDP-10 timesharing computer and was written in a primitive line-editing program called TECO. People generally used TECO for editing text files on an traditional paper-feed teletype or a "glass teletype." In fact, the name originally stood for "Tape Editor and Corrector." A TECO user would type a command to show a line of text from a file, then type a simple macro like "advance 32 spaces, delete 1 character, and add an 'M'." These macros were extremely dense and difficult to understand, and in fact, TECO was jokingly considered to be a "write-only" language, because once a program was written, it was nearly impossible to look at it and understand what it did. This, for example, is an actual TECO program that calculates the value of Pi to an arbitrary number of digits:

```
GZ0J\UNQN"E 40UN ' BUH BUV HK
QN< J BUQ QN*10/3UI
QI< \+2*10+(QQ*QI)UA B L K QI*2-1UJ QA/QJUQ
QA-(QQ*QJ)-2\ 10@I// -1%I >
QQ/10UT QH+QT+48UW QW-58"E 48UW %V ' QV"N QV^T '
QWUV QQ-(QT*10)UH >
QV^T @^A/
/HKEX$$
```

Paul's TECO program managed large text files containing the company's inventory information and the bills of material for the company's various modules and products. He wanted me to extend the program so that we could manage build schedules, forecast inventory consumption, and generate lists of items to reorder. And so I ended up writing what was probably one of the world's longest and most complex TECO macros. It was dozens of pages long and did all the tasks normally handled by a manufacturing resource management (MRP) product. We used this gigantic TECO macro for a few years, until the company grew and we purchased a real off-the-shelf MPR product. Along the way, I joined the American Production and Inventory Control Society (APICS) and became well acquainted with manufacturing software.

One day Paul came in and handed me a newspaper clipping describing VisiCalc, which was a new kind of software called a spreadsheet program. VisiCalc had just been released in 1979. It used the 24-line, 80 character-per-line display of the Apple II, and Paul thought that a spreadsheet program would be much better if it ran on the Perq's advanced bitmap display. This sounded like fun, so I got started on it, writing the program from scratch in the Perq Pascal language. I never actually used VisiCalc, and everything I knew about spreadsheet programs was what I'd learned from reading the

A screenshot from VisiCalc, the first spreadsheet program.

article. We called our program Pgrid. It was one of two programs used to demonstrate the power of personal workstations in general and the Perq in particular. Working on my own at first and later with the help of Jeff Stehle, we created an entire full-functioned spreadsheet program, including a graphics package and a large number of built-in functions. Along the way we got help from a number of people including Ed Fredkin, a noted MIT professor and investor in the company.

Ed would come to the office periodically, and was involved in business development as well as providing technical guidance. He'd occasionally drop by to see how I was doing. One day I asked him about a difficult problem I was working on with PGrid, having to do with parsing a formula in a spreadsheet cell. Ed listened, nodded, closed his eyes for a minute, then gave me an innovative and excellent solution to the parsing problem.

A couple of weeks before a big trade show Ed came to see me. He sat down at my desk and explained that he wanted something for the show that would impress people with how powerful the Perq was, even if the impression was far greater than the reality. This was a trade show, after all, where smoke and mirrors were part of the game. In fact, in the early days the company had actually demonstrated a Perq prototype at a trade show that was nothing more than a Perq monitor and keyboard attached to a PDP-10 computer hidden behind a screen. Now Ed was asking me to write a program that would answer any question on any topic by responding "YES," "NO," or "NOT ENOUGH INFORMATION." The trick was that when one of the Perq booth staffers typed in a visitor's question, they would not necessarily press the "?" key at the end of the question. They could also press the ">" key that was just to the left

128

of the question mark, or the ";" key that was just above it. The person asking the question would not notice which key the typists' pinky hit, because any of those three keys would display on the screen as a question mark. But the three different keys would result in the Perq responding YES, NO, or NOT ENOUGH INFORMATION. I wrote the program, and they told me it was a big hit at the trade show.

The first Perqs shipped in 1979, and they sold well. They were built in our small facility on Craig Street in Oakland. Initial customers included CMU, IBM, and the Department of Defense. The Perqs were also of interest to developers of advanced software, and I remember going up to Boston with the company's then-President Aaron Coleman, who as a young military engineer had helped develop the radar system that would have, had it been used properly, detected the fleet of Japanese bombers headed to Pearl Harbor in 1943. Coleman and I visited a startup company that had been working on a text editor that actually shifted text around on the screen as you typed; at the time this was a radical idea. We also sold several Perqs to U.S. government agencies - I remember being sent to Washington DC for an emergency tech support visit and staying up all night getting the machines working again. And we sold several to Martin Marietta Aerospace (later Lockheed Martin) in Colorado Springs who used them for managing inventory, though I never figured out why they needed $50,000 workstations when they could have just used regular timesharing computers like everyone else.

Encouraged by strong early demand, the company raised more money and moved to a much larger manufacturing and office facility in a nearby industrial park. They expanded their workforce and signed a partnership with a big company called ICL in the UK. However, in a scenario right out of Geoffrey Moore's classic book *Crossing the Chasm*, early demand from technology visionaries and early adopters does not necessarily lead to widespread acceptance from mainstream customers. The company went back to its first customers to ask about additional orders, and was generally told, "No thanks, we've got enough."

Being an early employee, I had been awarded a lot of incentive stock options, and based on forecasts of company growth and valuation I fully expected to cash in my options, reap a windfall, and never have to work again. Alas, that's not how it played out. Competition from other workstation manufacturers including Apollo Computer and Sun Microsystems cut into sales, and the Perq's $50,000 price point was unsustainable. Sales dropped, the company's high fixed costs led to huge losses, and eventually the most recent investors pulled the plug by refusing to invest more money. Because these later investors had preferred stock, they exercised their liquidation preference and took all the company's assets. Common stock holders (the founders) and option holders (the employees) received nothing but great memories and a useful education in the perils of the technology adoption lifecycle.

Personal Changes

By this time, Cheri and I had moved out of our apartment in the East Liberty neighborhood of Pittsburgh, and rented a house in Valencia, about a half-hour drive north of the city. I commuted every day down to the city to work at Three Rivers Computer, while Cheri worked at home weaving fabrics on her Glimakra loom. She was a terrific fabric designer, and was able to imagine a complex woven fabric, then order exactly the correct threads needed to weave the fabric. The threads would arrive by mail, she'd load them up on the loom, and the imagined fabric would take shape on the loom. She wove scarves, jackets, throw pillows and other similar things, and sold them at craft fairs. Sometimes I'd go with her to the craft fairs, sometimes she'd go on her own.

Our relationship started to deteriorate. Certainly part of the reason was the rushed way that we'd gotten forcibly married by her parents, well before we were really ready for the commitment. Also, she was home all day working at her loom while I worked long hours at Perq. At some point she went off to do a craft fair and met someone, another artist who lived in Tennessee. She decided that she'd had enough of the marriage, so she abruptly left and moved to

Jonesboro to live with him. I was a bit disappointed but not too much, having also been unhappy with the state of the marriage. I collected all the things that she'd left behind, stuffed them in the large freezer we'd bought, and shipped everything, freezer and all, down to Jonesboro.

The divorce was amicable and handled by one of Cheri's friends who was a lawyer. In fact, at one point Cheri invited me to come down and visit her in Tennessee. Her friends all thought that this was going to be an epic confrontation between the former husband and the current boyfriend, but that didn't happen. The two of us actually got along well, and he confided to me that living with Cheri was not as great as he'd expected it to be.

While visiting Cheri, I learned that there was a local controversy about the name of the town, which was originally Jonesborough but had been shortened to Jonesboro for no reason that anyone could remember. I designed a bumper sticker, "Put the UGH back in Jonesborough." The name was changed a couple of years later, and I will take full credit for that.

During this time I'd become close to Joan Scaglione. Joan was an Eckist and, like Cheri, an artist. She was working as a waitress at Café Steven B's in Shadyside. Joan and I became good friends. She was married to a musician named Steve Garb, but they broke up, leaving Joan single and available. There was a major Eckankar seminar in summer of 1980 that I planned to attend, along with Cheri who was coming up from Tennessee, and Joan, as well as quite a few of my other Eck friends. Cheri was delayed by a day for one reason or another, and Joan and I found each other. We began a relationship that didn't last long, maybe a few months, but it was intense. After it was over, we stayed close friends.

I'd moved out of the Valencia house and had rented a little house nearby, in the town of Mars. The owner had ignored the landlord's rule of never renting to a recently divorced man. One evening I was heating up some oil in a frying pan, getting ready to deep fry something for dinner. The phone rang. I went into the living room to take the call, forgetting all about the frying pan. After talking on the phone for ten minutes or so, the quality of light in the living room changed, it became sort of yellowish and flickering. I looked around and saw that there were flames coming from the kitchen. I ran in and saw a fountain of yellow flame coming up from the frying pan. Fortunately I did not burn the house down. Using a towel I was able to pick up the frying pan, burning oil and all, and put it down on the kitchen floor. The only damage was a circular burn mark on the linoleum.

Hawaii

Jim Coronato was a good friend. We'd met at CMU when he was a civil engineering Ph.D. student, and he'd shown some interest in Eckankar. His workload was huge, with tedious homework assignments night after night plus a thesis project. It was an exhausting multi-year effort, and when he finally graduated he wanted nothing whatsoever to do with civil engineering for a while. So we decided to go on a two week expedition to Hawaii in the summer of 1982, a week of hiking and camping in Kauai to be followed by a week of more civilized activities on the Big Island. He'd never done anything like that before, so because of my experience in Boy Scouts and other outdoorsy stuff I volunteered to organize the trip. We flew to Kauai, drove to a small local beach called Haena, parked the car and set out hiking on the Kalalau Trail which was the only way to get to the Na Pali Coast on the north shore of the island. We hiked several miles through a rain forest and arrived at Hanakapiai Beach, There we camped overnight, then hiked several more miles to Kalalau Beach.

Jim Coronato at the trailhead.

At one point deep in the rain forest we came upon a simple wooden platform made for tent camping. Someone had carved into the wood a famous quote from *The Far Country*, one of Paul Twitchell's Eckankar books:[1]

> "Man is a god clothed in rags, a master of the universe going about begging a crust of bread. He is a king prostrated before his own servants, a prisoner walled in by his own ignorance. He could be free. He has only to walk out of his self-constructed prison. None hold him but himself."

Kalalau Beach was completely isolated; the only way in by land was via the trail that we'd just hiked. Every fall and winter the ocean currents completely washed away the beach, then it was restored by different currents in the spring and summer. We stayed there for four days, camping on the beach near the cliffs (but not so close that we could get hit by falling rocks). It was magical. There were maybe a dozen other campers scattered along the beach. For fresh water there was a high waterfall that came down off a nearby cliff. We hiked in the forest, played frisbee in a water-carved cavern, swam in the ocean, and sat around a communal fire at night. Clothing was optional.

Frisbee cave at Kalalau Beach.

Later, I learned that our campsite was close to Taylor Camp, a hippie enclave of maybe 50 individuals who lived in a cluster of treehouses on a parcel of oceanfront land owned by the brother of actress Elizabeth Taylor. Some of the people who came to the evening campfires were resident of Taylor Camp, including a brown skinned blonde girl named Bobo. She was a recovering alcoholic who would regularly swim naked twelve miles along the Na Pali Coast to Kalalau Beach while towing a gallon jug filled with food and clothing and tied to her foot. She'd stay at the beach for a while, then hitchhike

---

[1] There is a nearly identical passage in *The Path of the Masters* by Julian Johnson.

back to town. (There's a great film called "Edge of Paradise" about the life and times of Taylor Camp.)

Taylor Camp, from the documentary "Edge of Paradise."

One night I slept out on the beach under the stars. I woke up in the middle of the night feeling some pressure on my stomach. Was it Bobo? I thought. No, something even stranger. A large sea bird had decided to take advantage of some free warmth and was roosting on top of me. When I sat up, it squawked and flew away.

At the end of the week, a couple of Zodiac boats came to the beach to pick up passengers, and we rode the Zodiacs back to our rental car at Haena. We stayed at an inexpensive lodge for a couple more nights, hiking around the island. Then we flew to the Big Island for a week. That week was uneventful, but I do remember one night when we were out in our car, trying to find someone's house for some reason. We were on a narrow winding road in dense fog. We couldn't see more than five feet in front of the car, so Jim got out and walked ahead to make sure I wouldn't drive off the road. There was a wooden fence on the side of the road, and a huge owl sat on one of the fence posts, just watching us.

Later, when we got back to Pittsburgh, Jim became involved with a much older woman, an Eckist named Connie Beedle White. Jim abandoned civil engineering and moved to Bemidji, Minnesota with Connie. He completely disappeared, leaving

This is probably Jim, circa 2022, fishing at Garrison's Resort. (TripAdvisor)

no trace of himself online, except for Connie's death notice in the Bemidji Pioneer. It said that Connie had changed her name to Saraiah Celeste White, and translated (an Eckankar term for died) in April 2014 and that her husband was James Coronato. The article said that in 1971 she bought a small fishing resort called Garrison's Resort in Shevlin in northern Minnesota where she launched many entrepreneurial ventures, from raising hybrid sows to planting seeds to selling new-age health supplements. I believe Jim still lives there.

Meeting Kathryn

In the fall of 1981, I was still single and unattached and a bit disappointed about my recent divorce. So I moved closer to the city and my job at Perq, leaving the rental house in Mars (with the circular burn mark still on the kitchen linoleum which cost me my security deposit) and renting a first floor apartment in the Bloomfield neighborhood of Pittsburgh. I was 28.

Still active in Eckankar, I was looking for a location to hold a small event and discovered the Center for Human Development, a small nonprofit in Shadyside that offered a variety of classes and events focusing on personal growth. I went in one day to ask about renting a room for an event, and wound up talking with Kathryn Katafiasz who was an administrator there in charge of such things. I liked her and she apparently liked me. Our first date was me going across the street to Minutello's Italian restaurant, picking up a couple of eggplant hoagies, and bringing them back to the CHD office for lunch.

Things did not get serious right away. I did rent the room for the Eckankar event. and I attended a couple of single mingle events that they held. At one of those events I met someone else. We went out a couple of times, but nothing came of it. But I continued to like Kathryn, so we started dating.

She had a different view of relationships than I did. Her main point was that a relationship isn't something that happens to you, it's something that you work at and make happen over time. This was a new concept for me, as all my prior relationships including my brief marriage to Cheri were of the "just happened" variety. Since none of them lasted long, I thought it would be interesting to see what would result from this different approach.

We continued to see each other frequently, including at my 30th birthday party at the house in Bloomfield. A short time later we decided to move in together. In summer of 1983 we rented the second floor of a nice house on Morrowfield Avenue in Squirrel Hill. Unlike my disastrous shotgun-wedding experience the last time I had a live-in girlfriend, Kathryn's family had no objection to this arrangement. I got along well with her mother Bea, her mother's longtime boyfriend Leonard, and her sister Karen.

Kathryn and me with Munchkin.

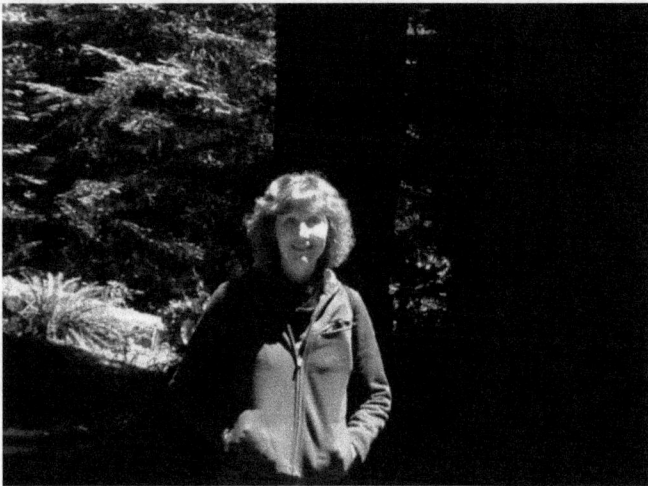

Wedding

We decided to get married, and set a wedding date of May 20, 1984. We planned it as a roll-your-own style wedding in our back yard on Morrowfield Avenue in Squirrel Hill. Mrs. Jacobson, the elderly landlady who lived on the first floor, was amused by this and told us that she had no objection as long as we didn't do any damage to her yard. So we fixed everything up for the wedding. The Pittsburgh Symphony was on strike at the time, so we were able to hire their harpist to play for us.

The ceremony was performed by Charles Limpar, the minister at the Allegheny United Church of Christ. Neither of us were members of his church, but he had been recommended to us as someone who was openminded about such things as vows written by the bride and groom, interfaith marriages, and so on.

Lunch was served outdoors afterwards by the caterers, all vegetarian.

It was a relatively small gathering. From my family: Mom, Dad, Aunt Floie, my sister Barbara, her husband Randy, and their two sons Peter and Keith. From Kathryn's family: her mom and Leonard, her sister Karen, and Karen's deceased husband's parents the DiDomenicos. Also a few close friends including Michael Cavallo, Joan Scaglione and her husband Denis Lehotay, Kathryn's friends Nina and Pat Carey, some of my Eckankar friends, and some of Kathryn's friends.

We had our rings made at Robert Hallett, a goldsmith in Oakmont. They were made of heavy hammered gold and turned out great. I wore mine on my ring finger for a few years, but because of rock climbing and hand drumming I

Joan and Denis.

switched to wearing it on a leather cord around my neck instead.

Then we headed west for our honeymoon. The highlight of the trip was a two day mule ride from the rim of the Grand Canyon down to Phantom Ranch, and back up the next day. We also visited Canyon de Chelly in Arizona on Navajo lands, and were there for a near-total solar eclipse on May 30, 1984.

After we got back, we had a reception on Long Island at the Maine Maid Inn on June 9 hosted by my mom, and another reception in Toledo on June 23 at Karen's house on Goodwood Avenue hosted by Kathryn's mom and sister.

Wedding pics.

Left: me after the wedding. Below: me, Kathryn, Mom, Kathryn's mother Bea, Dad, and Rev. Limpar.

*Wedding pics:
view from
balcony; Leonard
and Dad; Dad.*

Wedding pics: Kathryn's sister Karen; Jim Coronato with a champagne bottle; Jim helping to prepare the Toyota for our wedding getaway.

Honeymoon in
Arizona.

National Catering Systems

I was still working at Perq but didn't have much to do. Management had transferred me from my original job as IT Manager into sort of a technical sales support job where I assisted the sales team by providing technical information to customers while they did their relatively fact-free sales jobs. Unfortunately there wasn't enough work to fill the day. I found myself doodling in my cubicle.

One of my Eckankar friends, Don Vogel, was out of work and looking for something to do. We'd gone to see a movie together, and later over lunch we decided to start a company. We both thought that high end catering was a good opportunity, so we incorporated as National Catering Systems Inc., an impressive name for a tiny company. Don would do the day to day running of the company while I would be the savvy business guy, I think Don called me "the systems guy," who would make it all work.

We rented a small office in the Design Center building in East Liberty. The business concept was that we be sort of a virtual caterer – we would take catering orders, outsource the actual food prep to other vendors, then rebrand the food as our own and deliver it to customers. We lined up vendors for hot food, cold cuts and desserts, and Don's mother made radish roses for the cold cut trays. I wanted some good branding for box lunches, so my friend Joan Scaglione came up with idea and artwork for the Bistro Box, a cardboard container that held our box lunch. We went door to door visiting lots of large companies in downtown Pittsburgh. We got a couple of departments at CMU as regular customers for faculty and other sorts of meetings, as well as National Steel and some law offices downtown.

It was fun but we never really took over the world. Eventually Don got tired of having to work every day, so we shut down the business about a year after it had started.

Tech Startups

From the time when I felt things were wrapping up at Perq to when I started at my next job at Carnegie Group, I made a few attempts to start a tech business.

None of them gained any long term traction, but I learned a bit each time I did one.

Sleep Scoring. I became interested in what happens in the brain during sleep; this was probably related to my interest in lucid dreaming and attending an interesting talk on the subject by Stephen Laberge. I spoke with some people in the sleep lab at Western Psychiatric Institute and learned how they did "sleep scoring," which was the process of looking at an EKG printout and identifying the various stages of sleep such as alpha, theta and delta. This was a manual and time-intensive process which I felt could be automated by using some pattern-patching methods that I'd learned at CMU. I wrote a proposal for an automated sleep scoring system and submitted it to the department chair in January 1984, but it was not accepted.

Metacom. At CMU I'd become familiar with expert systems, and things called "production systems" that were rules that defined how an expert system would work. These production systems ran on top of a software layer that was usually written in the Lisp programming language. I thought that it would be a great idea to create a commercial PC-based product that would allow people to build their own expert systems without having to learn the details of computer programming. I came up with a name for the company, Metacom. The company's business plan described the first product, called KELT, as "an AI machine implemented in software, running on any computer that supports the Common Lisp language, that will transform its host computer into an environment for developing, debugging and running a knowledge-based system."

I wrote up a detailed business plan, even including a proforma profit-and-loss table that was created using the PGrid spreadsheet program that I'd written at Perq.

Never having started a tech company before, I needed some advice. So I went to Frank Demmler and John Freyhof at the Enterprise Corporation, a nonprofit economic development entity supported by CMU and located in the Mellon Institute building on Fifth Avenue. I remember wearing a suit, carrying my business plan documents, and walking up the long series of marble steps leading through the marble column façade and into the building.

Frank and John were helpful in critiquing the plan. They told me that my financial projections were overly optimistic, and that getting the product built and the company launched would require a lot more money than what I could raise easily.

Re-reading the business plan now, almost forty years later, it looks like a good plan. I think that if I'd ignored their advice and just built the thing on my own, there was a good chance that the company would have found some traction. The timing was good and the product idea was sound. However, I became discouraged and abandoned the idea.

Frank and John did say, however, that they were impressed with the plan and presentation that I'd made, and thought there was a good chance that I would succeed at something else.

JPCCS. Not giving up, in late 1984 I started Jeff Pepper Computer Consulting Company (JPCCS), a general purpose computer software consulting company. This was just a vehicle for me to do a variety of consulting projects. The tag line was "Fine Handcrafted Software." My first billable project (invoices #101 and #102!) was a project for my former employer, PERQ Systems, to make some changes to their "dp" drawing app. The second project was some training that I provided to the Center for Human Development where Kathryn worked.

When I started my next job at Carnegie Group, I discontinued the consulting company.

The Verona House

Since we were planning to start a family, it was time to move out of the apartment in Squirrel Hill and buy a house. We selected a real estate agent and told her that we were looking for some place that was out of the way, but still not far from Pittsburgh. A tough combination. She took us to see several houses, none of which seemed right.

Then she told us about a house for sale at the end of a winding, one-lane road in Verona, about 20 minutes east of downtown Pittsburgh. We saw it and knew almost immediately that it was the right place. We put in an offer a few days later, and bought it on July 11, 1985 for $64,000.

The house was a little bit run down, as it had been the home of Mr. and Mrs. Recklein, their four sons, and a grandmother who'd lived in a first floor room and suffered from incontinence, thus damaging the wood floors. But the house had a terrific location, and we thought we could fix it up.

Over time we renovated every room in the house. The biggest do-it-yourself project was renovating the upstairs bedrooms. There were three bedrooms, but the only access to the master bedroom was by walking through the middle bedroom. I redesigned the second floor to add a hallway to bypass the middle bedroom. The windows were small, the ceilings were low and covered with acoustical tile, the walls were dark paneling, and the master bedroom carpet was dark red and stained.

I came up with a new design for the master bedroom that exposed the roof joists by removing the drop ceiling and all the ceiling joists (after checking with an engineer to make sure the house wouldn't fall down when I did so) and replacing them with collar ties that did the same job but were much more attractive. I removed the small window in the back of the bedroom and cut a huge hole for a set of sliding glass doors, then installed the doors with help from Kathryn's friend Pat Carey. The glass doors opened onto a twenty foot drop to the ground below, but we were planning to add a deck at some point in the future. The only parts of the project that I contracted out were the drywall and electrical work.

I did the project over a couple of months in early 1986, working nights and weekends and then taking a couple of weeks off from work for the most intensive parts of the project. The space shuttle Challenger had exploded in January 1986, and I listened to live radio broadcasts of the hearings into the disaster in June 1986 while working on the project.

The house came with a half-acre of property and was surrounded on three sides by over a hundred acres of woodlands. In the following years we purchased four more parcels, expanding our holdings to just over ten acres. The first two parcels were wooded areas that we bought from Jeff Tyke, a neighbor and gas station owner. The third was the "ballfield," which we purchased from the Tykes jointly with Ron and Kathy Kozera in order to dissuade the Tykes from selling the ballfield to Verizon Wireless and allowing a cell phone tower to be built there.

The final purchase was a small bit of property next to our house that was owned by another neighbor, Dominic "Hawk" Carchidi. Hawk had given his friend Ed Connell permission to build a small house (really just a cottage) on the property, even though Hawk still owned it. Ed built the cottage close to our house, but he never bothered to get a building permit. One the house was almost finished he learned that he couldn't get an occupancy permit because new construction required a sewer hookup. There were no sewer lines in the area, so the cost of running a line up to his cottage would have been prohibitive. So Ed was stuck with a house he could not legally live in, on a parcel of land he did not own. I offered him a fair price to sell me the house if Hawk would agree to sell the property as part of the deal. They both agreed. For some reason Ed insisted in getting paid in cash. So I had to go to the bank with him, withdraw the entire amount of the purchase price in cash, put it in a shoebox and hand it to him. He and Hawk signed the papers and the cottage was ours. It has no running water or toilet, but it's good for storage. For a while there was a ping pong table and robot on the ground floor that I used for training. In the basement I'd built a nice adjustable rock climbing wall, and later I converted that area to storage for lawnmowers and other gas powered tools.

Carnegie Group

I was still bored at my job at Perq Systems. I'd heard that four CMU computer science professors had started an artificial intelligence consulting company, and that sounded interesting. So I interviewed and got a job as a programmer. I quit my job at Perq in 1986 and went to work at Carnegie Group (CGI). Their initial office was at Station Square in downtown Pittsburgh, and they moved later to one of the PPG buildings nearby.

My first job at CGI was working on a natural language processing product called LanguageCraft, a project led by Jaime Carbonell, one of the four founders. That was interesting but the funding for the project dried up. So I moved over to the more commercially successful area of diagnostic expert systems, working for Gary Kahn. We got a series of contracts from big companies to build rule-based expert systems for troubleshooting problems with machines and industrial processes. I worked on projects for a variety of customers, including Kodak (diagnosed problems with a large photofinishing machine), John Deere (agricultural machines), the US Army (the AWACS command and control system, the Apache helicopter, and the M-1 Abrams tank), and Ford Motor Company (car radios and service bay diagnostics for the Taurus). I did some software development, but I had better people skills and weaker programming skills than most programmers at CGI, so I focused more on knowledge engineering. This involved interviewing subject matter experts, extracting their expert knowledge about a particular field, and then encoding that in a knowledge base for use by the expert system.

Baby Katelyn

Katelyn Katafiasz Pepper was born on April 23, 1986. We'd been working with a midwife clinic throughout the pregnancy, but due to insurance issues they were not permitted to handle actual births. So we went to Magee Women's Hospital for the birth. After a long labor, Katelyn was born. She was healthy but a bit underweight. It soon became apparent that she had some severe dietary allergies. She could not breastfeed without getting sick, regardless of what Kathryn did or didn't eat. Standard baby's formula wasn't working either. Katelyn stopped gaining weight and was became a bit listless. The pediatrician just thought it was a case of colic. But after over a month of no progress, we

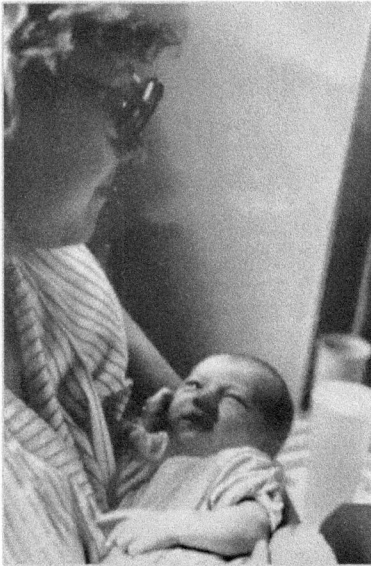

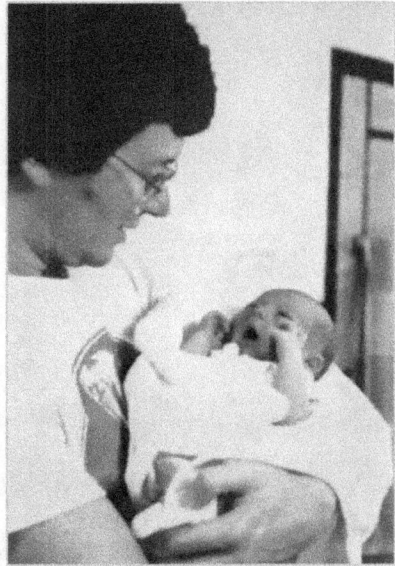

Kathryn with baby Katelyn; me with baby Katelyn.

went to Children's Hospital where we finally received some excellent care. The doctors suspected food allergies because she often cried after eating. They discovered what her allergies were and switched her to a special allergen-free baby formula. Finally she began to gain weight.

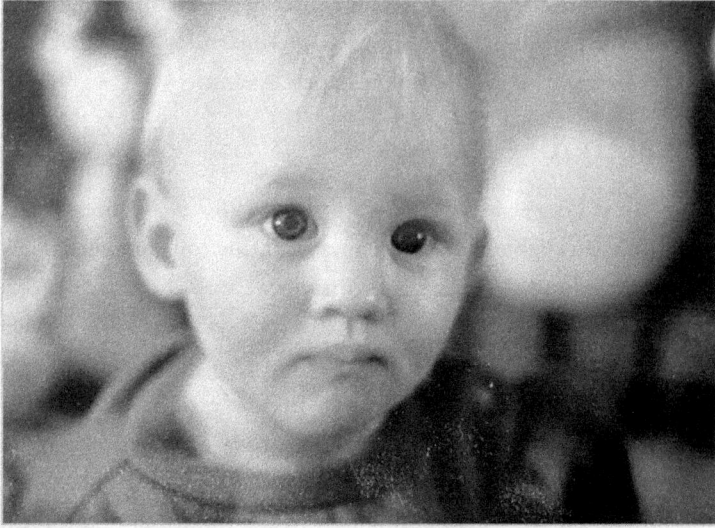

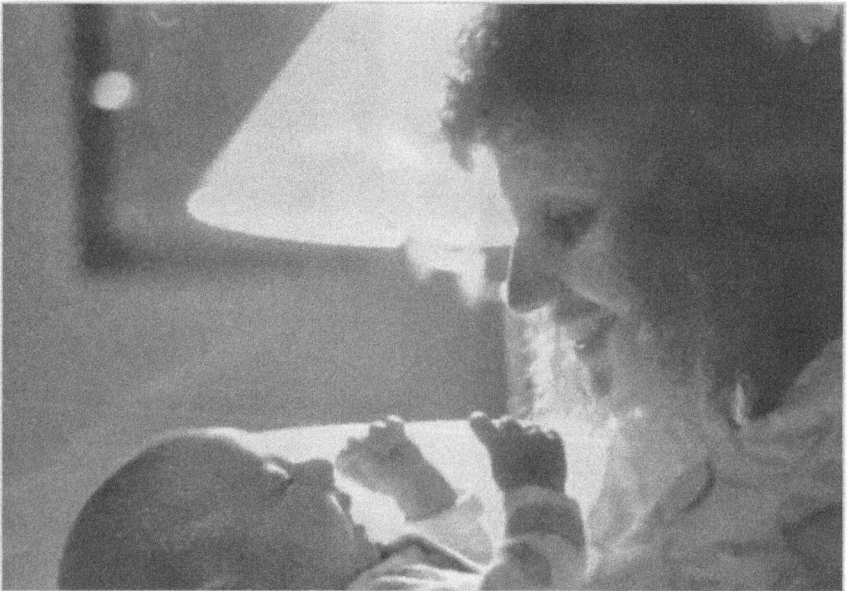

*Me with Kathryn and
Katelyn; Dad with Katelyn.*

Later that summer we went to Cape May, a coastal town in southern New Jersey, for a few days of vacation by the ocean. Katelyn was doing a little bit better but she was still underweight and crying a lot because of her digestive situation. We happened to be there for the Baby Day Parade on August 16. This was an annual event and a big thing for local families. Many of them created elaborate dresses for their kids. We just sort of showed up and walked along carrying Katelyn. To everyone's surprise, including us, they announced that Katelyn (or as they said, "Baby Katt-lin Pepper") was the winner. Apparently it was unusual for an out-of-towner to win the grand prize. But Katelyn was really, really cute. Still is.

Katelyn feeding a friend in a laundry basket.

Repair Strategies and Italy

Carnegie Group was closely tied to Carnegie Mellon University, and most of the senior staff had a background in academics. So lots of papers were published. I wrote or co-wrote several published papers, including "Artificial Intelligence Applied to Audio Systems Diagnosis" (1986), "GWW: A structured environment for building natural language interfaces" (1986, with Phil Hayes and Robert Joseph), "Building an Expert System That Works" (1987), "TEST: A Model-driven Application Shell" (1987, with Gary Kahn and Al Kepner), "Repair Strategies in a Diagnostic Expert System" (1987, with Gary Kahn), and "Towards an Integrated Maintenance Advisor" (1989, with Phil Hayes).

The repair strategies paper was the most interesting. Gary's team had developed a shell called TEST for rapidly building rule based expert systems. TEST was quite good at identifying the cause of a problem, but the human user also needed to know how to fix the problem afterwards. Turns out that fixing a problem can be quite tricky, with lots of different outcomes depending on what happens if you start the repair and fail to fix the problem on the first attempt. Gary challenged me to come up with a repair strategy for TEST that would complement the diagnostic strategy. I worked on this on and off for several months. I came up with several proposed solutions, but each time Gary, who had a Ph.D. in philosophy from the University of Chicago, told me that it was inadequate and that I hadn't thought deeply enough about the problem. So I kept at it, stepping back further and further to wrap my mind fully around the problem. Finally I came up with a strategy that worked in all cases. Gary was satisfied. I wrote the paper, it was accepted by the American Association of Artificial Intelligence, and I got to present it in person at their international conference in Milan. Italy in August 1987.

This was a great opportunity to see Italy, so Kathryn and I planned a major vacation around it. Katelyn was sixteen months old. We started off in Rome, including a visit to some ancient Roman ruins at the exact time of the worldwide Harmonic Convergence when the sun, moon and eight planets all aligned in a special way that was supposed to herald the arrival of an age of world peace.

Like a Moth

From there we drove north through Italy, stopping in Assisi, Florence, and other small cities, and ending up in Milan in time for the conference. Traveling with a one year old infant and all the diapers and other required stuff made it a bit of a challenge, but it was a fun trip. Katelyn was fanatical in her desire to learn words, so as we drove through the winding roads of the Italian countryside, she would sit in her car seat with a large Richard Scarry book, *Best Word Book Ever*, in front of her. She would point to a picture to ask what the word was. Kathryn would tell her. Then she'd point to another picture. And another. And another. This went on forever.

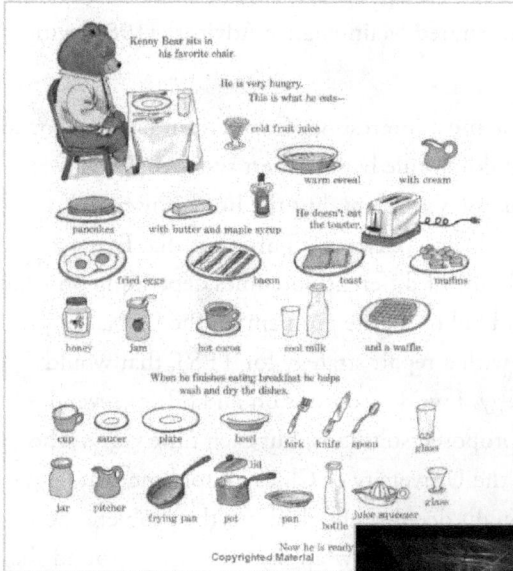

A page from Richard Scarry's Best Word Book Ever.

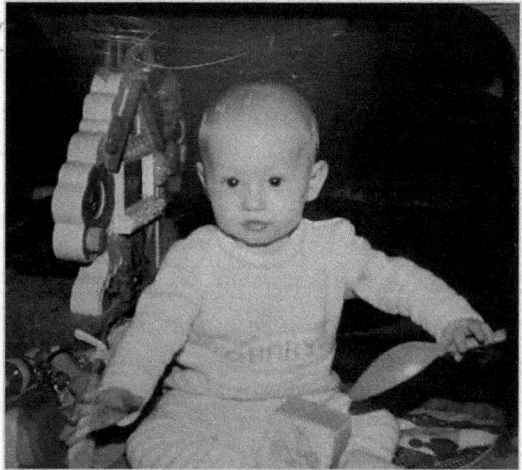

Katelyn with toys, around the time that we went to Italy.

We got to Milan and I presented my paper in a breakout session with perhaps 25 people in the audience. After the conference was over we set out for a day trip to Turin. We were standing in a subway car in Milan waiting for it to leave the station. A gypsy woman was walking around the subway car with a cardboard tray in front of her, asking for money. I didn't know it at the time, but this was a commonly used pickpocket assistive device that allowed the thief to reach under the tray and into the victim's pocket. The woman came up to me asking for money and I refused. She moved on, then quickly left the subway car. As she hurried away I realized that my wallet was missing. Just before the doors closed, I pulled Kathryn and Katelyn out of the car, then ran after the woman, shouting at her. She dropped the wallet and fled.

Dressed as hippies for Halloween.

Marketing and Management

Carnegie Group needed someone to be a product marketing manager for the TEST shell that we'd developed. Gary offered me the job. I protested that I didn't know anything about marketing. He tossed me a little book, *Marketing High Technology* by William Davidow, and told me to read it and get back to him the next day with a decision. I read the book that night and loved it. It was sort of like *The Art of War* but applied specifically to the rapidly evolving field of computer software and hardware. A quote from the book jacket:

> "Marketing is civilized warfare. And as high-tech products become increasingly standardized—practically identical, from the customer's point of view—it is marketing that spells life or death for new devices or entire firms."

I thought this would be a great fit for my skills and background. I took the job. That lasted for a year or so, until I was reassigned to an important new project, the Service Bay Diagnostic System that Carnegie Group was building for Ford Motor Company in Dearborn. This was an ambitious project intended to bring the power of artificial intelligence to the day-to-day work of troubleshooting cars in dealerships and repair shops. CGI was one of several vendors working on the project, and we were responsible for the expert system software that ran on the SBDS. Ford's project manager was a young up-and-coming manager named Leonard S. "Len" Tedesco, the chief subject matter expert was Gordy Kujowski.

Ford promo picture for the SBDS.

Ford committed a lot of money and manpower to the project, so CGI staffed up quickly. Gary put me in charge of the project. This was my first experience managing people. Gary was overseeing me at a director level, making sure I didn't make too many serious mistakes.

The project was in Dearborn, so I spent a lot of time there, working with the CGI and Ford teams. One of the CGI people on the project was Rajiv Enand, a bright and ambitious programmer. He volunteered to move to Dearborn, where he lived for over a year working on the project. Later, Rajiv and I would work together to build ServiceWare.

SBDS was considered a success by Ford. Carnegie Group completed its work and wrapped up their development in 1991. Support for SBDS was transferred in 1999 from the original prime contractor HP, to a new company started by a former HP employee. The new company, ERS Solutions, supported SBDS with parts and service for another seven years.

At my desk at Carnegie Group on a snowy day. On wall at left is the org chart for the SBDS project that I was managing.

The Age of Intelligent Machines

The four co-founders of Carnegie Group were all highly respected in the worldwide AI community. This helped to attract customers. But it also attracted media opportunities. One of these came in 1989 when Raymond Kurzweil, one of the world's leading AI researchers and thought leaders, contacted CGI. He was editing a large coffee-table book to be called *The Age of Intelligent Machines*, and he invited CGI to contribute a short chapter. The

The Age of Intelligent Machines

To Jeff,
Thank you for your important
contribution to this book.
With my best wishes,
Ray

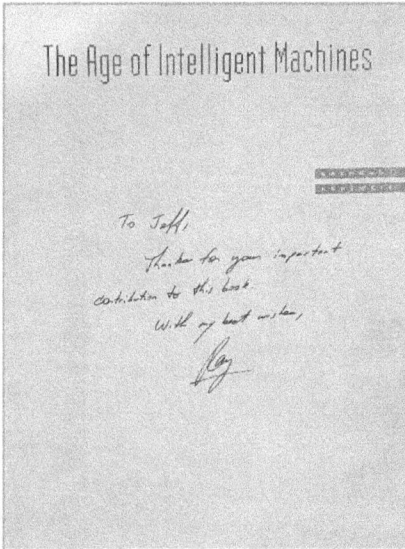

Ray Kurzweil's signature on my copy of
The Age of Intelligent Machines.

request was fielded by marketing director Chris Locke, who liked my writing style and offered me the opportunity to write the chapter. Of course I jumped at the chance.

At that time I was leading the Ford SBDS project, so I wrote the article, simply titled "An Expert System for Automotive Diagnosis."[2] It was a straightforward discussion of the project from a layman's viewpoint (i.e., very little computer science technical jargon). Kurzweil had asked all the authors to address the question, "Is your system intelligent?" In my chapter I responded that an expert system is nothing like a human expert. Human experts have an underlying body of knowledge about how the world works, and their diagnostic problem-solving is layered on top of that. Computer expert systems have no such real world knowledge, they just manipulate symbols (like "car" and "battery") with no real understanding of what those things actually are.

The article closes with this:

> Probably the best contribution I can make to this discussion is to digress a little and take you to the Carnegie Museum of Natural History. We go inside the museum, and we see an exhibit of the evolution of the horse. Over there is a row of horse skeletons ranging from the small doglike creatures of the ice ages to the modern thoroughbred racehorse. The small creature there on the far left doesn't look much like a horse at all. It is Eohippus, the "dawn horse." It was evolution's first experiment with this type of animal, and it was successful enough to survive and provide the seeds of evolution that have led to the magnificent creatures we know as horses today.

---

[2] *The full text of my article is here:* https://kurzweilai-brain.gothdyke.mom/articles/art0310.html

Perhaps SBDS and other similar systems are the dawn horses of intelligent machines. Although they are primitive in comparison to their human counterparts, they contain the seeds of intelligence. They are useful enough to ensure that they will spawn future generations, and their descendants will improve and deepen their methods of reasoning, perception, and understanding. Natural selection and strong evolutionary pressures will encourage this growth, one experiment giving way to another, until they evolve into the racehorses of AI, a future generation of truly intelligent machines.

Looking back 25 years, this was a surprisingly accurate prediction. The expert systems of the 1980's were, by today's standards, ridiculously primitive. Their underlying knowledge base was small and brittle, and the systems had no ability to reason from first principles or real-world knowledge. So by today's standards they barely even qualified as artificial intelligence at all. But they were a start, the "dawn horses" of AI, and the direct ancestors of today's amazingly intelligent machines.

Baby Kris

Kristopher Michael Pepper was born August 12, 1989. We worked again with the Birthing Center midwife group in Pittsburgh, and this time they were set up to do the actual birth onsite. Kathryn went into labor on August 11. We drove to the birthing center. Her labor slowed, so the staff there told us to take a break, maybe walk around a bit. The Shadyside Arts Festival was running that night on Walnut Street, so we went to the festival and walked around looking at the arts and crafts for sale. Later that evening Kathryn's labor sped up again, so we went back to the birthing center. Soon afterwards, Kris was born, in a comfortable and un-hospital-like room with the assistance of the midwife.

Katelyn and Kris.

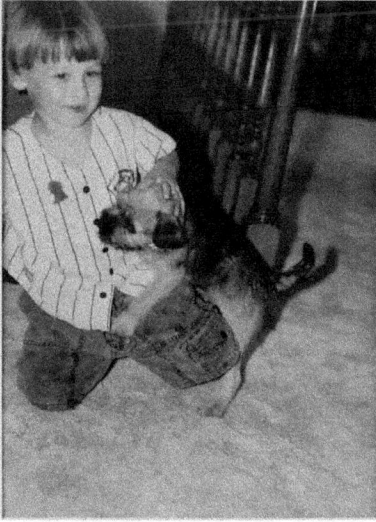

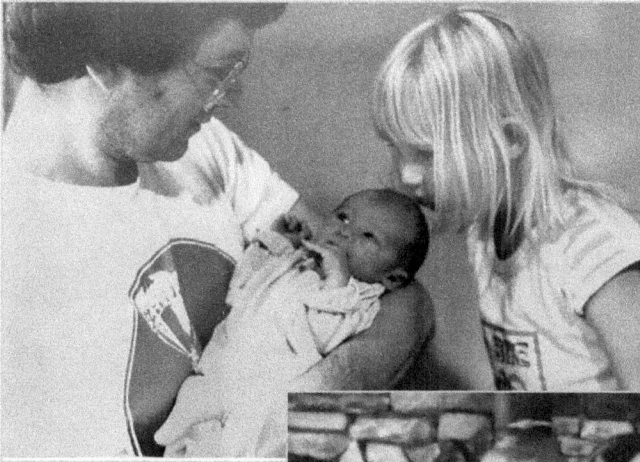

*From top left: Kris
with Mocha as a
puppy; Kris with
cake; Me with both
kids; Kathryn and me
with both kids.*

Kids in autumn leaves in front of the house.

The Lawnmower Incident

It was summer of 1990. Things were going well at my job at Carnegie Group. The Ford project was winding down and I'd started working on converting the TEST shell into a marketable product called TestBench, while also doing some knowledge engineering for customer projects. But once again I was getting restless.

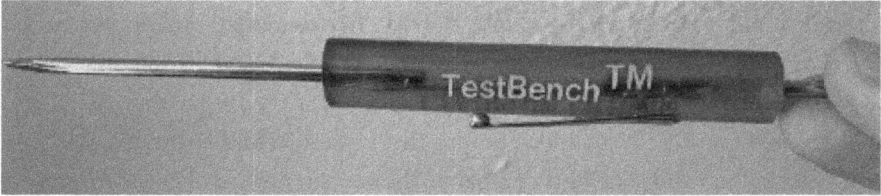

Part of the reason was that I'd gotten a new boss. Instead of Gary Kahn, I was now reporting to Mike Scally, the VP and General Manager. Mike was completely unlike Gary. He was a sales exec, a former jock, and a person who was not given to deep thought. Once I was walking past his office and I heard him actually dictating a memo to his secretary, a practice that I thought had died out in the 1950's.

In his favor, though, he was a good salesman and I did learn some important things from him. Probably the biggest lesson occurred one day when a major sales prospect came to the office. Mike was hosting the visit. My job was technical sales support for the meeting, so at some point I gave a presentation describing some of our technology. The customer said something that was incorrect. So I corrected him, as politely as I could. The customer didn't say anything but Mike was angry. Shortly afterwards he took me aside and simply said, "Jeff, it's not a matter of being right." In other words, in a situation like this, the purpose of speaking is not to say the truth, but to accomplish whatever goal you had when you decided to open your mouth. This was an important lesson.

Despite these occasional words of wisdom from Mike, I was definitely feeling that I wasn't learning anything from the people who were supposed to be my superiors; this included my boss Mike as well as the company's CEO at the time, Dennis Yablonsky.

One weekend I was in the yard, pushing the lawnmower and muttering to myself about my dumb bosses. Suddenly a thought popped into my head. "Quit," said the thought.

Well, that was unexpected.

I pondered this rogue thought as I continued to cut the grass, and decided it actually made some sense. I knew I was old enough (37) and experienced enough (ten years out of school) to start a company. And if I waited much longer, I might not be willing to take the risk. I knew several other people who were as smart as me if not smarter, but who hadn't had the nerve to quit their jobs and create something on their own. I didn't want to be like that. So when I'd finished cutting the grass I went into the house and told Kathryn I was quitting my job and starting a company. She was supportive of the idea, even though she must have known the financial risks involved. We had two small kids, a newly purchased house, and little or no savings.

The following Monday morning I went into work and told Mike I was leaving. To soften the blow a bit, I told him that I was willing to finish out the rest of the calendar year, supposedly to give the company time to hire and train my replacement. Of course, the company didn't really need six months to replace me. The real reason for the delay was that I had no idea what my new company was going to be and I needed time to figure it out. Fortunately, Mike and Dennis were ok with that arrangement.

I started to think about what the new company would look like. I'd read *Crossing the Chasm* and *Inside the Tornado* by Geoffrey Moore, as well as *Marketing High Technology* by William Davidow, and both authors stressed how important it was to dominate whatever market niche you are in. If you're a giant corporation like Ford Motor Company you can dominate the pickup truck market, but I would be just a guy in his basement with no funding, So I had to select a very, very, very small niche that I could define and dominate. Also, I didn't want to start completely from scratch, given that I had a family to support. That meant I needed to leverage what I'd learned from my time at CGI.

So I decided to focus on, unsurprisingly, expert systems for diagnostics. I knew the technology and I knew how to manage a project in that space. But since I had no product to sell and no resources to develop one quickly, it made sense to start as a consulting company rather than a product company.

Looking for some sage advice, I went to see Raj Reddy. He was one of my professors at CMU and had a reputation for excellence in both technology and business. I asked him how to establish my new company as the leader in this narrow niche. "Well," he said in his Indian accent, "to be the leader you have to be the expert." "How do I do that?" I asked. "You must write the book," he replied. "That will make you the expert." That made sense.

So I finished out the year at CGI, working on projects and sketching out some ideas for a book that might make me the expert. I converted our basement into an office with a cheap hollow-core door for some privacy and separation from the rest of the house, and a little brass plaque that read "ServiceWare Inc." The company was incorporated on January 1, 1991.

Later I got a zoning variance for the business, even though one of the neighbors had concerns about the increased traffic that would be on our street, probably imagining that we'd have a steady stream of customers dropping off their broken computers.

The original zoning notice for ServiceWare to be operated from our basement.

ServiceWare

Lots of talented people start companies, and most of those companies fail. ServiceWare was a spectacular success, and we had a few strokes of good luck that helped us get there.

The first bit of good luck was the first Gulf War, which was an awful thing for lots of people but worked out well for my new company. My previous employer Carnegie Group received an expedited wartime contract to develop diagnostics for the Apache helicopter. Rajiv Enand was still in Gary's diagnostics group, and he was in charge of the project. He didn't have anyone available to do the actual work, so he called me to see if I'd be available. He also offered me a lot of money. Since I was just sitting at home working on the book, I agreed quickly.

I put the book on hold for a while and headed to Fort Eustis, a U.S. Army base in Newport News, Virginia. I was at the base five days a week for six weeks working double shifts. During the day I would interview Apache helicopter pilots and mechanics to gather information about how they diagnosed problems, and in the evening I'd sit in my hotel room sifting through my notes and building a knowledge base. By the time the project was finished I'd created a good expert system, and by working sixteen hours a day I'd socked away enough cash to keep the company and the family afloat for a while.

We're Off to Seize the Wizard

Back at home, I began to work seriously on The Book. Since there was little chance of this being a best-selling paperback, I decided to write it for corporate decisionmakers. This would allow me to charge a lot of money. I also hoped it would lead to consulting gigs.

A few fun facts about the book. I called it *We're Off to Seize the Wizard: The Revolution in Service Automation.* The book was self-published, which was unusual because the print-on-demand industry did not exist at that time. I did it all from scratch in the basement with my Macintosh computer. I did all the research and writing. I located a terrific painting done by an early AI system and got permission to use it for cover art. I laid out the book using PageMaker. I conducted surveys (with help from survey expert Fred Bennekom), then

We're Off to Seize the Wizard:

The Revolution in Service Automation

Including: Results of the ServiceWare/AFSMI survey, Intelligent Systems in the Service Industry

How intelligent computer systems are transforming the service industry, and what you need to know to make them work for <u>you</u>.

by Jeff Pepper

analyzed and graphed the results with StatView. I found a downtown company to produce printing plates, then I delivered the plates to a small printer in Verona who printed the first run of 500 or so copies, not counting the 50 or so copies that I discovered had the pages assembled out of order and had to be scrapped. Finally, I distributed the book through two large trade organizations: Ron Muns' Help Desk Institute (HDI) and Joe Trpik's Association for Field Service Management (AFSM). I went to their events and gave talks on expert systems, and in a short period of time I built up a reputation for being, as Raj Reddy had predicted, the expert in the field.

Amazingly enough, it worked. The *Wizard* book was successful and got ServiceWare off the ground. It had a list price of $99 and I sold around a thousand copies, mainly through my two trade organization partners. And even better, it led to several good consulting contracts with large companies who heard about the book, ordered it and read it, could not decide how to proceed with their projects, and hired the expert (me) to help them figure it out.

The book also won the Service Publication Book of the Year award from AFSM, and to my great surprise, was listed as required reading for a course at Indiana University of Pennsylvania!

> - 1991 revenue: $70,000, mostly from book sales
> - 1991 headcount: 1

Consulting and Conferences

In the second year revenue started to take off as the consulting business got going. The company had three employees at year end: myself and two programmers who were brought on temporarily to help with projects.

I did lots of onsite consulting for clients. The most unusual was the time I was invited by the University of Alaska at Fairbanks to spend a week on their campus, in January. The sun didn't appear for the entire week, but I did see the northern lights one night. The consulting work went well. As an added bonus, that weekend one of my clients, Jay Beavers and his wife, took me on a drive 150 miles north of Fairbanks for an overnight stay at Circle Hot Springs, located in the tiny hamlet of Circle. It was bitter cold of course, and the pine trees surrounding the hot springs were coated with several inches of ice from the rising mist.

One of the cool things we did in 1992 to grow the business was to put on a pair of events focused on advanced technology in customer service. I called them the *Wizard* conferences, using the book title as a way to brand the event. We ran two conferences, one at Seven Springs Resort outside of Pittsburgh and the other at Keystone Resort in Colorado. We had a great lineup of speakers from the industry. In September 1991, I printed and mailed out 14,000 flyers, mainly to HDI and AFSM members, promoting the events. Kathryn greeted the attendees as they arrived at the airports, and I hired someone to do registration at the events. Both events sold out, mainly to customer support managers at large companies. Reviews were positive, and the events helped to solidify the reputation of ServiceWare and me personally.

Midway through the second year, I felt I was ready to scale up the company, so I approached Rajiv to see if he'd be interested in leaving CGI and joining me at ServiceWare. He was definitely interested, being just as ambitious as I was. We haggled for a while in my back yard over the terms of his joining the company, and we finally settled on him getting a 40% stake in the company if he hit certain aggressive revenue goals in his first year. He joined me in the basement in January 1993, and he quickly hit his targets and became a co-owner of the company.

- 1992 revenue: $210,000, mostly from consulting
- 1992 headcount: 3

The First Product

In 1993 we hired our first permanent employee, Eric Heiger, to be our office manager. Soon afterwards we moved out of the basement into a small office in Oakmont.

Rajiv and I knew that if we wanted to grow fast and increase the company's value we had to be a product company and not a consulting company, and we debated what our first product should be. There already were lots of software companies in the customer support industry and we didn't see an opportunity for another entrant, especially one as small and underfunded as we were.

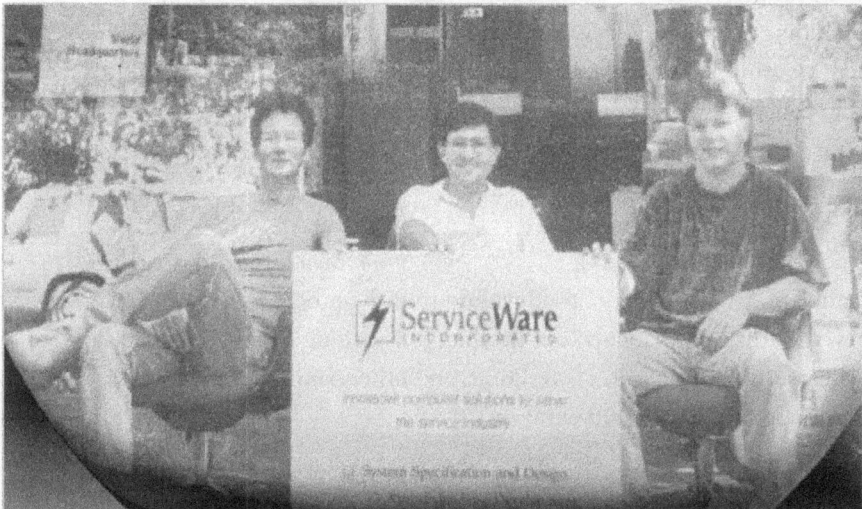

Me, Rajiv and Eric Heiger on the day we moved out of the basement.

That's when we met Scott Webber, the CEO at Software Artistry. His company was one of the leading software companies in the customer support industry, and their product had the ability to use knowledge bases to provide answers to help desk staff who needed to help people use their PCs. We suggested to Scott that we could provide him with pre-packaged knowledge bases, so that his customers could simply install our knowledge bases and instantly have answers to thousands of questions. Scott was intrigued, and said he'd like to come out to Oakmont to visit us.

Yike. This was a great opportunity, and we had to be ready. Our office, if you could call it that, was just a handful of desks, and our staff was just the four of us (Dennis Whalen had joined us as our first software developer). Time to scale up, and fast. I headed to a used office furniture store and bought a half dozen used desks. We put computer terminals on them, and spread papers and technical manuals on them to make them look like they were in use. We asked some of our friends to come down and pretend to be ServiceWare employees. And of course we put together a slick demo showing how our knowledge base worked with Scott's Expert Advisor software product.

Scott came to visit, liked what he saw, and signed a deal where they would sell our product, which we called a Knowledge-Pak. We hired a couple more people including Renate Godfrey, our first knowledge engineer. The first Knowledge-Pak was shipped on September 30, 1993. It covered about five hundred things that could go wrong with Microsoft Windows 3.1. List price was $5,000 per help desk seat (that is, per user).

We were off and running, and well on our way to becoming a product company.

Software Artistry sold the product and split the proceeds with us. Over the next few months we broadened our product line, adding new Knowledge-Paks for Microsoft Word, Excel, PowerPoint, and other common office software tools. Each one sold for $5,000 per user.

Once we had Software Artistry up and running, we approached their competitors and signed distribution deals with several of them. Since we didn't want to have to build separate knowledge bases for each partner, Dennis developed a conversion tool, sort of like a compiler, that automated the process of converting Knowledge-Paks into the proprietary formats required by each of our distribution partners. This kept our costs under control and enabled us to stay profitable even with our rapid growth. Eventually the toolkit that Dennis built evolved into Knowledge-Pak Architect, our first software product.

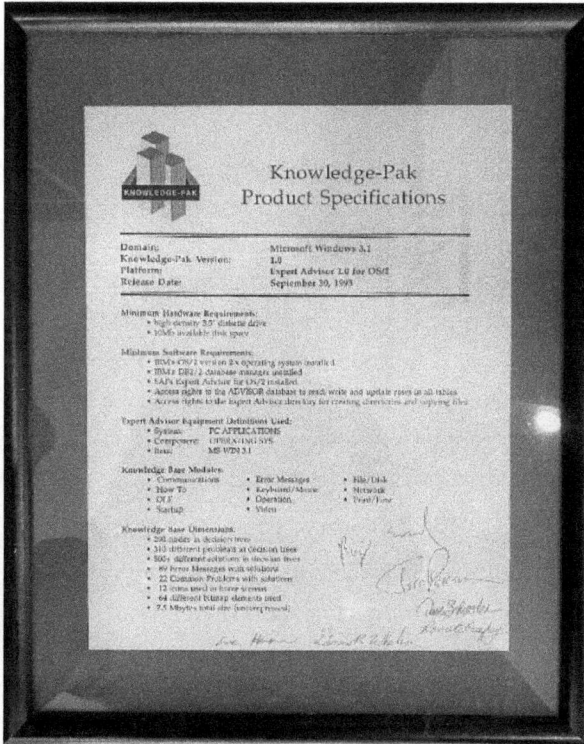

The info sheet for the very first Knowledge-Pak, signed by everyone at ServiceWare: Rajiv Enand, me, Dave Schroeder, Renate Godfrey, Eric Heiger and Dennis Whalen.

It was for Microsoft Windows 3.1 and only ran on the Expert Advisor help desk product. It shipped on a 3.5" diskette and required 10 mb of free disk space.

We also ran another seminar, HelpDoc '93 near Boston. The keynote speaker was Avron Barr, an old friend from my AI days at CMU. I gave a talk about the different types of technologies used for help desk troubleshooting, Rajiv spoke about the implementation process, and there were a dozen other speakers. It was also a sellout, at $795 per person.

I started writing a monthly column for Call Center Magazine, a project that continued for two years. Each month I tried to find a topic that was entertaining and thought-provoking. Sometimes to get in the right mood I'd read some of Dave Barry's humor columns that he wrote for the Miami Herald. One of my favorite columns was the one I wrote in October 1994 titled "Let's

Get Horizontal" where I talked about horizontal integration versus vertical integration. Not the most exciting topic in the world, but it did give me the chance to coin a few new words. Horizontalization was defined as the trend towards layered help desk solutions. The opposite trend was, of course, dehorizontalization. The backlash against this was antidehorizontalization. And someone who believed in this could be said to be a antidehorizontalizationist. Presto, a new and very long word.

- 1993 revenue: $58,000, mostly from Knowledge-Paks
- 1993 headcount: 7

The Crazy Price Cut

In 1994 we successfully leveraged our relationship with Software Artistry to sign similar deals with several other distribution partners. Business was good, but I was starting to see trouble ahead. The good news was that our product was unique, which allowed us to charge a high price. But how many customers would be willing to pay us many thousands of dollars per help desk staffer? It didn't seem like a recipe for long term sustained revenue growth.

I talked it over with Rajiv, and we agreed that we needed to cut our prices in order to increase sales. The obvious problem, though, was that if we simply cut our prices without rapidly increasing the number of units that we sold, we'd soon be out of business. Well, I reasoned, what if we changed our business model? Instead of selling Knowledge-Paks to one customer at a time, what if we told our distributors that they had to include our product in *every* product license that they sold? That would make their product much better but it would increase their costs. Therefore, we had to make our product so cheap that they'd be willing to absorb that cost in order to gain a competitive advantage, or prevent others from gaining competitive advantage over them.

Ok, so how deep a price cut were we talking about? Fifty percent? Ninety percent? Not deep enough, our distributors would never go for it. We finally decided on a 98 percent price cut. That's right. Our products would go from $5,000 per user per Knowledge-Pak down to $100. But in order to get that price, our partners had to include *every* Knowledge-Pak with *every* product license that they sold. These were big companies, we were tiny. So in essence, we were the little tail about to wag the big dog.

We approached our distribution partners and told them our new strategy. They screamed, they complained, they haggled, but eventually nearly every one of them accepted our terms.

- 1994 revenue: $1.2 million
- 1994 headcount: 21

Jeff Pepper: The Pursuit of an Idea

The key to Jeff Pepper's success was not necessarily the result of a single idea, but rather the courage to abandon his original idea in pursuit of "something better."

In 1984, Jeff developed a business plan to start a company that created a PC-based shell for building expert systems. While he found the concept interesting, there were many other entrepreneurially minded developers building similar products despite little market demand.

"I always wanted to do something entrepreneurial," Jeff admits. "I had the technological background, but not the business knowledge. So, I went back to work to gain the experience I would need to someday start my own business."

Thus, Jeff abandoned his original plan and began working with the Carnegie Group, a company that helps transform university-based artificial intelligence (AI) research into commercial products.

"I learned a great deal about the marketplace and how high technology companies operate," Jeff says. "It took years to find the right idea and market segment and to prepare myself, personally, before I was ready."

When Jeff decided to give entrepreneurship another try, he knew it was finally time. In the summer of 1990, Jeff was mowing his lawn as he had probably done a hundred times before. On that day, however, the sensation to leave his job struck so strongly and instantly, that when he returned to work on Monday, he gave his six month notice.

"At that time," Jeff adds, "I knew I wanted my business to focus on the field I knew best: applying advanced technology to customer service. I didn't want to jump prematurely into an expensive and risky product development cycle, though. So I

decided to launch ServiceWare as a consulting firm, maintaining a tight market focus but being totally open to exploring various technology options for our clients."

Jeff started his first year by researching and writing a book, *We're Off to Seize the Wizard*, on advanced service technology, and began lecturing around the country at industry conferences and ServiceWare sponsored seminars.

"The *Wizard* became a best seller and the kernel around which the consulting business grew," Jeff says. "It wasn't until two years later that I felt I had a deep enough grasp of the

Jeff Pepper of ServiceWare shows his Help-Desk software

Article in Enterprise Magazine showing me holding a Knowledge-Pak, fall 1994

First VC Round

The dot-com boom, or what is now called the dot-com bubble, began around 1994. This was our second huge stroke of luck. It changed everything about how one ran a company. Concepts like profitability and sustainability became archaic, and businesspeople who still believed in those things were told bluntly, "You don't get it." This was not just an insult hurled by young entrepreneurs at older ones; it was actually true. Instead of companies being valued at a multiple of earnings (that is, based on profit), they started being valued based on a multiple of revenue, or even, in some cases, at a multiple of eyeballs or page clicks or something equal non-monetary. So the correct business objective at the time was not to make a profit, but to grow as fast as possible.

ServiceWare began several years before the dot-com boom and we were self-funded. Initial funding came from my personal credit cards and a $13,000 loan from my dad in August 1993, so profitability and positive cashflow were critically important to us. All that changed in 1994.

Early in the year, Rajiv and I went to an AFSM trade show. As usual, we rented a small truck and hauled everything to the venue and set it up ourselves. We had our little 10' x 10' trade show booth in the low-rent district around the periphery of the trade show floor. We were promoting our Knowledge-Paks and working on attracting new distribution partners. A woman named Susanne Harrison was wandering around the trade show floor chatting with vendors and looking for interesting companies. Someone suggested that she should talk with us, as we had a product that was unique and showed promise. She came over, we talked, and she was interested.

It turned out that she represented a small venture capital firm on Long Island named POLY Ventures. The firm was founded by her husband Shelley Harrison who'd made a fortune by founding Symbol Technologies, the company that made the barcode ubiquitous. Susanne was a partner in the VC firm, and there were a couple of other partners. She invited me to come to visit them at their office in Farmingdale and make a pitch.

In early July 1994 I flew to New York with my laptop computer and my portable LCD projector. I rented a car and drove out to Long Island to the address she gave me. It was a classroom building on the campus of SUNY Farmingdale. I went in, wandered up and down the halls for a while, and finally found their little office in a remote corner of the building. Susanne greeted me. I set up in a small conference room and began my pitch to the partners. I sketched out the landscape of the market we were in, described our business model, described our product and how we would dominate the market and crush the competition, and finished by making some wildly optimistic projections. This was all standard investor pitch stuff.

It seemed to fall on deaf ears. The people in the office were, without a doubt, the rudest people I'd ever met in business. Although Susanne sat and paid attention through the 20 or so minutes of my talk, the rest of them wandered in and out. They took phone calls, they made calls, they talked to each other about things that had nothing to do with my pitch, and they only occasionally glanced my way.

I thought the trip was a disaster. I packed up my stuff and left. The next day Susanne called me and said they were prepared to invest a quarter of a million dollars in ServiceWare.

Our first venture capital investment.

By today's standards this was a microscopic investment, the kind of thing an angel investor might kick in just for fun. But for us, it was a game changer in more ways than one. The money itself allowed us to ramp up our growth rate without having to worry about running out of cash. This, in turn, led us to change our mindset about the goals of the company. No longer worried about profit, it was all about growth. (Of course, venture capital is like a drug, and the more you use the more you need, as we learned later.)

Beyond that, though, our new board member Susanne brought a new level of experience and hard-headedness to the company. She'd served on several other boards and knew quite a bit about the lifecycle of a high growth company. This was generally useful. However, her advice wasn't always terrific, and one of her decisions cost Rajiv and me several tens of millions of dollars, but that came later.

A year after taking the initial round of investment from POLY Ventures, we were approached by another firm in New Jersey called Geocapital Partners. In

June 1995 they invested another $1.1 million at a much higher valuation. We kept growing and kept hiring. We moved to larger offices across the street, and our landlord began construction of a three-story corporate headquarters building for us in Oakmont.

We continued to add more Knowledge-Pak topics and more distribution partners. We also entered the software business by converting our internal knowledge engineering toolkit into a knowledge management product that we called Knowledge-Pak Architect. This would enable customers to build their own knowledge bases instead of just buying them from us. Our revenue tripled. But for the first time, the company spent more money than it took in. We were hooked on venture capital.

- 1995 revenue: $2.8 million
- 1995 loss: $0.7 million
- 1995 headcount: 65

Fame and Fortune

In April 1996 we took our third and final round of venture capital investment. Norwest Venture Capital a Silicon Valley firm, invested $2.5 million. They also purchased another $3 million of stock from Rajiv and me. This allowed us to take a little bit off the table and reassure our spouses that this tech startup thing would actually pay off. Kevin Hall made the investment decision for Norwest and joined our board. Revenues grew to just over $5 million. We were also losing money, but nobody seemed to care as long as we were growing fast.

Because the company was now controlled by the three VC firms, the goal was to make as much money as possible for them through a "liquidity event" which entailed either being acquired by another company or by going public through an initial public offering (IPO). In either case, stock was converted to cash and everyone got a payday.

During the dot-com boom, IPO valuations for tech companies were typically calculated as a multiple of revenues, not profits. A 3x or 5x multiple was common, but a 10x or 15x multiple was not unheard of. This led to some strange math. A company might decide to sell a product to a customer at below cost, say selling it for $500k even though it cost $700k. That sale might be unprofitable, but that $500k would increase the value of the company by a couple of million dollars when it was sold or went public. Our senior team understood this and played the system effectively.

Japan

In the 1990's, Japan was a highly respected player in the technology world, especially in artificial intelligence, and their economy was strong. So part of our 1996 plan was to establish a master distributor in Japan. I took this on as a project.

After several explorations we selected Sumitomo, one of the handful of Japanese *keiretsu*, the Japanese equivalent of conglomerates. We signed an agreement whereby Sumitomo would "localize" our Knowledge-Pak Architect software and our Knowledge-Pak content for the Japanese market. Shigeo Kakuno was the business development executive who was assigned to the ServiceWare account. We met several times in Pittsburgh. One time I took him out for dinner, and

ServiceWare Inc.

Founder

For the last six years, Jeff Pepper has worked to build his company from a one-person basement startup to one of the major powerhouses of the international customer support industry. ServiceWare has grown by over 7,000 percent in the last four-and-a-half years.

Mr. Pepper started ServiceWare in 1991 when he wrote and also self-published a groundbreaking book addressing the shift of customer support from a traditional labor-based activity to its new role as a knowledge-based activity.

Jeff Pepper — That book, "We're Off to Seize the Wizard: The Revolution in Service Automation," became a best-seller and won the 1992 Patton Award for best support industry publication of the year.

Mr. Pepper has continued to be a prolific writer, contributing a monthly column to Call Center Magazine and publishing more than two dozen technical articles and papers.

He was a guest contributor to The Age of Intelligent Machines by Raymond Kurzweil, selected by the Association of American Publishers as the Most Outstanding Computer Science Book of 1990.

He has also contributed to the design and development of hundreds of knowledge-based system projects in the last 15 years, in both commercial and military applications, and co-holds one of the few U.S. patents granted for knowledge-based system architectures.

Before founding ServiceWare, Mr. Pepper spent six years with Carnegie Group Inc., where he co-developed the patented Test-Bench diagnostic system technology.

Mr. Pepper holds a bachelor's degree in mathematics from Carnegie Mellon University, where he also served as an instructor in the computer science department from 1978 to 1980.

Article in Pittsburgh Business Times, June 1996.

as a cultural experience we went to a play afterwards. Unfortunately I'd selected *Annie*, which was set in 1930's America and included some racist and anti-Japanese sentiments. A bit embarrassing, but Mr. Kakuno had his polite face on and didn't react at all.

I traveled to Tokyo in spring of 1996 to kick off the partnership. The event was held at a prestigious hotel near the Imperial Palace. It was hosted by Sumitomo and attended to dozens of high ranking executives from other Japanese keiretsu and smaller companies. Great quantities of whiskey were consumed, bows were performed, and speeches were made. I spoke in English and it was translated for the audience, few of whom understood English. Mr. Kakuno stayed by my side, translating between Japanese and English for me. One of the speeches was given in an unusual dialect of Japanese with Mr. Kakuno did not understand. So another manager translated that speech into ordinary Japanese, whereupon Mr. Kakuno translated it for me in English.

The next few days were spent meeting with the Sumitomo team who were tasked with localizing and selling our products. We also went out every night for business dinners, sometimes including potential customers. I was a vegetarian by this point, but decided that it would be impossible (and impolite) to try to maintain that during the trip, so I just ate whatever they put in front of me and washed it down with whiskey.

Japanese society was (and probably still is) extremely formal. Social interactions are so polite and ritualized that it's difficult even for Japanese people to know what the other person is really thinking or saying. As a result, a safety valve involving alcohol consumption has evolved. Two people, say a boss and his subordinate, or a salesman and his client, will go out after work for drinks. Conversation is polite as always, up to a certain point. At that point one or both of the participants will begin acting extremely drunk, and that gives them social permission to say whatever is really on their mind, without fear of reprisal or breaking social taboos. I experienced this once, when Mr. Kakuno and I went out for dinner and drinks at Kiku, a local Japanese sushi restaurant in Pittsburgh. We ate sushi, we drank sake, and at some point he began slurring his words and told me some things that needed to be said about my interactions with his team in Japan. I knew what he was doing, so I just listened and nodded my head. He finished, and seemed to sober up with remarkable speed.

At a dinner reception in Tokyo. From left: Mr. Aoki, head of SSD; me; Miko Ishiyama, President of Sumitomo Metals System Development; Eiichi Ueda, Managing Director of Sumitomo SED; Shigeo Kakuno, Manager of Sumitomo SED Market Research; and Mr. Yamashita, the manager who ran the Knowledge-Pak business.

 I visited Japan several times over the next few years to maintain relationships with my Sumitomo counterparts and to assist with their sales efforts as I could. These visits were always in Tokyo or one of the nearby big cities, and I never had a chance to experience traditional Japan. So on my next-to-final visit in 1999, I told my hosts that I wanted to see that side of Japan. They were happy to oblige. So on my last visit, after the last business meetings were concluded, they escorted me to a Tokyo train station. I took a train to another city, then changed to a smaller train on a narrow-gauge railroad. That train took me to a small town in rural Japan. I got off the train and was met by the owner of a nearby *ryokan*, a traditional Japanese guest house. It turned out that I was the only non-Japanese person at the ryokan and possibly in the entire town. Nobody spoke any English, and I spoke no Japanese. Despite this, it was a wonderful visit. I slept on a tatami mat on the floor. I was not allowed in the main dining room because they were hosting a gathering of Japanese businessmen, so the staff brought meals to my room. Outside my window was a rice paddy – a real rice paddy! – and I watched a farmer planting rice while I worked on my laptop computer.

High Growth

Flush with VC money, Rajiv and I accelerated the company's growth. We assembled a terrific senior management team – Ted Teele as VP of Sales (later promoted to President), Paul McDermott as VP of Finance, Suzy Nicastro as VP of Marketing, and Rick Joslin as Director (later VP) of Knowledge Engineering. We promoted Dennis Whalen to CTO and hired an older ("seasoned") executive, Carl Swartz, to run the software team. Those executives filled out their respective teams. Our sales grew, and our expenses grew faster.

Our Sales VP Ted Teele was probably the most brilliant salesperson I've ever met. He understood the key to successful sales, which is to never try to just close the sale; you need to create a need, preferably a desperate need, in the mind of the customer. Once that's established, closing the deal is easy. Shortly after Ted joined us he discovered that we were short of cash and only a few months away from not being able to meet monthly payroll. So being the guy in charge of producing revenue, he looked around for the biggest deal he could find. He found an entrepreneur, Unni Warrier, who was assembling a company called Cybermedia with the goal of going public quickly and making a windfall profit. Ted convinced Unni that he needed a Knowledge-Pak deal to make his company successful.

Once the guy was hooked, Ted began to reel him in. Ted made him an offer that gave Cybermedia exactly what Unni was convinced he needed, but Ted's offer expired at the end of the calendar quarter. In order to get the deal, Unni had to wire us $1,125,000 by the next business day. At the time, Rajiv and I were at a trade show in California while Ted was in Pittsburgh on the phone with Unni. Unni refused to do the deal or wire the money. Ted said fine, you won't be able to achieve your goals without us, and he hung up the phone. A few minutes later Unni called back. They talked, and talked, and talked. Unni hung up a few more times. Ted was relentless. He sent us email updates every hour or so. Finally, after something like ten hours of the phone, Unni finally caved at 2:30 am Pittsburgh time, which was 11:30 pm Pacific time, just before the deadline. Ted closed the deal, Cybermedia wired us the money the next day, and we had enough funds to meet payroll.

A full page Call Center ad June 1996 listing our partners

By this time we had more than outgrown our second floor office space. Employee cars were parked on both sides of Allegheny Avenue, blocking traffic and annoying the local merchants. Finally the new building was ready and we moved in. The building at 333 Allegheny Avenue built for us by Jim Siciliano, a tough old-school Italian contractor and landlord. To save money he avoided all exterior decoration, leading some locals to call the building the Berlin Wall of Oakmont. And he designed the first floor so that if we went out of business, which was always a possibility with a software company, he could easily convert the first floor to retail.

To save money and space, we didn't have a large meeting room or a lunchroom. For meals we used the Brugger's Bagels located on the first floor. And we held our company meetings in the Oaks Theater across the street, renting it out for the afternoon and giving everyone free popcorn and candy. I refused to take a corner office, instead taking an office in the middle of the third floor facing the parking lot. The office at the third floor corner was designated a conference room.

Our new headquarters on Allegheny Avenue in Oakmont, under construction.

The ServiceWare team in the excavation that would become our new corporate HQ.

We kept hiring. At one point I calculated that the average tenure of employment for a ServiceWarian was around 3 months.

I was President and CEO and very much enjoying the job. Rajiv had a variety of titles depending on what he was working on at the time, including VP of

Business Development. Morale at the company was high, and we went years without anyone quitting even though everyone worked long hours. We had a quarterly employee-produced newspaper called The ServiceWarian. We had social events in the parking lot. We rented large venues for holiday parties. Some of us formed a cover band called The Gigs, with me playing guitar. Davis Raborn on drums, Chris Evans on bass, Ken Zalesky on lead guitar, and Deanna Dean on vocals. I wrote a song called Hotel ServiceWaria, set to the melody of Hotel California, the Gigs played it at a company party, and it became the company theme song.

Me, playin' in the band.

Hotel ServiceWaria

Jeff Pepper and Don Henley

Heading east on the Parkway, cold rain in my hair
Warm smell from the steel mills, rising up through the air
As I pulled into Oakmont, I saw an interesting place
Drove around for an hour and a half just to find a parking place

There they stood in the lobby, gee they sure looked swell
And I was thinking to myself 'this could be Apple or this could be Dell'
and they led me up the stairway and they showed me my cube
Trained me for a day and said
　　　'Now you're a knowledge engineering dude'

Welcome to the Hotel ServiceWaria
They risk heart attacks, building Knowledge-Paks
Plenty of room at the Hotel ServiceWaria
Any time of year, you can find them here

They got their corporate customers, they got their odds and ends
They got their pretty Premier Partners that they call friends
How the salespeople sell it, all day long
Some sell to hit quota, some sell to hit the gong.

So I went to a TG and said, 'Please bring me my pop'
They said, 'it's all free here, you can drink it nonstop'
And still those voices are calling from far away
Read my email in the middle of the night, I thought I saw it say...

Welcome to the Hotel ServiceWaria
They work night and day, building KPA
Livin' it up at the Hotel ServiceWaria
Get your parking tag; bring your sleeping bag...

Last thing I remember, I was heading for the door
I had to find the passage back to the place I worked before
'Good night,' said Margie, 'You look well rested.
But you can't leave for three more years, 'cause your options aren't vested!'

*The Gigs playing
at a ServiceWare
TGIF.*

*Lyrics to Hotel
ServiceWaria.*

We had a large brass gong on the second floor where the sales team was located. Whenever anyone closed a big deal, someone (usually Ted) would bang the gong and announce the new deal.

The gong.

Our marketing team was always running promotions to drum up interest in our Knowledge-Pak Architect software product. Once they ran a contest, and the grand prize was a new Harley Davidson motorcycle. Any customer who purchased Knowledge-Pak Architect in the prior three months was eligible. I thought it would be fun to show off the bike at a company meeting in our new building. So the marketing team bought the bike and stashed it in an office just adjacent to the large meeting room on the first floor. The company meeting started, I fired up the bike, and rode it into the company meeting. Fortunately nobody was run over. I have no idea how we ever delivered the bike to the contest winner, or whether his employer allowed him to keep it.

- 1996 revenue: $5.2 million
- 1996 loss: $1.0 million
- 1996 headcount: 90

Me riding a Harley into a company meeting. Ted (in striped shirt) is applauding.

Ants

I don't have a degree in business and never took a business class in college. Everything I know about starting and running a company comes from trial and error, listening to good advice, and reading occasional books on the subject. The closest thing I have to a business philosophy is "Try to think clearly and don't do anything stupid. And if you do something stupid, don't be afraid to change course." This actually isn't as obvious as it seems. I've met lots of CEOs who where so overconfident that they couldn't admit that they were doing something stupid, nobody was willing to tell them, and they were too arrogant to change course afterwards.

I've already mentioned a few business books that affected me, but one of the most important ones was not about business at all. It was about ants.

When I was at CMU, the only thing that mattered was how smart you were (as opposed to, say, in high school, where the most important things were social skills and wearing the right clothes). So as a result of my education there I just sort of assumed that the key to a successful business was hiring the absolute smartest people I could find and giving them wide latitude to identify and solve problems. However, although that approach probably works fine in a small tech startup, it wasn't scaling up well. We were hiring a lot of people, and as our

186

headcount crossed the 100 mark I found myself frustrated at their lack of creativity.

Then I read *The Ants*, a Pulitzer prize winning book by Edward O. Wilson and Bert Holldobler. The book was fascinating as simply an exploration of the dominant life form on earth – someone once said that to a first order of magnitude, every animal on earth is an ant. But I got something else from it. The authors describe how successful ant colonies are, even though nearly all of its members are just following simple instructions. An individual worker ant does not understand the overall architecture of the nest. It just does what it's programmed to do. Every ant follows a set of simple instructions, and the colony thrives. (Actually the colony's queen is also following her own simple set of instructions, but that's another discussion…)

This got me thinking about my experience doing some projects for the military, including the U.S. Army. The Army is in many ways like an ant colony, with a large number of foot soldiers playing a similar role to ant workers. The soldiers don't need to understand the complexity of logistics or battle strategy. A soldier succeeds, at least from the Army's point of view, if he understand the rules that he's supposed to follow and has the discipline needed to follow those rules even in stressful conditions.

If ant colonies and military organizations can be so successful by having large numbers of individuals following basic instructions, why not a software company? This completely changed my view of my company. I didn't need a hundred queens or a hundred four-star generals. I needed a few of them, to be sure. But for the majority of people in the company, all I needed was for them to do their jobs well, follow instructions, avoid being disruptive, and exercise a reasonable level of creativity.

Of course the company didn't need dumb drones. But it didn't need geniuses either.

As a result, I became much more comfortable having people in the company who had a range of abilities. And I wasn't upset anymore when the guy in the shipping department couldn't write good code or understand a financial statement.

Long Distance Decision

With things going well, I went on a family vacation to Hawaii. One of our stops on the trip was a drive to the top of Mt. Haleakala, one of the largest volcanos in the world. The morning of the trip up the mountain, I got a call from one of the senior managers informing me that the guy who was our VP of sales at the time was trying to assert more authority than he actually had, and was causing a major disruption in the company. It seemed one of those "when the cat's away" situations. This person had shown similar tendencies earlier, so I believed the story that I heard. Something had to be done, but I was five thousand miles away.

I set up a conference call with all the senior managers except the sales VP to talk things over, and this confirmed the story. So I called up the sales VP and fired him, effective immediately. Then I asked our IT guy to set up a speakerphone link so I could address the entire company at a certain time. When the time came we were at the top of Haleakala. I drove about halfway down the mountain to a spot that had decent cellphone reception, pulled off the road, and let everyone in the company know what had just happened.

High Visibility

We were now becoming large enough and successful enough (in terms of growth anyway) to attract notice. Our rapid growth placed us number 76 in the 1997 Inc. 500 list of the fastest growing companies in the United States. Later that same year I won the 1996 Entrepreneur of the Year award, an event sponsored by Ernst & Young and the Pittsburgh Technology Council. And I was invited to serve on the board of directors for the Pittsburgh Technology Council. Shortly afterwards I was invited to be a member of the executive committee, a much smaller group of board members who made many of the key decisions.

Provides internetworking training svcs.			
74. Solutions Consulting Canonsburg, PA Provides systs.-integration consulting svcs.	2,343	15,735	644
75. Capricorn Systems Atlanta, GA Provides computer-software consulting	2,324	19,049	786
76. Serviceware Oakmont, PA Sells prepackaged knowledge bases	2,276	5,037	212
77. Equipe Technologies Sunnyvale, CA (9) Mfrs. robots used in prod. of computer chips	2,228	34,988	1,503
78. Dentrix Dental Systems American Fork, UT (78) Develops clinical & practical mgmt. systs.	2,222	10,355	446
79. Universal Fabric Structures Quakertown, PA Mfrs. portable fabric structures	2,184	16,902	740
80. i Market Waltham, MA Develops & distr. target-marketing software	2,136	11,963	535

Our listing in the 1997 Inc. 500, showing revenue growing from $212k to $5.03 million, an increase of 2,276% in three years.

Liquidity Events

As the dot-com boom heated up, several of our distribution partners went public. These IPO were successful, where "success" occurred if the share price going up immediately after the IPO and staying high for a reasonable time. Everyone who owned stock in the company made out well through the IPO, including company management, early angel investors, later stage venture capital firms, and of course the underwriter that handled the IPO itself. There were also "friends and family" shares which was a way for company management to bestow gifts and share the wealth by selling chunks of common stock to friends, family members and other insiders at the initial offering price of the IPO. When the stock jumped in value immediately after the stock opened, as it almost always did, one could flip those shares and make a tidy profit. I had a good enough relationship with the senior management at these companies that they invited me to purchase some shares. I did this at least twice that I can recall, one with Clarify and again with Vantive. The Clarify IPO provided enough profit for us to add a nice deck onto the kitchen side of the house. The Vantive IPO provided another cash windfall that was used, in part, to pay for a major extension on the house.

Of course we were always on the lookout for our own liquidity event. Our first opportunity came when our major competitor, Primus, approached us. They were based in Seattle. Rajiv and I met their CEO Mike Brochu and one of his

In 1997, ServiceWare hit $10 million in annual sales

co-founders over dinner at Kuleto's, a famous Italian restaurant and techie meeting place near the San Francisco airport. Shortly after that meeting they approached us about a merger. Primus was larger than we were. They had already raised $34 million in venture capital (compared to only about $5 million for us), and their revenue was about twice ours. As a result, they were closer to being able to go public on the Nasdaq exchange. Primus focused on software, whereas our specialty was content (the Knowledge-Paks), thus making the two companies complementary. Mike offered us a merger deal where the Primus shareholders would get 2/3 ownership of the resulting company and our shareholders would get the other 1/3. After a bit of haggling he agreed to a 60/40 split. Rajiv and I both thought this was a good deal. We took it to the board and asked them for their approval.

Most of the board members were uncertain, but Susanne was adamantly opposed to it. She insisted on getting 45% or no deal. The rest of the board went along with her, and we had no choice but to agree. We took that back to Primus. They rejected it, and that was the end of that. Two years later they had a successful IPO at a valuation of over $100 million. Had we done the deal and taken the combined company public, the valuation probably would have been in the $150 million range, and our shareholders would have walked away with something in the range of $60 million. At the time, I owned forty percent of the company.

We were getting ready to close the books on 1997, and revenues was looking like $9.9 million. I was willing to go with that, as it showed nearly 100% annual growth. But Ted wanted us to cross the $10 million threshold. He sat down with our CFO, reviewed all the revenue recognition decisions we'd made, and successfully got the books (legally) rejiggered so that we showed just over $10 million in revenue for the year.

In the lobby of our building we had a big 3D bar chart. It was on the wall facing the front door so visitors couldn't avoid noticing it. Each year starting with 1991 had a vertical metal bar that showed the revenue for that year. The growth curve was steep, and by 1996 we had run out of room for the vertical bars. So for 1996 the vertical bar reached the ceiling and then continued onto the corresponding wall on the second floor. For 1997 the bar reached the third floor.

- 1997 revenue: $10 million
- 1997 loss: $1.6 million
- 1997 headcount: 150

Boardroom Battle

Rajiv and I were heading back to Pittsburgh after another business trip in early 1998. I'd been running the company for seven years. It had been an exhausting trip and I was a bit tired at the time. I said something to him about how nice it would be to take some time off. This was all Rajiv needed to hear. He told me that he was ready and eager to have, as he put it, "his turn" as company CEO. I knew that Rajiv was bright, a terrific strategist, and had big ambitions. And he'd been waiting in the wings for five years for this opportunity.

In retrospect I should have realized that Rajiv would have a difficult time moving into the CEO job. I didn't have any management experience when I started ServiceWare, but I was fortunate enough to be able to grow into the job over several years as the company grew from a one-man basement startup to a 200+ person enterprise. Rajiv, by contrast, had never actually managed a large team, generally operating as a lone wolf or the leader of a small team. Could he jump in and take the reins? I had a great deal of respect for his abilities and thought that he did deserve a shot at the CEO job. So I agreed that it probably was time for him to replace me.

Meanwhile, Ted Teele had been promoted to President and was doing an excellent job of running the company's day-to-day operations. Ted had a Harvard MBA and several years experience leading large teams. Ted was a natural leader, in contrast to Rajiv who was a brilliant strategist but didn't have Ted's strong leadership skills.

When Ted heard of the planned transition, he reacted strongly. He made the case that he was much more qualified than Rajiv to be CEO. Ted's opinion of Rajiv was that "he couldn't lead ants to a picnic." After talking with him I realized that he had a point, but I'd already offered the job to Rajiv. And so began a classic boardroom struggle that lasted several weeks, though it seemed to last much longer. My office was in the middle of a row of window offices on the 3rd floor. Rajiv's office was on one side and Ted was on the other. For days on end I met with one, then the other. Ted and Rajiv refused to meet directly on this subject, though of course they had to see each other on regular company business. Our CFO, Paul McDermott, saw what was happening. He became worried and began polishing his resume, expecting the worst.

The struggle between Ted and Rajiv continued. For the most part the board members did not have a strong preference either way, but they were alarmed at the dysfunction that had suddenly blossomed in a company that they thought was well-managed. We began to lose their confidence, which is the end of one's career in a VC-controlled company.

After a few weeks of this, we scheduled a major board meeting for July 9. I submitted a set of options for how to move forward. They were: (1) Rajiv becomes CEO (Ted thought this was a terrible idea); (2) Ted becomes CEO (Rajiv thought this was a terrible idea); (3) I remain as CEO for 6 months while Ted transitions to the CEO job; (4) we retain a search firm and hire a new CEO from the outside; (5) we seek to be acquired by another company with Ted remaining as President; or (6) we merge with our competitor Primus with their CEO taking over. I recommended option 2 or 3, essentially handing control to Ted.

On June 30, ten days before the big board meeting, the most violent storm in recent memory hit Pittsburgh. It was called the "microburst" and was supposedly caused by a freak weather event that briefly brought the high altitude jet stream down to ground level. It hit in the middle of the afternoon, turning an ordinary rainstorm into a hurricane. We looked out the windows of our office building and saw large tree limbs ripped from their trunks and flying down Allegheny Avenue. Rick Joslin, our risk-averse VP of Knowledge Engineering, told everyone to go and shelter in the basement. I stayed on the third floor with some other people to watch the storm.

Then the power went out.

This would have been an inconvenience no matter when it occurred, but it was the last day of the calendar quarter. Ted and the sales team had revenue targets to hit, and the building was dark. Jay Levino, our IT manager, jumped in his car and drove down to the local Home Depot and bought the last gas-powered generator they had in stock. He brought it back to the building and got the computers back on line. Ted sent everyone in his sales team home so they could work on closing deals before the end of the day.

I went home late that afternoon and found that the narrow winding road to our house was completely blocked by a dozen fallen trees. I grabbed a chain saw and joined other neighbors as we cut the trees and unblocked the road. Because we lived on top of a hill, our yard was hit harder than most. Several large trees, including some very large catalpas, had been blown down. Fortunately, there was no damage to the house. A news crew from local station WPXI TV came to the house, pointed a video camera in my face, and asked me how bad it was. "Oh, not bad," I replied, standing in a pile of huge fallen trees. Greatly disappointed, the crew turned off the camera even before I finished talking, and walked away.

Working from their homes, Ted and his sales team successfully hit their sales targets for the quarter.

The microburst was the catalyst for a major waterfall project at our house, more on that a bit later.

Back at the office, there was only a week until the big July 9 board meeting. Rajiv knew that I was going to recommend that Ted be named the new CEO, so he began actively working to block this. As a major shareholder he had quite a bit of leverage. He managed to get a couple of board members on his side. I reluctantly agreed to this change in plan, and so prior to the July 9 board meeting the three of us sat down together. I told Ted about the decision. Ted saw that he was checkmated, with no way to reverse the decision. He accepted it and offered to stay on as President. I thought that was a great idea and a gracious way to concede defeat. Rajiv was noncommittal.

The changeover occurred at the end of June 1998. Rajiv became CEO. I remained Board Chair. We had a big company party in the parking lot. The

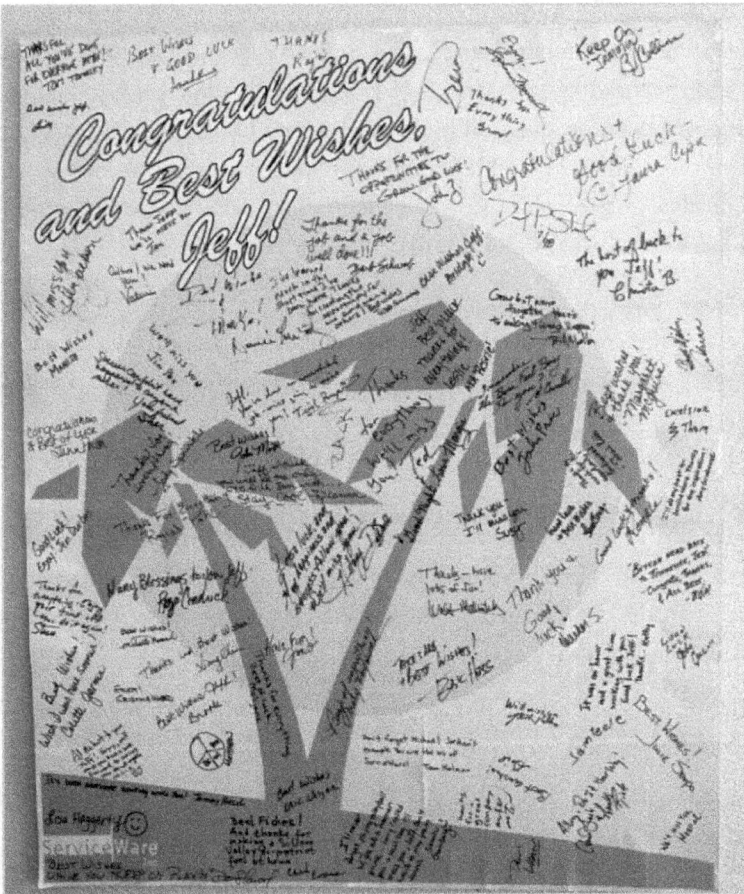

My giant going-away card.

Gigs played. I was given a large "Congratulations and Best Wishes" card signed by everyone at the company.

Sadly, my concerns about Rajiv's role as CEO provide to be well founded. Within a few months, Ted resigned from the company. Our CFO Paul McDermott also resigned. And most of the rest of the senior team quit or were fired by Rajiv.

My going-away party in the parking lot. Rajiv and me at the going-away party. Note that my blue ServiceWare hat has been replaced by a sombrero.

- 1998 revenue: $12.9 million
- 1998 loss: 3.8 million
- 1998 headcount: 200

Preparing for the IPO

While all this was going on, we had already started the complicated, time consuming and expensive process of becoming a publicly traded company.

Several Wall Street underwriting firms had visited over the previous couple of years to pitch themselves as the firm that would take us public. We invited several of them to come in and make their final case, and of those, we selected Alex Brown as the lead underwriter and Piper Jaffray as the secondary underwriter. Both were reputable companies, big enough to do the job but small enough to be interested in a little Pittsburgh startup like us.

On March 13, 1998 we informed the rest of the company that we were officially starting the process of becoming a public company. We entered the "quiet period" between this announcement and the actual IPO, where everyone with inside knowledge of the impending IPO had to say nothing. This was to prevent any information leaking out, which might bring down the wrath of the Securities and Exchange Commission on us. Somehow word of the impending IPO leaked out anyway and was reported in the local Pittsburgh Business Times. I never found out who leaked it, and fortunately no damage was done.

It was my job to coordinate the IPO process, even though I had resigned as CEO and was not actually running the company when it happened.

Going public takes a huge amount of time and money, with no actual commitment from the underwriter that they would actually go through with it in the end. However, Alex Brown assured us that there was virtually no chance that they would pull the plug. So we got started on it. We switched law firms to one with more experience in these things. Our new law firm, Morgan Lewis, began preparing the prospectus, a 100+ page document that described our company and the offering. They set up a war room in their office in downtown Pittsburgh, and a team of lawyers and associates led by attorney Marlee Myers worked day and night, literally, for a couple of months on this. Their legal bills ran into six figures. At least one of their people quit, exhausted from the project.

While this was happening, the air began to slowly leak out of the dot-com bubble. Stock prices for tech companies were at astronomical levels, but the companies themselves often were losing cash at an unsustainable rate. Despite this, more and more tech companies were having successful IPOs as they all rushed to cash out while they could.

When a company goes public, the early investors, primarily the venture capital firms, make large profits because the value of the stock price increases greatly. Founders become billionaires, early hires become millionaires, and the underwriters who handle the IPOs, and their friends, all make tidy profits. The financial fuel for all this is (or was) the money invested by thousands of individual investors who buy the stocks of these tech companies on the open market. Everyone was clamoring to buy newly minted stock in tech companies.

All of us at ServiceWare, including the investors and senior management, were excited about the financial payoff that came with a successful IPO. So we remained committed to moving forward. And company performance was still on track, with Q1 revenues and profits right on plan.

But in early June, just as the prospectus document was ready to go to the printer, things began to unravel. Our lead underwriter Alex Brown pulled out. They cited the poor climate for tech IPOs, especially for small unprofitable companies like ours. We protested that they'd told us that there was virtually no chance of them doing that, but it was no use. They saw too much risk. We had no choice, we had to put the IPO on ice.

We began frantically casting around for another underwriter to replace Alex Brown. Finally a small New York bank, Unterberg Towbin, stepped up. They had gotten to know us during a pre-IPO financing round that was intended to improve the company's balance sheet and allay any investor fears of the company running out of money. They agreed to underwrite the IPO for us, but they wanted us to hit certain goals before they'd take us public. They also recruited three other underwriters including Bear Stearns to co-underwrite the offering.

Management Crisis

By this point I was no longer playing an active role in running ServiceWare. I was spending less time in the office and was focusing on my new venture, ElderVision. But then I received an anonymous and disturbing email on April

16, 1999. It probably came from someone in the software development team, though I never learned exactly who sent it. The writer pointed out that the company had missed its numbers for three quarters in a row and is running out of cash. It ended with, *"I'm worried that you and the board are not paying attention to how the company is operated and how badly Rajiv works with his management team... Please help turn things around and make this company fun and successful again."*

Jeff Pepper

From:	Anonymous [nobody@anon.olymp.org]
Sent:	Friday, April 16, 1999 8:55 PM
To:	pepper@serviceware.com
Subject:	worries about ServiceWare

Dear Jeff,

I hear you are off doing virtual reality for old folks. It sounds fun.

But while you are having fun, I worry about if you are paying much attention to ServiceWare. I'm sure you know we've missed our numbers three quarters in a row, that last quarter we had only a handful of new software customers, that we are running out of cash and so on.

But have you also heard that half of development has resumes on the street and that we've got a betting pool about how many of the senior managers will have quit by mid summer? This used to be a cool company, everybody from Product Management to Sales to Software Dev is pretty depressed about how badly the company is being managed. I'm not sure it is safe to stick around to see what happens when The Cloud is launched. If Mark or Carl leaves, I'm sure I'll bail.

I'm worried that you and the board are not paying attention to how the company is operated and how badly Rajiv works with his management team. I certainly hope you are guarding the value of my options, but I haven't even talked to you for more than a year.

Please help turn things around and make this company fun and successful again.

The anonymous email.

Although I didn't want to get involved again in ServiceWare operations, and really, really didn't want to second-guess Rajiv, I felt that I had no choice. The future of the company was at stake, as well as the financial wellbeing of myself and everyone else in the company. So I set up meetings with nine members of the team, including some senior managers and some mid-level and nonmanagers whose opinions I trusted. Nearly everyone I spoke to reported serious problems. To make things worse, the company was in serious trouble financially. Sales bookings had fallen 60% short of plan, and software license renewals were down 89%. Overall, the feeling was that the company was spinning out of control and failing.

After finishing these nine interviews as well as conversations with several board members, I invited Rajiv over to the house to talk things over. It was a sunny day in May. We sat outside on the deck next to the garage. I told him bluntly that although everyone liked him personally, there were concerns about his performance as CEO. I then went through a systematic review of what the team had said, going point by point and citing examples of each one. Rajiv did not concede any of it. He told me that after he took over the CEO job he was shocked at how bad the situation at the company was, and that he was trying his best to turn things around. I countered that there are always serious problems in any organization, and the job of a leader is to have a clear idea of where the organization needs to go, sell that idea to everyone, and motivate and mobilize everyone to get there. I told him that he was not articulating a vision, was not motivating people, and was missing his business targets.

Nothing was resolved, but I felt that I needed to ask the board to make some changes. We had a stormy board call in late May. I outlined all the issues that I saw with Rajiv's performance and the company's problems, and pushed for the company to name a new CEO. Kevin Hall from Norwest and Susanne Harrison from POLY Ventures were very concerned and asked a number of probing questions. Larry Lepard, the board member from Geocapital Partners, reacted immaturely and started talking about legal action to protect his firm's investment. Eric Cooper, CEO of Fore Systems and a highly respected outside board member, said nothing, but he resigned from the board the next day.

The venture capitalists who controlled the board decided that major changes were required and they took over. They held a series of phone calls among themselves, cutting me and Rajiv out of the loop. They fired Rajiv and installed our VP of Sales, Mark Tapling, as CEO. Mark was not particularly brilliant or strategic, but he looked good in a suit and had a stable and likeable personality. The board members and the underwriter thought that he could solve the company's revenue problems and would also be an good face for the company when it went public.

- 1999 revenue: $17.7 million
- 1999 loss: $9.9 million
- 1999 headcount: 250

Going Public, Staying Public

As we entered 2000, the IPO climate continued to cool. On March 20, 2000, a cover story appeared in Barron's, an influential business magazine. It was titled "Burning Up. Warning: Internet companies are running out of cash – fast." The author looked at the unsustainable cashflow of the leading public dot-com companies and predicted that most of them would soon face bankruptcy within a year.

A couple of weeks later, as the Barron's predictions started to come true, the Nasdaq lost 25% of its value in a single week. By April the Nasdaq had dropped from 5,132 to 3,043.

It was in this climate that ServiceWare and our underwriter Unterberg Towbin pushed ahead with the IPO, even though the three other underwriting firms that had been recruited to assist with the IPO all pulled out.

The big day was August 25, 2000. We were one of the last small unprofitable tech company to get "out the door" before the collapse of the dot-com bubble. We sold 4.5 million new shares of common stock. Initially the stock was supposed to be offered in the range of $10.50 to $12.50 per share. As the underwriters saw softening demand for the stock they lowered it to a range of $8.00 to $9.00. The final offering price was $7.00 per share, which raised about $31 million for the company.

Thanks to the reduced price, the IPO was successful, meaning that the value of the stock remained stable. The stock price actually rose a bit in the following weeks, reaching a high of $10 per share. I owned about 4 million shares of stock, so on paper the stock was worth $40 million. However, SEC regulations prevented insiders from selling any stock until one full year had passed since the Barron's IPO, so I could not sell any of the stock I owned.

The company had increased spending rapidly but revenue growth was tapering off. We were rapidly burning through the $31 million raised in the IPO.

SUBJECT TO COMPLETION, DATED JULY 18, 2000

PROSPECTUS

4,500,000 Shares

ServiceWare

Common Stock

This is the initial public offering of 4,500,000 shares of common stock of ServiceWare Technologies, Inc. We are selling all of the shares of common stock offered under this prospectus. We anticipate that the initial public offering price will be between $10.50 and $12.50 per share.

There is currently no public market for our shares. We have applied to have our common stock approved for listing on the Nasdaq National Market under the symbol "SVCW".

Investing in our common stock involves a high degree of risk. See "Risk Factors" beginning on page 4 to read about risks you should consider carefully before buying shares of our common stock.

Neither the Securities and Exchange Commission nor any other regulatory body has approved or disapproved these securities or passed upon the adequacy or accuracy of this prospectus. Any representation to the contrary is a criminal offense.

	Per Share	Total
Public offering price	$	$
Underwriting discounts and commissions	$	$
Proceeds, before expenses, to us	$	$

We have granted the underwriters a 30-day option to purchase up to an additional 675,000 shares of common stock from us at the initial public offering price less the underwriting discounts. The underwriters expect to deliver the shares on or about   , 2000.

Bear, Stearns & Co. Inc.   **SG Cowen**

Wit SoundView

C.E. Unterberg, Towbin

The date of this prospectus is   , 2000.

The front cover of a draft of the IPO prospectus document.. In the final version, only C.E. Unterberg Towbin was listed as an underwriter.

Serviceware IPO up 25%

August 25, 2000: 5:52 p.m. ET

Software firm is last IPO in slow week, which featured only three new issues

NEW YORK (CNNfn) - Software provider Serviceware Technologies Inc. rose 25 percent Friday as the last initial public offering to begin trading this week.

Serviceware Technologies gained 1-3/4 to 8-3/4 after raising $31.5 million ahead of its IPO. Serviceware is the only new issue to trade Friday and the third this week.

The new issues market has nearly ground to a halt this week, with only three IPOs debuting raising $99 million, according to data from CommScan, a New York-based investment banking research firm.

No new issues are expected to begin trading next week. The slowdown is typical of the IPO market, which breaks a few weeks ahead of the Labor Day holiday, and IPOs are not expected to surge back to life until the second week of September. O2Micro Inc., which surged 131 percent on Wednesday, emerged as this week's clear winner.

Serviceware Technologies sold 4.5 million shares at $7 each, the low end of its targeted range, via underwriters C.E. Unterberg Towbin. The deal's price range has been cut twice.

The company originally filed 4.5 million shares at $10.50-to-$12.50 a share, later cut to $8-to-$9 a share and then to the present range of $7 to $8. Bear Stearns, SG Cowen and Wit Soundview were originally slated to be underwriters but pulled out, leaving only Unterberg to lead the deal.

Article in CNN Money, August 25, 2000.

- 2000 revenue: $17.8 million
- 2000 loss: $22 million

The Meltdown and the Aftermath

A couple of quarters after the IPO, ServiceWare missed its quarterly revenue targets and came in below analysts' profitability expectations. There were problems at the senior management level, there was competition from other well funded companies, and the "irrational exuberance" of the dot-com era was rapidly fading. When the company missed its financial target, investors headed for the exits as fast as they could. The stock price fell. As it kept dropping, fewer and fewer people were interested in buying it. Eventually the stock became illiquid, meaning that there were not enough buyers and sellers to create an actual marketplace for the stock. By the time my one-year lockup had expired, there was simply no marketplace for the stock. I was now legally permitted to sell, and I approached the brokers at Unterberg Towbin about selling a block of my stock, but there were simply no buyers for large quantities of the stock. The price continued to drift downwards, to less than a dollar per share.

In an effort to stem the cash drain, the company conducted three major layoffs in 2001, reducing the number of employees from its peak of 250 down to just 54. In March, an article in the local Tribune Review said:

> With its stock price sagging and its bottom line dripping red ink, Oakmont-based ServiceWare Technologies Inc. wants to focus on its growing software design business and sell its older Internet self-help business. "We have an ironclad commitment to become profitable for 2001," said Mark Tapling, ServiceWare's chief executive, on Thursday. "We owe it to our investors and our customers."

In a misguided attempt to streamline the business, Tapling sold off the Knowledge-Pak business to ServiceWare's CFO Mark Finkel and some former executives at Magic Solutions, for practically nothing. Finkel left ServiceWare to help run the new company, now called RightAnswers.com. ServiceWare was now a software-only company.

Tapling was fired in September and was replaced by Kent Heyman, an experienced business executive and a steady hand on the tiller. Revenues dropped in 2001 for the first time in the company's history, to just $12.4 million. Despite Tapling's "ironclad commitment" to become profitable in 2001, the company lost a staggering $31 million, which was more than $12 for

Article in Pittsburgh Tribune Review, March 2, 2001.

every share of stock. The stock was trading at just 26 cents per share. The value of my own investment had dropped from $40 million to just over $1 million.

As the stock price plunged and the company's financial situation worsened, the company was moved from the Nasdaq National Market to the Nasdaq Small Cap Market on April 25, 2002. It was delisted completely from the Nasdaq a year later, on May 5, 2003, due to its low price per share and lack of liquidity. It spent the next four years listed on Nasdaq's over-the-counter bulletin board, the final home for penny stocks and delisted companies.

Revenues in 2002 fell again, to $10.1 million. The layoffs had the desired effect of trimming spending, but the company still lost $6.8 million, burning through more cash. On the OTC bulletin board the stock price bottomed out at 11 cents per share. By now the stock had lost 99 percent of its peak value, and my founder's stock was now worth less than a half million dollars.

ServiceWare brought a patent infringement suit against its main competitor Primus in October 2003. The suit was settled a year later, with Primus agreeing to pay ServiceWare $800,000 in cash plus $850,000 worth of stock. After legal fees and other expenses, net revenue to ServiceWare was about $1.3 million, making it the most profitable deal the company had closed in years.

In 2004, the company was renamed Knova. The CEO was Bruce Armstrong. None of the original senior team remained.

| | For the Year Ended December 31, | | | | |
| | 2004 | 2003 | 2002 | 2001 | 2000 |
		(In thousands, except share and per share data)			
STATEMENT OF OPERATIONS DATA					
(Prior year amounts reclassified)					
Total revenues	$ 12,502	$ 11,511	$ 10,158	$ 12,427	$ 17,800
Net loss from continuing operations	$ (1,694)	$ (2,979)	$ (6,825)	$ (31,486)	$ (21,781)
Net (loss) income per common share, basic and diluted					
Continuing operations	$ (0.33)	$ (1.23)	$ (2.85)	$ (13.00)	$ (16.53)
Discontinued operations	—	—	—	0.73	1.52
Net loss per share	$ (0.33)	$ (1.23)	$ (2.85)	$ (12.27)	$ (15.01)

Knova financial summary, 2000 – 2004.

On December 7, 2004, the stockholders approved a 1-for-10 reverse stock split. This reduced the number of shares by a factor of 10 and increased the price per share by a factor of 10. The stock price at the time had recovered a bit to 36 cents per share, so after the reverse split the price was $3.60.

On February 8, 2005, Knova merged with Kanisa, a software company that had already acquired several other companies including the Ask Jeeves search engine. Company headquarters moved to Kanisa's offices in Cupertino, California.

Finally in March 2007, the board chair Kent Heyman arranged a cash sale of the company to Consola, a knowledge management software company. As a result, Knova was taken private. (Later, Consola merged with another company and was renamed Aptean.) Shareholders received about 50 cents per original share. For the people who had started and built ServiceWare, this was the final payoff and the end of the road.

The software side of the business, what was once called Knowledge-Pak Architect, changed names and owners several times and has now disappeared from the software world entirely.

However, there is one bit of happy news at the end of this story. While researching and writing this, I discovered that the original content product, Knowledge-Paks, is still alive today over thirty years after RightAnswers was spun off from ServiceWare in 2001. The company had grown slowly and steadily for sixteen years until it reached $6 million in annual sales. In 2017 it was acquired by Upland Software for $17.2 million in cash. But after all that, the Upland website still proudly proclaims that

> "Knowledge-Paks are an invaluable asset for any IT support organization, with more than 30,000 accurate knowledge articles to the most common issues your users have, on more than 400 of the most widely used off-the-shelf software applications. Whether to support agents or give users access to quality knowledge through self-service, Knowledge-Paks are your plug and play solution for reliable IT support."

RightAnswers Knowledge-Paks®

Save time and money with prewritten IT support content.

RightAnswers started out creating knowledge for IT technical support, so we know a thing or two about writing great knowledge articles. Our Knowledge-Paks® library sets the standard for professional IT knowledge bases.

From the Upland Software website, 2023.

Meanwhile

During ServiceWare's wild ride, life continued at home. Running a rapidly growing startup company was a tremendous amount of work. I traveled out of town almost every week, going to visit customers and attend conferences and trade shows. A typical workweek was probably 60 to 80 hours, and things really didn't settle down until after I wrapped my CEO job several years later.

Rafting with Kris (left) and his friend Alec Silberblatt.

Katelyn and Kris got along well together. They played all sorts of games. One of them was "stairs game" which involved them climbing up a few stairs on the outside of the railing, then jumping onto a pile of sofa cushions. We had a big back yard with a zipline that ran down the hill. There was also a large treehouse that I built for both kids, although Kris was the main tenant.

Both kids were exposed to lots of books and stories. Every night either Kathryn or I would tell them a bedtime story. I made up two characters named Goofer and Suzie, who lived in a zoo and had lots of adventures, and just about every night that I was in town, I'd tell them a Goofer and Suzie story. They also listened to bedtime songs including Gordon Lightfoot's "Pony Man" and Vaughn Monroe's "Ghost Riders in the Sky."

Once our financial situation improved we began taking vacations, including several in the Caribbean. The kids (and their parents!) were fortunate enough to see a lot of the islands during the time I was at ServiceWare. We went to Omega Institute's Kids Week nearly every summer, and we went several times to North Myrtle Beach. I also began a tradition of father-and-son ski trips with Kris, which we continued every winter for maybe 10 years, until he was old enough to ski on double black diamond trails that terrified me.

Skiing with Kris at Vail in 2003.

The Waldorf School

Our house was in the Penn Hills school district, which was not one of the best by a long shot. So with two young kids, Kathryn and I were thinking about education and not liking what we saw locally. We'd heard about an alternative education method called Waldorf that was created in the early 1900's by Rudolf Steiner, at the request of the owner of the Waldorf-Astoria Cigarette Company in Germany. The company's owner wanted a holistic approach to education that he could offer the children of his employees. Steiner developed a completely new system based on his esoteric philosophy called Anthroposophy. It was successful, and there are now over 2,000 Waldorf schools worldwide.

Like a Moth

A kickoff meeting was held in Pittsburgh in 1992, and soon afterwards, the Pittsburgh Waldorf Initiative began. We joined and became active in helping to start the first local Waldorf school. By the time Katelyn was ready for kindergarten it still wasn't ready to take students, so we sent her to school in the local Penn Hills lower school. Results were disappointing. So for first grade we transferred her to McEwan School (now Kentucky Avenue School) where she stayed for lower and middle school before transferring to Winchester Thurston for upper school.

By the time Kris was ready to start kindergarten the Waldorf school was ready, so we enrolled him in preschool. Things went well for Kris in the early grades, but the school was small and didn't offer higher grades at that time. So we needed to find another school for him.

We visited several private schools in the Pittsburgh area. Waldorf education was unusual in many respects, and one of their most radical ideas is that kids should learn how to read much later than what's normally taught in other schools. As a result, Kris couldn't read. Some teachers at other schools were appalled at this and thought Kris was some sort of unschooled wild child. When we realized that this could be a problem, we started teaching him to read at home (or rather, we allowed him to teach himself). He rapidly caught up and exceeded the reading level required of him, and he was accepted at Winchester Thurston where he started in the second grade.

Neural Network Project

One of my fun side projects while I was at ServiceWare was a neural network for medical diagnosis that I did with Denis Lehotay, a biochemist and Joan's husband. I'd already learned something about neural networks when Dave Hornig and I did some early experiments while we were at Carnegie Group. I thought the idea of a self-learning network was cool, so I was always on the lookout for something interesting that I could do in that area.

Denis worked at the Hospital for Sick Children in Toronto, specializing in diagnosing inborn errors in metabolism. These are genetic diseases such as PKU that are inherited. A skilled diagnostician like Denis could look at the numbers in a blood test and tell if a newborn was likely to have any one of several common genetic disorders. I thought this was an interesting skill, so I asked Denis if there was a standardized way to identify the disorders from looking at the numbers. He told me that it was just sort of a learned skill, not something that had really been formalized. Maybe we could teach a neural network to learn how to do it, I suggested. We decided to collaborate on a project to do that.

We wrote up a grant proposal in 1995 and submitted as a Phase 1 SBIR (small business innovative research) project under the US Department of Health and Human Services. The abstract says it all:

> This project will assess the ability of neural network based computer systems to assist physicians in diagnosing inborn metabolic disorders in children, including phenylketonuria (PKU), maple syrup urine disease, cystinuria, homocystinuria, urea cycle enzyme defects, organic acidopathies such as methylmalonicacidemia, and lactic acidemia. The project will result in the creation of a PC-based system comprised of expert systems, online documentation and other supporting software, which will form the basis for a supported diagnostic product available to physicians and medical laboratories.

HHS approved the project and gave us $75,000 to do it. I built the system with help from a contract programmer, using training data supplied by Denis. We trained the system on several hundred samples of blood samples plus the diagnostic conclusions reached for each one, then we tested it on a second set of samples. The system performed really well.

The system's neural network ran on a tool called NeuralWare, and one of its cool features was that you could actually peer into the network connections and get an inkling of how the network self-organized itself. In other words, if the system learned something unexpected, you could actually see what connections led to that. Examining our network, we found several surprises; these were combinations of blood markers that, the system discovered, made it likely that an infant had a certain disorder. I showed these to Denis and he was surprised and impressed that the system had discovered these patterns.

We completed the project and wrote up the results. Denis and I talked about taking the project further and turning it into a product, but that never happened, mainly due to some interference from the administrators at the hospital where Denis worked.

The Waterfall and the Garden Tour

I already mentioned the intense microburst storm that occurred in late June 1998, and the effect it had on our efforts at ServiceWare to hit our revenue targets for the financial quarter. But it also resulted in some major changes at our house.

Our house is on a hilltop, four hundred feet above the Allegheny River. So we get high winds during normal thunderstorms. When the microburst hit, it knocked down several large trees in our yard. After we cleared away the downed trees, Kathryn and I saw that we had an opportunity to do something interesting with the yard on the south side of the house.

We thought it would be nice to have a little stream running down the hill. So we contacted Richard Liberto, a landscape designer. He brought in Jim Lampl, who had a reputation for building beautiful and complex water features. Jim came to the house, walked around the yard, asked us what we were looking for, then told us what he wanted to do. He wanted to build a large water feature that would include seven individual waterfalls, a several thousand gallon pond at the bottom, and a recirculating pump system to keep it all running.

It was way more than we had in mind. But sure, we said. Go ahead.

He started work. He had one helper, a young but willing guy with little experience. Jim brought in some large construction equipment including a full sized backhoe. He spent a couple of weeks excavating the pond and streambed. Then he laid down sand, cement and a layer of rubber to waterproof the streambed and pond. Then he started adding rocks. Every day he'd arrive with one or two large boulders in his truck, and he'd spend the entire day placing and adjusting the boulder.

The largest boulder we called Grandfather Rock. It overhangs the stream at a point where the stream cuts to the left. Placing it was a delicate and difficult matter. Jim's helper was working underneath the boulder while Jim operated the equipment to lift and place the boulder. The helper had just pulled his hands out from underneath the boulder when the cable snapped and the boulder dropped into place, never to move again. Shortly after that, the helper quit. His replacement was our landscape designer Richard Liberto, who helped Jim finish the project.

It was a huge project, taking something like four months to complete. But it was worth it. It's been in place for almost 25 years and there hasn't been a single leak or other problem with the entire system. We have replaced the water pump several times, mainly because I'd let it run throughout the winter a few years and the pump burned out due to low water levels during cold snaps. But other than that, the rest of the system has worked flawlessly.

A few years after the water feature was finished, the Pittsburgh Botanical Garden was planning a summer garden tour of water features. Someone told them about us, and we were included in the tour. The other homes featured on the tour were mostly in more posh neighborhoods like Squirrel Hill and Fox Chapel. Our house was in the working class town of Verona, so most of people looking at the brochure figured we just had just some little puddle with a bubbler and some plastic ornaments.

We did get a few visitors anyway. And as the day went on, more and more people came. They told their friends. Interest continued to build. Sometime in late afternoon, a bunch of people were on the tour bus heading to a location in North Hills. Someone announced to the group that they really need to see this water feature in Verona. So they all decided they'd rather visit our house. They hijacked the bus and told the bus driver to take them to Verona. In total, we had over a hundred people come to see Pepper Falls.

Pepper Falls in summer, looking up from the pond.

Dad's Trip to China

In early 1989, Dad told us he was going to visit China. A tour company was offering a "last chance to see" trip down the Yangtze River to visit places soon to be inundated by the massive Three Gorges Dam then under construction. It was supposed to be the trip of a lifetime, and it turned out to be just that.

As the departure date approached there were increasing reports of unrest in China, with thousands of students protesting political restrictions. Dad wasn't worried. Having lived through World War II, he probably assumed this couldn't possibly be worse. And as he told Barbara and me, "I'm already 75 years old. If something happens to me, so what?"

On May 20, the Chinese government declared martial law and brought in 300,000 troops from outlying provinces into Beijing. But for some reason the tour was not cancelled. Dad flew to Beijing for the beginning of the tour, arriving in the early morning of June 4. He went to the hotel with the rest of the group. After resting for a few hours, he went out in the evening to do a bit of sightseeing with some of the other tourists. They walked over to Tiananmen Square, which was being occupied by the students. He chatted with a few of them, then headed back to the hotel for dinner and bed.

At 8:30 that night, Chinese military helicopters appeared in the sky. A couple of hours later, troops attacked the protesters, killing hundreds or possibly thousands of them, with thousands more wounded.

All communication was cut off. We heard about the massacre and knew Dad was in Beijing, but we had no way of knowing if he was ok or not. Later we learned that he was staying in the same hotel as most of the Western journalists, so he was relatively safe. He told us later that they spent the next day looking out the window and watching the tanks roll by.

They waited in the hotel for a couple of days. One of the tour guides went to a nearby airport and, as we heard the story, bribed a pilot to take the tour group out of the country. This sounds far fetched, but given the confusion at the time, it's still possible. The guide rented a bus to take the tour group to the airport, then they flew in the "borrowed" plane to Tokyo. The tour operator managed to salvage the tour by sending the tourists to Thailand for a few days. But regardless, it was a trip to remember.

Dad's Final Years

Dad was living by himself in an apartment in Long Island but was having trouble taking care of himself. I suggested that he move to Pittsburgh to be close to our family. He agreed. He came out to see what living options were available. His first thought was to rent a condo in an over-50 community a few miles from our house. But I convinced him not to do that because he might need medical care in the coming years. We looked at some continuing care retirement communities in the area, and he liked Sherwood Oaks in Wexford, about a half hour north of our house. He moved there in 1990. On moving day I drove him from Long Island to his new home in Wexford. We talked for a long time, and some of our conversation is included in Appendix 1.

Dad seemed to enjoy living in the retirement community, even though he was from out of state and probably the only Jewish resident. I tried to visit him on weekends, though work and family commitments made that an on-and-off sort of thing. We'd drive there, spend some time chatting, then go out for dinner. One of our favorite restaurants was a nearby Chinese place. The kids were young, and Kris would make something he called "bad guy stew" from all the condiments available on the table. (We found out much later that there's actually a song called Bad Guy Stew by a group called Eyeball Skeleton, but it was written in 2005, well after Kris stopped making his restaurant concoctions.)

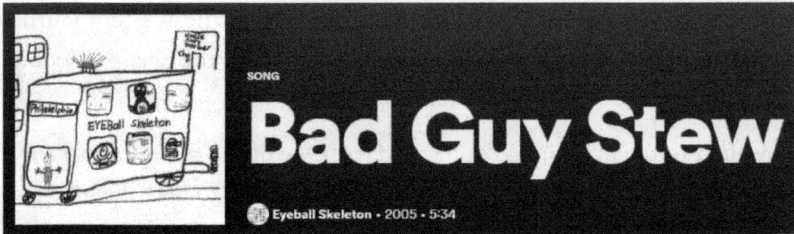

As Dad got older, he could no longer live in his apartment at Sherwood Oaks. He was able to stay in the community but moved to the assisted living unit where he could receive some help with his daily living needs. Sometimes when I asked him how he was doing, he'd just shake his head and say, "Jeff, I feel lousy." Occasionally he'd ask me how his long-deceased mom was doing. Finally, as his Alzheimer's progressed, he moved to a dementia care unit.

On the morning of January 15, 1998, I was at home when someone called from the hospital where Dad had been for a few days. He'd just passed away. I'd known that his condition was deteriorating but had no idea that he was so close to death. Or maybe I was just distracted by work and didn't want to consider the possibility.

He had a Jewish funeral on Long Island, where he'd lived most of his life. We found a young rabbi who agreed to do the service even though he'd never met Dad. The service was sparsely attended, because Dad had moved away several years earlier, and most of his friends had died or also moved away. After the service, we drove an hour to Calverton National Cemetery where the coffin was interred.

ElderVision / Touchtown

In Dad's final years, I was often struck by the difference in our daily living situations. I was immersed in an incredibly complex and stimulating lifestyle, running a fast-growing tech company and traveling around the world seeing people and doing deals. Meanwhile, Dad was living a boring life. He was no longer working of course. He didn't play golf anymore, and his day-to-day life consisted of eating in the dining halls, watching TV, and sitting with his friends.

What if, I thought, there was some way to bring some of the richness of my everyday life into Dad's world in the retirement home? The more I thought about it, the more interesting the idea became.

By the time Dad died, my work at ServiceWare was just about over. I had time, I had money, and I had a great deal of confidence (perhaps overconfidence was a better word) in my ability to accomplish just about

Jeff Pepper, president and CEO of Eldervision

anything. So I decided to start another company that would transform the lives of elderly people.

Unlike ServiceWare, though, I really didn't know anything about the business I was planning to get into. I knew almost nothing about the long term care industry or the needs of elderly people except what I'd observed firsthand. And I didn't know much about the technology that I had in mind, which was just starting to be called "virtual reality." So I had a lot to learn.

In February 1999 I incorporated a new company which I called Eldervision.Net. My vision was to create a virtual world that would be accessible to elderly people and would provide them with easy access to a variety of interesting experiences. The stated goal was to overcome "social isolation," an industry buzzword. But really, I just wanted to give elderly residents a chance to have some fun and reconnect with friends and family.

In my ElderVision office.

Since I had no idea what I was doing, the first thing I did was to form an advisory board consisting of a variety of people who were experts in fields where I needed to learn. I approached a half dozen people, and they all agreed to join the advisory board. They were: Judy Comer, CEO of Sherwood Oaks where my dad had lived; Pete Lucas, president of Maya Design Group and an expert in human/computer interface design; Dr. Jules Rosen of Western Psychiatric Institute, an expert in geriatric care; Randy Pausch, associate professor at Carnegie Mellon University and creator of CMU's virtual reality program; David Bianco, co-founder of ElderHostel; and Joe Garlington, VP of interactive projects at Walt Disney Imagineering. Since ElderVision was a corporation I also needed a board of directors, so I asked Susanne Harrison, the first VC investor in my previous company, and Ron Muns, founder of the Help Desk Institute, to serve on the board. They both agreed.

To gain another point of view, I also created an Elders Advisory Board comprised of residents of Sherwood Oaks retirement community where Dad had lived: Willard McCown, Arthur Croll, Dottie Freedman, Doug White,

Martha Estabrook, Eloise MacQueen, Melvin Judkis, Dick Longini and Olive Tiller. These folks were interested in technology, and many of them were former teachers, engineers and scientists. We gave each of them 5,000 shares of ElderVision stock, and conducted several interviews and tested several software and hardware prototypes with them over the next few years.

Next, I really need to learn something about virtual reality. Randy Pausch, one of my Advisory Board members, was teaching a legendary course at CMU called Building Virtual Worlds. His students created VR games and immersive experiences. The course was so famous that the end-of-semester presentations were done in a packed auditorium and were attended by game developers and senior staff from major entertainment companies including Disney. Randy became world-famous a few years later when he developed terminal pancreatic cancer and gave the famous "Last Lecture" at CMU which was made into a best-selling book.

With the ElderVision interns after playing laser tag.

I asked Randy if I could audit his class, and he readily agreed. He also agreed to accept a few thousand shares of ElderVision stock, not because he needed the money but because he thought it would be "a really cool thing" to own stock. I sat in on nearly all of his classes. At the end of the semester he let me give a 20-minute pitch about my new company, where I described what we were doing and offered to hire a bunch of his students as summer interns. One student, Karyn Graff, came up to me afterwards and said she really wanted to be

Randy Pausch giving the Last Lecture at CMU, September 18, 2007.

part of this project. I hired her, and she became the team leader for the summer interns. She also stayed with the company for years afterwards, making major contributions to product development and marketing.

At this point I moved the company from its interim location at my house, to offices on the second floor of 215 Allegheny Avenue in Oakmont, a space once occupied by ServiceWare in its early days.

ElderVision Park

In the month or so leading up to the start of the summer intern period, I worked on the concept for ElderVision Park. It was to be a large multi-person 3D virtual reality space where people could wander around, explore, play games, and interact with other people. Each user would have an avatar which they would move with a simple joystick. Whenever they came within ten virtual feet of another person, an audio link would automatically open up, allowing them to have a conversation with that person.

I hired Davis Raborn who had worked with me at ServiceWare, and he built much of the underlying tech for ElderVision Park. I came up with the design for the park by scribbling on scraps of paper. An early sketch is on the next page. The final sketch was drawn on a large whiteboard and hung up on a wall in the office.

 ElderVision Park had lovely landscaped streets, a movie theater, a café, a post office, a music pavilion, and much more. Every user had their own virtual house where they would "wake up" every time they logged in to the system. We

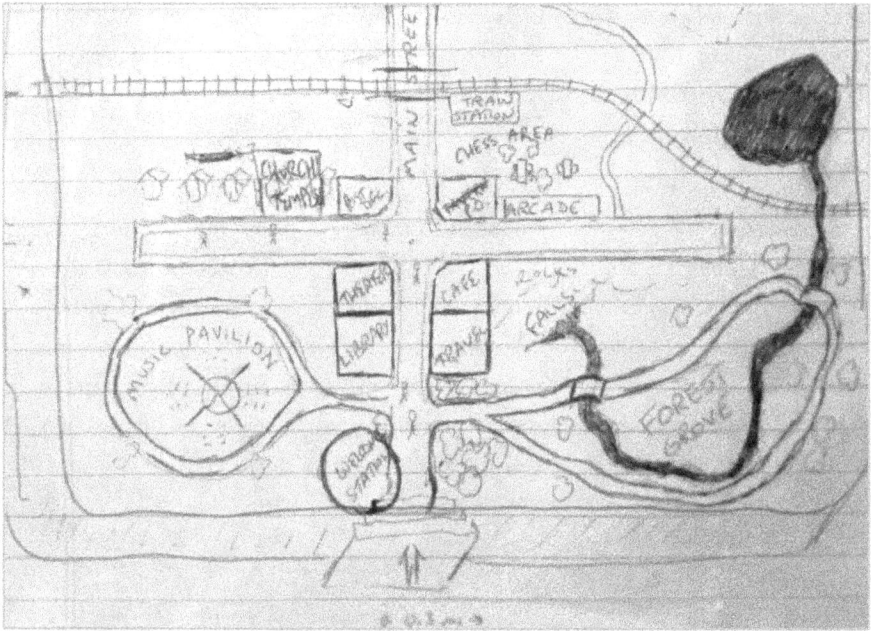

An early sketch of ElderVision park.

even created a few hidden places called "nooks," which were interesting little spots that did not appear on the official map but which a user might stumble upon if they went down a certain street or alley.

To make all this work, we also cobbled together a bunch of hardware – a large computer monitor, a scooter-like chair with a joystick mounted on it, and a headset with a speaker and microphone. The complete product that we intended to sell was a combination of this hardware, our virtual reality software, and support services. We eventually called it Touchtown, the winning suggestion in a company-wide naming contest held a year later.

Full of confidence, I went to our first industry trade show in late 1999. Visitors got demonstrations of the immersive VR experience we were promoting. We got lots of enthusiastic comments, but at a price point of $50,000 per seat we had no buyers.

Realizing that we too far ahead of the adoption curve, I went back to the office and talked with the team, which at that point was Karyn, Davis, and a couple of other people we'd hired after the summer interns had left. The problem, I said, was that there was too much stuff. Senior living communities were just not willing to convert one of their common rooms into a VR hall with a bunch of large immersive VR rigs. We needed something smaller, cheaper, and less disruptive to the operation of the community.

At the time, the Apple iPad was still ten years away, but I felt that a tablet-like computer was exactly what we needed. A tablet was much more compact than the full-on VR rig. I felt that by eliminating the keyboard and mouse and just using touch and voice, we would have something senior friendly and more marketable. So we began work on our second prototype product, a custom made tablet computer. He re's an early concept sketch by Jerry Boyle, our newly hired marketing director, and one of the early designs for the display, showing a virtual phone and a window into a scaled down and less immersive ElderVision Park.

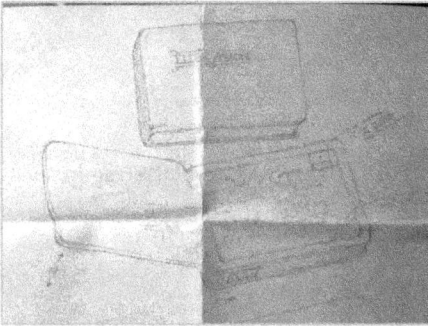

Left: an early concept of the ElderVision tablet. Right: user interface sketch for the ElderVision tablet display.

We hired Maya Design to design and build the hardware, and we wrote our own software. The result was one of the first tablet-like devices ever sold anywhere, and certainly the first in the senior living industry. It was big and heavy, but we designed it to have easy-to-grab handles on both sides. It also had a touchscreen, which was unusual at the time. The information displayed on the touchscreen was large and easy to read. A big phone icon on the left side could be used for audio communications, and the rest of the screen showed a handful of useful apps like email, news, and internet access. There was also a "town" button that provided access to ElderVision Park.

A marketing flyer for the senior tablet.

Confident that we had a winning product on our hands, and flush with cash from the ServiceWare IPO, I started building up the company's staff. I went to recruiting events and hired a bunch of top-notch programmers, designers, marketers, and salespeople. I even hired a terrific customer support director, Kathy Campbell, even though we had no actual customers for her to support.

Before we had actually sold any product, we'd reached a headcount of 25 and we were burning over $300,000 a month.

Angel Investors

With Karyn at a recruiting fair.

It was no fun writing personal checks every month to fund the company's operations, so I looked around to see if I could scare up some early stage investors. Two local veterans of the tech scene, Tom Canfield and Chet Fisher, had just formed a company called Equity Catalysts to bring together angel investors to fund companies like mine. I signed up with them, came up with a pre-money valuation for the company of $6 million without any real justification, and started making pitches to the investors who they'd gathered. There was still a surprising amount of enthusiasm for tech companies despite the dot-com crash (one group of early investors optimistically called themselves "Bucks Unlimited"), and I was one of the few entrepreneurs in the region who'd actually built a successful tech company and made money for investors. So without too much difficulty Tom and Chet pulled together a $1,275,000 investment in ElderVision. Because of the high valuation I'd put on the company, this only required me to give up about 18% ownership.

One small snag was that Tom and Chet had neglected to go through all the necessary steps required to set up their firm, such as taking required tests and obtaining a license from the SEC. The SEC could have shut them down and forced us to return all the investors' funds, but they were lenient. They allowed Tom and Chet to complete the necessary paperwork, and we got to keep the investors' money.

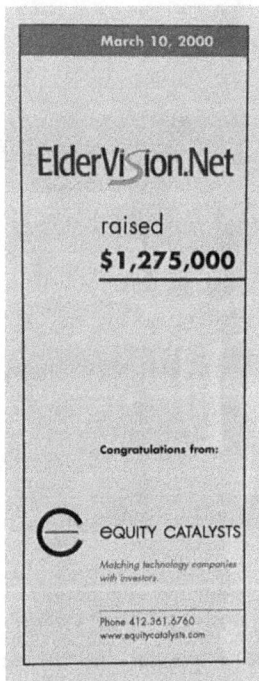

The "tombstone" for the Equity Catalyst investment.

When our homegrown tablet proved too expensive and difficult to manufacture, we redesigned the product again. This time we came up with a device with a smaller footprint and a more realistic phone – that is, it was a phone that you could actually pick up and use like a cordless phone.

Around this time we hired a marketing firm called MarchFirst. They created some slick marketing campaigns for the new product and billed us for over a quarter of a million dollars. They even shot a video with real directors and actors. Here's a screenshot from the video and an accompanying brochure, showing the "grandma" character pretending to use our third-generation device to talk with "Joey," her grandson.

One of the actors in our ElderVision video production.

MarchFirst sent us monthly invoices and we made a few relatively small payments. Then, fortunately for us, after they finished all the work we asked them to do they went bankrupt. Their assets were purchased by another company which made a half-hearted attempt to collect on the receivables. But for some reason they never contacted us, and after a few years I just wrote off the debt.

Bulgaria

One of the programmers I'd hired was a bright young guy from Bulgaria named Anton Hristov. We were sitting around one day talking about how hard it was to hire good software developers. Anton was really good, so I asked him jokingly, "Are there any more like you in your home village?" Anton replied, "Yes, there's a whole country full of people like me." It turned out that Bulgaria was the Silicon Valley of the Eastern bloc during the years when the USSR controlled most of Eastern Europe. The country had an educated work force and a good exchange rate.

This sounded like a good business idea, and a lot of fun. Working with Anton, I came up with a list of 40 potential software development partners in Bulgaria, which I whittled down to six final candidates. I set up a trip for myself, Dennis Whalen (who had joined me at Touchtown after finishing up his work at ServiceWare), and Anton. In November 2000 we visited those six potential partners in three days, plus a couple of days at either end for jet lag and tourism. The trip was really fun. For some reason I'd expected Bulgaria to be some depressing Soviet-style collection of factories and drab apartment

With a couple of our software development partners, performing the traditional Bulgarian debugging dance.

buildings, but I was pleasantly surprised at what it was really like. Beautiful countryside, good food, and friendly people.

We selected one of the six companies, and they did most of our software development for a few years afterwards, with Anton serving as liaison between our office and theirs.

Cash Crash

During this time I'd been funding the company myself, using the funds that I'd put away from my time at ServiceWare and confident that the pile of ServiceWare stock that I owned was quite valuable, even though it was still locked up and I was unable to actually sell any of it.

Then on January 9, 2001, ServiceWare announced that it had missed its earnings targets. By a lot. Rajiv called me to give me the bad news. The stock price plunged to $1.87, wiping out much of my net worth. I spent most of that day talking with ElderVision's advisors and board of directors. We explored a few options, but it became clear that no matter what the long-term plan for the company, we could not sustain the daily expense of keeping such a large staff. In fact, it seemed increasingly obvious that since we had no income and no product, it made little sense to have any staff at all.

One option would have been to simply declare bankruptcy and shut down the company, but I didn't want to do that and give up the "elder vision" that I had. Also, I felt that I had an obligation to my investors to try and make the company successful so they wouldn't lose the investment they'd made in it, and me.

So I suspended the company's operations and laid off nearly all of our staff. In a letter to our angel investors I said that the suspension was the result of the collapse of ServiceWare's stock price, which had wiped out my ability to continue funding ElderVision's operations and eliminated the possibility of me using that stock to guarantee loans to the company. At that time the company had $150,000 in the bank but owed about $550,000 in payables and short-term debt, not including money owed to me personally. The company was losing about $300,000 a month. My cash investments and loan guarantees already exceeded $1.8 million.

The following morning I came to the office and gave everyone the bad news. This was inconvenient and disappointing for some of the younger staff, but terrible news for some of the older folks who had mortgages to pay and families to support. I could not give them any severance pay at the time, but promised to give them a couple of months' severance when and if the company got up and running again. (We kept these debts on the company's books and they were eventually paid, with interest, ten years later.)

Although I laid everyone off, about half of the team stayed on anyway on a volunteer basis, to get the product to the point where it can be handed off to someone else. At the time I said to a reporter,

> "Having always been successful up until last week, I just believed that anything I did would succeed. But in that first half hour last Wednesday, I suddenly realized that this could happen to anybody. As an entrepreneur, you have to be able to create a certain reality and impose it on the rest of the world. That process is really close to the process of denial because you're basically saying that this is the way the world is no matter what anyone tells you. The successful entrepreneur learns how to promote a certain view of the world and if you successfully do that, your company succeeds because investors, employees and customers buy into it. It was a difficult process to suddenly let go of that and have it all come crashing down."

Eat What You Kill

For a while after the layoffs, I really didn't know what to do. I kept going to work every day. Talking with the remaining staff, we tried to figure out how to get things restarted. I continued to feel that the company's mission was still worthwhile, even though it was clear that we'd have to completely replace the product and strategy.

To make some money and take my mind off ElderVision, I took on some unrelated consulting projects. The biggest one was serving a stint as interim President for a bizarre rollup called Media Holdings that was engineered by a finance guy named John Whitehill and a local lawyer named George Medved. John and George had purchased out of bankruptcy a 40-year old film processing lab in Crafton called WRS, and they'd also bought a small document processing company called Digital Encoding Factory located underground in an Iron Mountain facility in northwestern Pennsylvania. They wanted me to run both companies and somehow make the combination profitable. They didn't pay me a salary but offered me a generous cut of whatever profits I could generate from the two companies. Or as John put it, "You can eat what you kill."

However, the two new owners had gotten themselves into a complicated legal and financial situation, and were involved in a blizzard of lawsuits. As a result, they had little or no money to give the companies to buy the materials they needed to do their work. So the idea of eating what I could kill turned out to mean that I didn't eat much. George would occasionally write a check for a couple of thousand dollars whenever he thought I might be getting discouraged, but that was all I ever got.

I became friends with the guys who worked at the film lab, and was shocked at how badly they were being treated by the new owners. The staff really believed in what they were doing, to the point where they sometimes used their own personal funds to buy materials needed to do the work that their customers had contracted them to do. So I stopped working with the document processing company and focused all my efforts on helping WRS get back up and running.

The film lab guys despised the new owners (with good reason), and they initially saw me as a paid stooge of the owners. In reality I was an unpaid stooge. But regardless, I worked hard to gain their trust and to turn things around at the film lab. This led to some interesting moments. In one incident, George had promised to write the lab a check for a few thousand dollars to buy some blank film it desperately needed for a contract. Then he became wishy-washy about the commitment. "Where are you now? I'm coming to pick up the check," I demanded on the phone. He told me. I jumped in my "yellow bird" Subaru SVX sports car, with the lab manager Russ Scheller sitting beside me. We raced down to the industrial park where George was. I saw him pulling out of a driveway, and I physically blocked him with my car. I asked him (nicely) to get in the car with me, and together we went to the bank to get the funds that the lab needed.

Overall, though, the new bosses had created a hopeless situation, and my skills were not enough to save the lab. By the end of the summer I reluctantly quit. I believe the film lab was shut down shortly afterwards, and the staff was all let go.

Frugal Restart

Back at ElderVision, I was absorbing a few important lessons. First of course, one should have a good working product before investing in growing the company. In retrospect this might seem obvious. But during the boom times the business mantra was "get big fast," based on the idea that there was a pot of gold out there and if you spent enough money fast enough, you'd reach it before the other guys. Now, though, things had changed. There was no pot of gold anymore. So instead of trying to race to some finish line, my new goal was to build a profitable, self-sustaining company while spending as little as possible.

Second, I realized that it's easier to create a good product if you know what your customers are looking for. The initial product ideas came from my own imagination. Sometimes this works (think of the iPod), but more often it doesn't. So I decided to get serious about listening to and learning from customers. I contacted the CEOs of 16 leading senior living providers and invited them to be part of the Senior Connect Partnership. This gave them a voice in defining our new product, a chance to participate in early testing, and a deep discount if they decided to purchase it later. For us, of course, it gave us a free source of good advice and a ready-made customer base. All of them agreed to be part of the Partnership.

With this buy-in from so many major players, we went to work on our next generation product, which was software-only and accessible via the Web. An early version was ready in a couple of months. I wanted to show it to customers but didn't want to spend our limited funds on booth space at the annual AAHSA conference in San Diego. So I took a small suite at a hotel across the street from the conference, and invited several dozen potential customers (including the members of the Partnership) to come to the suite for private demos. I had to pay for the hotel suite, but I used my frequent flyer miles to get to San Diego and back.

Our low-budget trade show exhibit

For some people, it might be difficult or painful to make such a drastic reversal in strategy. But for me that's one of the great joys of being an entrepreneur. I really like the process of recognizing that something's wrong, seeing a new path, and discarding the old stuff in the course of zeroing in on the new solution. Whether it's a 98% price cut or a completely new product concept, the act of changing course is very satisfying. Especially if it works.

Senior Portal

Our new product was simple. It was an easy-to-use web portal for residents of senior living communities. It offered email, bulletin boards (local and national), games, and tools for the community's staff to get announcements to the residents. Instead of developing email and bulletin board system from scratch, we used existing open-source systems and just wrote senior-friendly front ends for them.

Our first software-only product, running on a laptop PC.

It was a minimal product that ran on ordinary PCs. This was good because it could be easily integrated into the "computer rooms" that were popping up in senior living communities at the time.

One drawback was that the product didn't actually make money for the buyers, and didn't save them money either. It was a "nice to have," which mean that we couldn't charge much for it. As our advisor Jules Rosen famously told me, there are three types of products: oxygen, food, and vitamins. You want to be selling oxygen, not vitamins.

Using that metaphor, we were selling vitamins, and so our price point had to be low enough for the purchase to make sense. We sold the product for $5 per month per account. Clearly this was not going to make us a multi-million dollar company overnight, but we had to start somewhere.

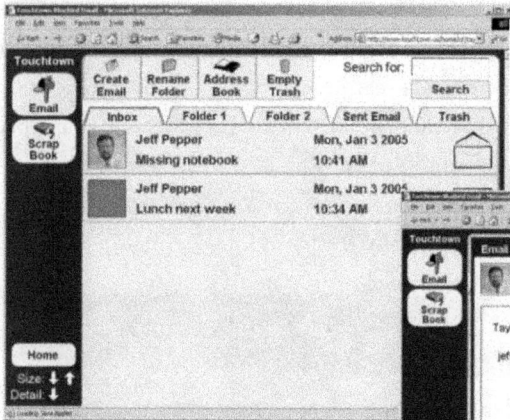

Two screenshots of "Bluebird," one of the two senior-friendly email clients that we offered our users.

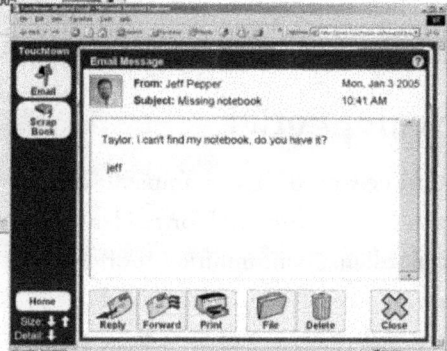

Name Change

There were a few problems with the company name, ElderVision.Net. The "Elder" part was intended to evoke wise elders of a village or tribe, but the similarity to "elderly" caused some backlash. The "Vision" part led lots of people to think that we sold eyeglasses. And the ".Net" was outdated.

So I ran a little contest to see who in the company could come up with a new name. Matt Kambic, a musician and filmmaker who at the time was working as a graphic designer for us, came up with "Touchtown" which I thought was the perfect name. So we changed the product name to Touchtown, and in March 2003 we changed the company name to match. At the time, we had 35 customer organizations.

Matt Kambic

Scavenge R. Hunt

One of the fun things I did during this time was writing a weekly scavenger hunt puzzle for Touchtown's user community. I created two characters, Scav (short for Scavenge R. Hunt) and his traveling companion Sirrah. Scav and Sirrah were always visiting interesting places and coming up with puzzles for each other. The puzzles were not particularly difficult to solve, but they did require expertise in navigating the internet and using search engines. Hundreds of people played the game every week. Here's one sample, selected more or less at random from the 100 or so that were published.

Sirrah is full of enthusiasm and ready to pose another puzzler to her traveling companion Scav.

"Scav," she says, "this week we're going to bounce around the United States, starting off in the North, visiting the South, and ending up back in the North again. Are you ready?"

"Okay, Sirrah," he replies, "I've got my traveling shoes on. Hit me with the clues!"

"We'll start off at a restaurant located at 6 Forest Street in New Canaan, Connecticut. The first word of the restaurant's name is evocative of a Pulitzer Prize-winning novel.

"Now you need to create a six letter word, by stringing together the first three letters of the author's first name plus the first two letters of the author's last name plus the third letter of the novel's mythical location.

"Once you have that word, you'll recognize it as the first of a two-word name for a well known American corporation. The second word of this corporation's name is also the name of a small college in the South.

"Find out the name of this college's Director of Careers Office. It's the same as an American President. We are looking for this President's birthplace."

Email the name of the birthplace to scavengerhunt@touchtown.org by Saturday morning, 9:00am Eastern Time. Make sure to include your name and mailing address. We'll post the names of everyone who sent in a correct answer. We'll also select one winner to receive a gift tin of a dozen Classic McAroons from www.mcaroons.com. Anyone can play and win, but to be eligible for the prize you must be a Touchtown member and not have won a prize in the last two months. Enjoy!

The answers, in case you're interested, are:

- Tequila Bar & Mexican Restaurant
- To Kill a Mockingbird by **Har**per **Lee**, set in Maycomb
- Har + le + y = Harley, => Harley Davidson
- Davidson College
- Director, Careers Office: John Adams
- President John Adams, born in Quincy MA

Senior Friendly ISP

In an effort to broaden our customer base, I got the idea of starting a dialup ISP (internet service provider) service for seniors. Nationwide, dialup was being replaced by broadband, but I felt that older people would be slow to switch to broadband and might be attracted to a senior-friendly service. We did a bit of software development to tailor an existing ISP platform to our needs. I hired a guy who was a ISP veteran to run the business. We ran some billboard ads locally, as well as print ads in Senior News, a monthly magazine with nationwide distribution that was geared towards seniors.

We also offered large organizations the chance to sell a branded version of our product to their members. Our biggest deal there was AMVETS, the veterans organization. They promoted our ISP service, which was rebranded as an AMVETS service with their logo and lots of red, white and blue artwork.

We also did a similar but smaller deal with the Seniors Coalition, which appeared at first to be sort of like AARP but turned out to be a shady lobbying firm financed by the pharmaceutical industry and which was once investigated by the New York State attorney general's office for participating in a "pattern of fraud and abuse."

The service was inexpensive, generally $14.95 per month. The biggest problem we ran into was that older computer users were voracious consumers of technical support. We constantly got phone calls from our ISP customers who were having trouble with email, or word processing, or spreadsheets, or resetting their passwords, or whatever. Some of them would simply call us to chat about whatever was on their minds. After a year or so of this, I pulled the plug on the ISP business.

Touchtown was growing and marginally profitable, but still small. I'd been at it for five years and still didn't have much to show for all investment of time and money.

Then everything changed.

The Nashville Show

We'd been selling our senior-friendly web portal nationwide and gotten a few large customers, enough to be almost profitable. One of the biggest was Westminster Retirement in central Florida. We had a great relationship with them. They were also using a product from another company called VCTV which gave them their own private television channel. The VCTV product let a retirement community remove a commercial channel from their cable bundle and insert their own content on that channel instead. This content was just a series of slides, like a PowerPoint slide show but more primitive. It let them deliver announcements, birthday wishes, and so on to their residents. The residents simply had to tune their in-room TVs to that particular station and they got a continually running slide show of local information.

Like a Moth

One day I got a call from Lisa Bloder, my contact at Westminster Retirement. She had an idea. Since Touchtown provided information via computers and VCTV provided it via televisions, maybe the two companies could integrate their products to better serve their common customers. She introduced me to Jim Sheedy, VCTV's founder and CEO.

I spoke with Jim. He seemed interested in partnering. We worked out a general framework for cooperation, and agreed to make a joint announcement of our partnership at the upcoming 2004 AAHSA show in Nashville.

I went to the show, set up the booth, and started to promote our product and the VCTV partnership. Jim's team did the same at their booth. Jim and I planned to meet for dinner the first night of the conference to hammer out the details. I went to his hotel. When I got there, he informed me that he was changing the terms of the deal, making it much more favorable to his company. He told me that VCTV would own the customers, blocking us from working with them directly. I was shocked, and walked away from the meeting without agreeing to anything. The next morning I got on the phone with our software team, which at the time consisted of Dave Hornig, Evan Ruiz and Karyn Graff. I told them about the collapse of the planned partnership.

Evan, a brilliant software architect and engineer, had already spent some time looking at the VCTV product in order to do the integration work. He said that he was profoundly unimpressed with what he'd seen. He said that the VCTV product was based on old pre-internet technology, was poorly organized and missed some important features. "We could build something better in three months," he said. I jumped at the idea.

The next three months were a blur of activity. Evan and Dave designed the new product and wrote the code. Karyn did the user interface design and wrote the documentation. I handled the legal stuff, wrote the marketing materials, and started to line up our first customers. Within three months we had a brand new product that we called Touchtown TV+. It was much better than what VCTV had. Shortly after we launched the product in March 2005, Westminster Retirement cancelled their VCTV contracts and bought Touchtown TV+ for all of their locations. Shortly thereafter we sold 63 systems to Merrill Gardens, another national chain. Within a year we had sold several hundred TV+ systems. We were in business.

A key feature of TV+ was a "smart designer" that designed a slide based only on the text entered by a user. So if someone wanted to promote a bingo game, they

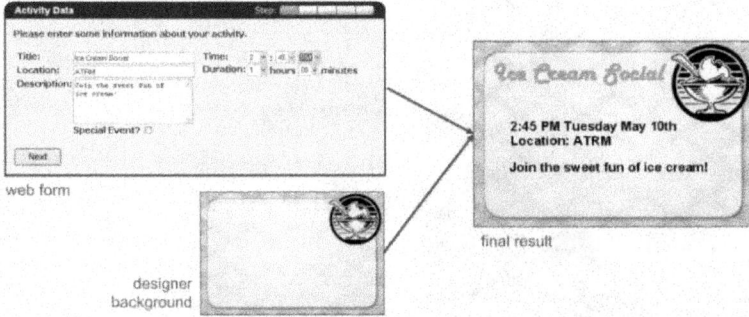

The Touchtown TV+ "smart designer" which combined textual information with a stored template to create a final slide for display on residents' in-room' TVs.

just had to type in "bingo" plus the date, time and location, and TV+ would create an attractive slide for them including the graphics. It would also schedule the slide to show according to some simple rules, such as "show the slide every 15 minutes, starting three days before the event."

VCTV had nothing like this. And amazingly enough, they *never* developed it. They continued to compete with us for another sixteen years, until Jim retired and we finally acquired the company in 2020.

There was also a hardware component to TV+ but it was relatively simple, consisting of some rack-mounted off-the-shelf hardware. This was called the Broadcaster. We created a new department called Systems Engineering to build and install the Broadcasters.

We also had a Network Operations Center (really just a PC on someone's desk) that continually monitored all the Broadcasters in the field, making sure every one of them was working properly. Initially we dispatched someone to the customer's facility to install their Broadcasters, but that proved to be way too expensive and time-consuming. So Tim Parrish, head of Systems Engineering, developed a method for having customers do their own installations.

At left: the broadcaster. Above: our monitoring
software to keep track of the status of all
broadcasters installed at customer sites.

Within a couple of years, we had over 25,000 residents using TV+.

Quarterly growth of
installed Touchtown
TV+ systems.

Expanding the Product Line

We already had our earlier product, which we renamed Touchtown Web Portal. We linked the two products, giving our customers the ability to share information on TVs and via the internet. Soon we added two more products in the family: Touchtown Digital Signs and Touchtown Calendars. We now had a family of four fully integrated products. We applied for a patent. In August 2005 we were awarded a provisional patent for "Method and system for creating, managing and delivering community information," and a year later we were finally awarded U.S. Patent # 7,930,722.

Unlike some software patents, this actually did us some good, as it effectively blocked VCTV from copying our multi-platform approach. In fact, we heard through the customer grapevine that VCTV avoided doing anything that would put them in violation of our patent.

This was Touchtown for the next few years. We ramped the company up, staying focused on our family of products for community engagement. The company was modestly profitable.

Dancetown

One day, Katelyn brought home Dance Dance Revolution (DDR). This was an arcade game where a player dances on a 3x3 dance pad while listening to music and following stepping instructions displayed on a computer monitor. Katelyn said to me, "Wouldn't it be great if your customers could do this?" I agreed. I also thought it would be an interesting project (since I'd never designed a game before) and a nice addition to our product line. And so, Dancetown was born.

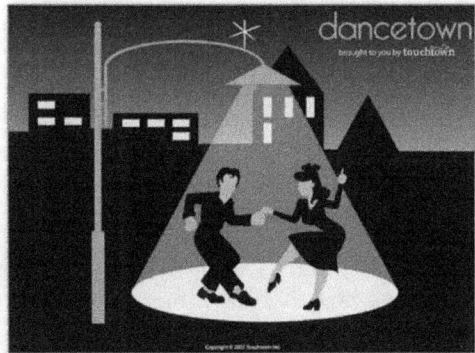

Developing the project was a lot of fun, and the project grew quickly. Eventually it involved over 40 people. I was the game producer and architect. UK-

Dancetown artwork by Camilla Kidland.

based game developer TickTock wrote most of the code, while another software team in Pakistan built the website. Camilla Kidland from Randy Pausch's Entertainment Technology Center at CMU developed the game flow and visual design. Dr. Stephanie Studenski of the Claude Pepper (no relation) Center at the University of Pittsburgh did research and field testing and observed major weight loss and strength improvement for older women who regularly used the product.

For the software platform we used StepMania, an open-source software package that was similar to DDR, and modified it to our needs. Here's a before-and-after comparison of a post-game screen from the original StepMania and our modified senior-friendly version:

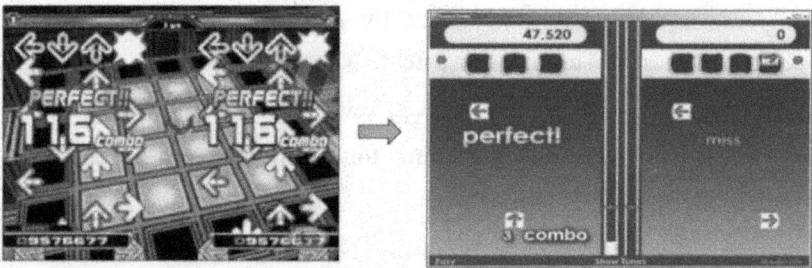

We purchased heavy-duty dance pads from Cobalt Flux and added sturdy metal railings on three sides to prevent falls. And we wrote all the usual user management, reporting and analysis tools needed to turn it into a product that would be attractive to a senior living provider.

A 2008 article in GameDeveloper magazine cited some research and had a good quote from me:

> Thirty-one older women who played DDR 30 minutes twice a week lost up to 20 lbs. The more they weighed, the more they lost, and their blood pressure dropped up to 20 points. "Traditional retirement home culture is bingo, birthdays and crafts," said Pepper. "Very traditional. Keep people occupied, but don't rock the boat. Nothing dramatic... they might hurt themselves! There's a resistance to doing anything out of the box. Existing fitness programs tend to be lame - chair exercises: get up, grab the back of the chair, lift your legs. No emotional investment... you do these exercises like you take medicine."

Two residents of Longwood at Oakmont using Dancetown.

For music, we used tunes from 1960 to 1975 from the Beatles, Elvis and Michael Jackson, as well as some show tunes. For each song we created "stepfiles" which defined the steps needed to dance to the song at each level of difficulty. This was a tricky process, but fortunately we found some professional step file creators who did much of this work for us.

Each song had five step files which gave users five difficulty levels to choose from. This encouraged competition and intergenerational play, because two people could dance to the same song at different levels of difficulty.

We got lots of publicity in the game world as well as the senior living industry.

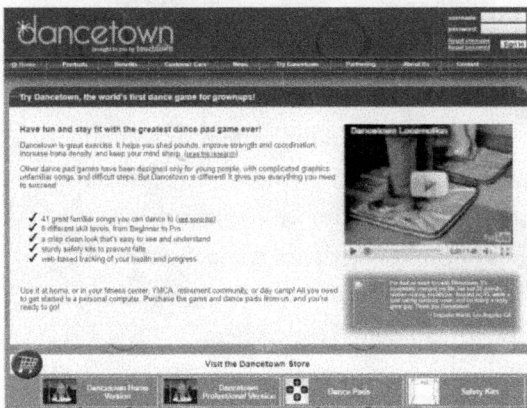

The Dancetown.us home page.

Even now, fifteen years later, there are dozens of DanceTown articles, videos and slide shows on the web.

The game was featured in a WQED television program, and the video is still available here: youtube.com/watch?v=Gh-ywkqx7Wk.

We partnered with the giant healthcare company Humana, which was just starting a Games For Health initiative. They funded some of the work. When they were satisfied with the game they installed it in six locations around the country. They're quoted as saying,

> "Research has shown that Dancetown participants experience significant improvements in their ability to climb stairs and walk more than a mile, as well as reduced overall pain and lower depression levels."

The Dancetown launch event at Longwood at Oakmont.

We rolled out the product at Longwood at Oakmont retirement community and sold it to a couple of dozen other communities. We signed up two resellers in what was called the active gaming industry. And we brought the game to some trade shows, where I had lots of fun doing dance competitions with people who stopped by the booth. There's a great YouTube video of me doing a dance-off with Leo Novsky, CEO of Golden Wellness here: youtube.com/watch?v=wrp1VY9ida8.

This my first and only experience building a computer game, and I really enjoyed it. We had a great team, and all of us had fun designing, building and playing the game.

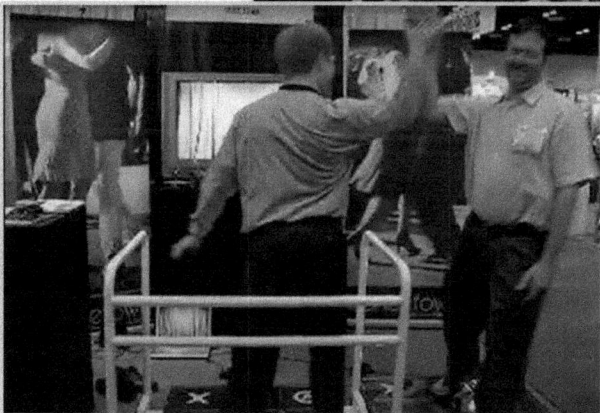

A Dancetown dance-off at a trade show.

In the end we only sold a few dozen systems, so based on product revenue the product was not successful. But fortune smiled on us yet again. After the game was on the market for less than a year we were approached by Cobalt Flux, the company that was supplying us with dance pads. They were trying to move up the food chain and become a provider of complete games, not just dance pads. They were also eager to expand their business into senior living. They asked me to quote a price, I threw out a number of $200,000, and they said yes. So I spent a couple of days in Salt Lake City teaching them everything I knew about the game and introducing them to the various vendors who helped us develop the game.

Cobalt Flux did almost nothing to sell the game as it was, but they hired TickTock to make some major revisions. Eventually they re-released the game as an eight-mat wireless multiplayer game called BluFit. This was launched in 2009, but the company went out of business two years later.

The Swamp Dream

One morning I woke up with a vivid dream recall. In the dream I'd been driving a pickup truck down a winding mountain road. I'd taken all the curves in the road with no trouble and was nearing the base of the mountain where the road ended. I could see the goal, it was just around a bend. There was a swamp between me and the goal. It would have been easy to stay on the road, going around the swamp. But instead, I gunned the engine and tried to race across the swamp water. I got halfway across, then the water pulled me down.

The dream was powerful because it wasn't as if things were happening to me. The dream had given me a choice. After all that I'd gone through to get near the end, I could achieve success by taking the safe and sure road, or I could risk it all. There was really no logical reason to take the risk, but in the dream it seemed like the natural thing for me to do. I realized that this explained a lot about me. And as we'll see, it was prophetic.

From Vitamins to Oxygen

Things at Touchtown were going well. We were selling TV+ systems, making money, and growing steadily. We had a great company culture, everyone was having fun. We had never lost a customer and never had a customer fail to pay us for what they'd bought, two things that were almost unheard-of for a tech company.

But I was feeling a bit impatient. Just like in the early days of ServiceWare, I felt like we didn't have enough room to grow. Yes, our products were selling, but to use the Jules Rosen analogy, they weren't oxygen. Maybe they were food or maybe they were vitamins. Either way, I wondered: was there a way to get us into the oxygen business? Was there an opportunity in senior living for a product that had a higher price point and a higher sense of urgency?

There were already lots of products that focused on resident safety. Generally called "nurse call" systems, they alerted staff if someone had a medical emergency. It seemed like a mature and crowded space that I didn't want to get into. But I knew that we were really good at senior-friendly user interfaces.

Perhaps by focusing on what we were good at, we could create a new kind of safety product.

We also had a potentially disruptive technology: wireless mesh networks. These were just starting to come into being, and were touted as a near-miraculous new kind of network. You didn't have to run wires through a building or a campus. You didn't even have to design the network. You just placed enough network nodes (called "locators") around the area you wanted to cover, and the network organized itself. The network would figure out on its own the best way to pass packets of information from one node to another, bypassing failed locators if necessary.

There were several different competing mesh network technologies, but something called Zigbee seemed like the most promising.

And so, our life safety product was conceived. Originally called Touchtown At Your Service (a weird name coined by Don Lazzari, our VP of Sales), we soon renamed it as the much simpler Touchtown Safety. It had a 7" color LCD screen and some controls and it was hinged on a base. It ran on A/C power but was backed up with six "C" batteries.

The original Touchtown Safety device.

One cool feature was the unique user interface that I'd designed: an easy-to-grip vertical slider on the left selected the app that you wanted, and a few big selector buttons on the touchscreen were used to give commands. There was also a big red "HELP" button at the bottom which served as sort of a nurse-call button.

We got design help from Daedalus, a local hardware design firm that was good but less expensive than our previous partner, Maya Design. We found a company in China that made a touchscreen display that was just the right size.

Once again we were in the hardware business. We designed the circuit boards and had them manufactured for us. We contracted to have a company make the plastic parts. We bought all the other various innards of the device, and assembled and tested them at our office. We needed more room for all this, so we moved to a larger facility on Ann Street in Oakmont.

Of course, things got complicated. The mesh networks were unpredictable, they didn't have the bandwidth that we were expecting, and they didn't self-organize quite as well as promised. We got some consulting help from some Zigbee experts and solved the problem well enough that the product could be sold and delivered.

A number of customers showed interest but initial sales were disappointing. The most common reason we heard from customers was that they already had a vendor that they were working with for other safety-related needs such as nurse call, and so they were reluctant to have multiple unrelated safety systems.

The Second Sneaker

In 2008 I was invited to contribute to that year's Carnegie Bosch Institute program at Carnegie Mellon University, where executives from around the world came to learn new ways of problem solving. They wanted me to present Touchtown as a case study. Did I have a problem that needed to be solved, they asked. Did we ever.

So I became part of the two-week Bosch program. A small group of executives, mostly from big companies in Germany, formed a team to work on Touchtown's business challenge. We met frequently as they worked on the problem. When the program was nearly over, one of the CMU faculty from the theater department told the team that they needed to present their findings not in the traditional stand-up-at-a-lectern way, but as a stage play (actually more like a skit). They had already been getting some basic acting lessons, so they were enthusiastic about this change in plans.

I came to the performance, accompanied by Bill Rooney, a board member and one of our early investors. The skit's plot, if you could call it that, revolved around a man who only had one sneaker. He liked his sneaker but could not run because he was unbalanced. After some adventures he was presented with the opportunity to get a second sneaker. He got it, became well balanced, and happily ran offstage.

Me with a roomful of Safety devices going through burn-in testing.

Clearly this was not going to win a Tony award, but the moral was clear. Just to be sure, the actors told me directly after the skit was over: Touchtown's product was like one sneaker. It didn't solve a complete problem. We needed the second sneaker, which in this case was nurse call.

And so our life safety business, which had already cost us a ton of money and diverted attention from our core business, got even more complicated. We not only needed to have the original tablet device and the plug-in Zigbee locator, now we also needed a battery-powered nurse call device (a pendant), a wall-mounted nurse call device (a pullcord), and lots more software. All the new devices had to be designed and manufactured to meet strict FDA requirements for life safety devices, which increased the complexity and cost to design and build. There was endless paperwork, endless testing and endless rework to get the devices approved. For example, we spent many months working to get the locator approved, repeatedly tweaking the design of the three brass prongs that connected the locator to its wall outlet to make sure they could withstand enough pulling force without coming out of the wall.

Expenses for product development and initial manufacturing ran into the millions of dollars. Our prosperous little company was suddenly buried in a huge pile of complexity and debt.

Visit to China

Our first few circuit boards were built by a small and dirty factory outside of Pittsburgh. Later we switched to Epic, a more professional contract manufacturer in Ohio. But they were expensive. So I asked the guys at our design firm Daedalus if it made sense to outsource the manufacturing to China. They thought this was a good idea, and put me in touch with SUGA, a small company in Shenzhen not far from Hong Kong.

We began working with them. Communication was a bit spotty, and the project was not large enough for us to put a full time employee in China to keep an eye on things. So I thought it would be a good idea to go visit them. Also, I liked the idea of visiting China.

In March 2012 I flew to Hong Kong. I met with their management team there, then crossed the border in to mainland China and spent a couple of days visited their factory in Shenzhen.

With the SUGA team in Hong Kong.

One interesting outcome of the visit was that I'd made an effort to learn a bit of Mandarin Chinese before the trip. I found a nice elderly blind lady in Squirrel

Hill who taught me a dozen or so basic words, how to tell time, and how to count to 12. I didn't realize that in the part of China that I was going to, the common language is Cantonese not Mandarin. And even if I'd learned the correct language, it would have been completely impossible for me to understand any spoken Chinese or read anything.

Here's my favorite example of "Chinglish." It's a sign in my Hong Kong hotel that is a hilarious attempt at translation from Chinese to English.

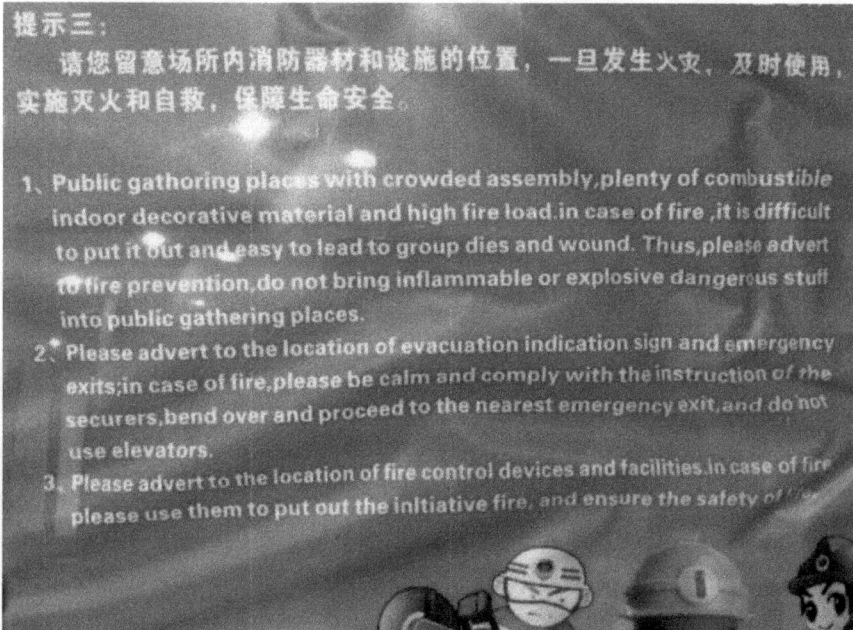

提示三：

请您留意场所内消防器材和设施的位置，一旦发生火灾，及时使用，实施灭火和自救，保障生命安全。

1. Public gathoring places with crowded assembly,plenty of combustible indoor decorative material and high fire load.in case of fire ,it is difficult to put it out and easy to lead to group dies and wound. Thus,please advert to fire prevention,do not bring inflammable or explosive dangerous stuff into public gathering places.
2. Please advert to the location of evacuation indication sign and emergency exits;in case of fire,please be calm and comply with the instruction of the securers,bend over and proceed to the nearest emergency exit,and do not use elevators.
3. Please advert to the location of fire control devices and facilities.in case of fire, please use them to put out the initiative fire, and ensure the safety of life.

A public safety warning message in the lobby of my Hong Kong hotel.

However this got me interested in learning the Chinese language. Shortly after returning home, I started taking language classes at the Pittsburgh Chinese School. More on that later.

Complete Product Line

In theory, we now had a complete product line for senior living. Our overall concept, what's called the value proposition, was "enter information once, from any browser anywhere, and deliver it across multiple platforms." This was unique. We had competitors who could do one or maybe two of these things,

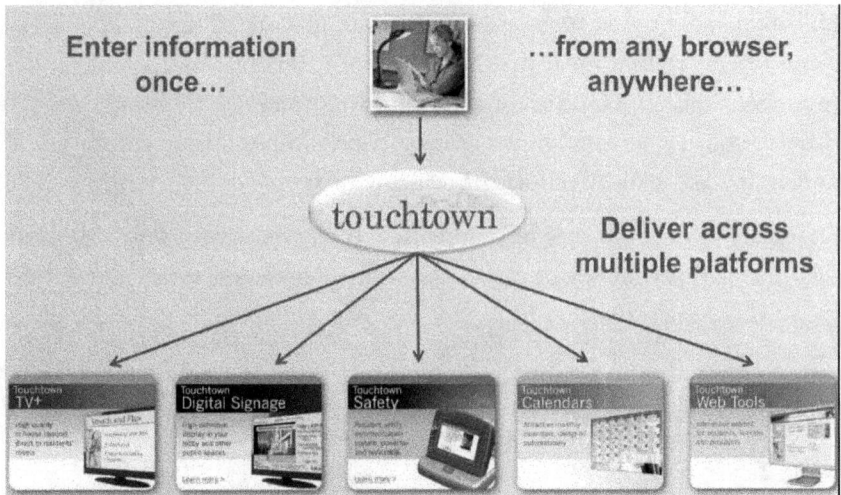

Enter information once... ...from any browser, anywhere...

touchtown

Deliver across multiple platforms

but Touchtown was the only company with a complete resident-facing solution. This gave us a strong competitive advantage, which we used to close deals with major chains. By 2013 we had grown to serving over 1,200 locations throughout North America. Of these, 99% were using the core product line, only 1% had Touchtown Safety. But the fact that we offered such a broad solution made the core product even more attractive.

Safety Customers

The value proposition for Touchtown Safety was also compelling: "get all the benefits of a nurse call system, plus the interactive features of our tablet, plus a self-organizing, self-healing network that required little or no wiring." Even so, it was tough to close deals for a major expensive product like this. Nobody ever wants to be the first buyer for anything, and risk-averse senior living communities didn't want to be the first to buy a system that could, if it failed, lead to the death of a resident.

So to allay the fears of customers, I took a big risk: I offered an unconditional money-back guarantee: if they were unsatisfied with the product for any reason, *ever*, we would fix the problem at no charge. And if we couldn't fix the problem, the customer could cancel the contract and all get their money back. This was a persuasive argument and it got several customers to agree to buy the system. Unfortunately for us, I had neglected to put a time limit on the unconditional guarantee, and that came back to bite us later.

I also sweetened some of the larger deals by giving Touchtown common stock to some of the larger customers. This had the effect of discounting the price of the system by 10% to 20%, and it also aligned the customer's interests with our own, making them shareholders and less likely to do anything to harm us.

Thanks to these two sweeteners and our company's reputation for delivering quality products, we sold around a dozen complete systems over the course of Safety's lifetime. In three of those deals we gave shares of stock to the customer. Some projects were relatively small, covering one or two floors in a building. The largest was for Garden Spot Village, a huge retirement community in central Pennsylvania, that sold for over $700,000.

A Touchtown kickoff meeting at a large Erickson Retirement community.

The product was complex, with lots of administrative features lurking behind the extremely simple user interface. And the Zigbee network technology turned out to be less reliable than we'd been led to believe. Some customers, especially those in large spread-out campuses, encountered mysterious drop-outs in coverage. This meant that a resident who went out for a walk on a garden path might find themselves out of range of the network. If they ran into a problem and pressed their nurse call button, nobody might get a notification. Fortunately for everyone, we never heard of any resident who was actually harmed by system unreliability, but it certainly made some customers unhappy.

One weekend in October 2011, we had a deadline to meet for a customer delivery, and a huge amount of work to do. I asked everyone to come in that weekend for a "Safety Blitz" and we managed to get all the devices built, tested, and packed up for delivery.

The Safety blitz: testing and packing up Touchtown Safety devices.

The Partnership From Hell

One of the most exciting opportunities that came from the Touchtown Safety project came as a result of a phone call from Direct Supply Inc. in 2011. DSI was a giant company that provided just about everything needed by a nursing home, assisted living community, or any other senior living community. They were the Wal-Mart of senior living. The company had started off with a little mail order catalog filled with low-cost items like mops and brooms, but they grew to offer thousands and thousands of different products. The "Direct" part of their name mean that they were a virtual warehouse. They stocked nothing. Customers placed orders, and DSI arranged to have the manufacturers drop-ship the products directly to the customer.

DSI wanted to move up the food chain and offer bigger-ticket items, including nurse call systems. They also were interested in having their own private-labeled products. They'd heard about Touchtown Safety, and were interested in possibly branding it as a DSI product.

Well, it sounded like a great idea at the time. Later I'd heard a story (possibly true, possibly not) that the legendary investor Warren Buffett would keep track of which companies were invited by Walmart to partner, and he'd bet *against* those companies. The idea was that Walmart would offer huge potential rewards to the other company, but then push all the risk onto them. If the rollout failed, which it usually did, Walmart walked away unhurt but the other company got badly burned.

This, in a nutshell, is what happened to us. DSI invited us to literally dozens of meetings in Milwaukee, sketching out a grand strategy for the partnership and promising huge returns for us. They told us what changes they wanted us to make in the product, and they demanded lots of demos before moving forward. They never made any commitments.

We made all the product changes they asked for. We even rented out a vacant assisted living building near Milwaukee and set up a complete Touchtown Safety system there for them to test out. We spent over two years making a compelling case for them to private-label the product. But after we'd done everything that they asked of us, there were some internal reorganizations at their company. The managers who were our biggest cheerleaders were reassigned. The project was abandoned. We had lost a great deal of money and effort that could have been invested elsewhere.

The End of Safety

Despite the challenges and financial losses, I remained committed to Touchtown Safety. In August 2013 I split the company into two divisions. The Lifestyle Division focused on our core products of TV+, Digital Signs, Calendars, and the new Resident Apps. The Innovation Division focused on new product development as well as maintaining and extending Touchtown Safety. Kim Kessler was a hardworking and loyal employee and well respected by the rest of the team, so I tapped her to run the Lifestyle Division, while I ran the Innovation Division and remained as President and CEO for the overall company.

Business was good on the Lifestyle side, but problems continued to plague Safety. One customer discovered that some of the "C" batteries in their tablet devices were leaking and damaging the tablet, and they used that as a reason to invoke the cancellation clause in the contract. We had ninety days to fix the problem or we'd have to give them a full refund. We ran a crash program to design an external battery pack for the tablets using off-the-shelf components and a small custom circuit board. We built hundreds of these external battery packs and delivered them to the customer just a few days short of the ninety day deadline.

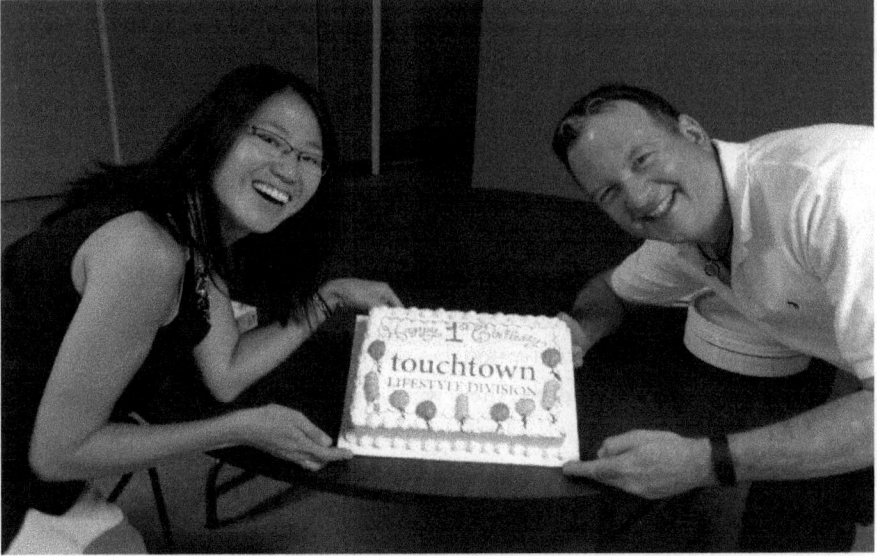

With Kim, after her first year running the Lifestyle Division.

This, plus other problems at the dozen or so Touchtown Safety customer sites, convinced me that it was, finally, time to phase out the Safety product line. We didn't make a big announcement. We just scaled back on our manufacturing so we had enough devices to replace ones that went bad at customer sites. We stopped promoting it through our marketing and sales. And we worked out a couple of informal partnerships with competitors, giving our existing customers an affordable way to discontinue using the Safety product.

New Management, Part 1

In 2014, with Touchtown Safety fading off into the sunset, I felt it was time to move on. I'd been running the company for almost fifteen years. It looked like the "core products" were going to remain profitable and dominant in the industry, but given my personality and appetite for risk, I had a hard time getting excited about selling and incrementally improving the products. So I began looking for a way to exit.

Kim Kessler was running the Lifestyle Division and seemed to be doing a good job. She was young and inexperienced, but she had a great deal of poise. She was comfortable talking with just about anyone, she had good judgement, people liked her, and she had no major character flaws. So I offered her a promotion to President of the company, effective January 2014, with me staying as CEO and Board Chair.

She accepted without hesitation. Lacking experience, she didn't quite understand the difference between being President and actually running the company. At the big company meeting when we made the announcement, I introduced Kim and told everyone what we were doing. After the announcement and a bit of Q&A, she asked me if I could step out of the room so that she could talk to "her team" without me. This was surprising to me, since it was still my company. I refused as nicely as I could. Afterwards we sat down and I explained to her exactly what the difference was between what her job really was and what she might have thought it was. In retrospect, to avoid confusion I suppose I should have given her a more accurate title such as Chief Operating Officer.

Things went well for a while. Then a few months after the promotion, Kim and I were at a big trade show. She got to talking with a guy named Fahad Aziz, founder and CEO of CareMerge. His company was a competitor to Touchtown, also focusing on resident engagement in senior living. They were flush with cash, having raised a lot of VC money. Kim introduced him to me. My impression of Fahad was that he was a smooth talker, a typical tech industry guy who made grandiose predictions about the inevitable mindblowing success of his company. It seemed like a familiar line of bull to me, the sort of thing he (or I) might say to a potential investor. But Kim was enthralled by the picture he painted for her of how CareMerge was going to revolutionize health care. I was unimpressed. I told him that I couldn't see any way for us to collaborate. It turned out that he stayed in touch with her. Later that year he made her an offer to leave Touchtown and join CareMerge as VP of Product.

This was, I believe, the first and only time that a senior manager at one of my companies had ever left to join a competitor. I was really annoyed, but couldn't do much about it. Kim had signed a nondisclosure and noncompete agreement, but the noncompete portion was not legally enforceable.

New Management, Part 2

So I was stuck without a company President. I could have gone back and taken the job myself, but really didn't want to. Fortunately (for me, anyway), my good friend Ted Teele was available. He and his wife Suzy had been running a successful software startup, but the VC investors were impatient with the rate of growth. They fired Ted and Suzy without warning. Bad for them, but it

Ted and me with the Touchtown team at the new building on Third Street in Oakmont. I had designed and fabricated the brushed steel sign on the wall.

meant that Ted was on the market.

Ted started in January 2015 as a consultant serving as interim VP of Sales, with the intent of converting to President and CEO in mid-year. For that, we negotiated a compensation package where Ted got a generous salary (about twice what I'd been paying myself), plus a bonus which was a percentage of the increase of the company's value from when he joined to when it was sold. We calculated the then-current value of Touchtown, after deducting all of its debts, at $700,000. Not much for fifteen years' work.

Ted's first day of work was a Saturday, when everyone came in to prepare to move the office from the big warehouse-style space on Ann Street to a more comfortable building on Third Street in Oakmont. This building was the former home of a circuit board manufacturer, converted to offices per our specs. So everyone got to meet Ted as we packed things up, crushed cardboard boxes, and tossed things out at the old building.

Ted applied his systematic and proactive approach to management at Touchtown. He continued to phase out Touchtown Safety. He fired several longtime employees who were personal friends of mine but who didn't perform at the level that Ted was expecting. He hired some talented young people. He also immersed himself in the senior living marketplace. He went to conferences and trade shows, striking up friendships with industry influencers and looking for large sales opportunities.

Over time, his approach paid off. In 2018 the company showed a profit of $1.2 million on revenues of $5 million. It was growing and was paying down its debts.

The newly landscaped Touchtown office building on Ann Street in Oakmont.

My office in the Ann Street building. On the far wall, Lightning Dreaming aboriginal art by Malcolm Jagamarra Maloney, 1989. At far left, an old mechanical calculator that I picked up in a junkyard and restored. The desk and chair were the original used items purchased for a few dollars when I started ServiceWare 25 years earlier.

Sale to Uniguest

Throughout the time that Ted was CEO, he was always exploring possible acquisition possibilities. Most were dead ends, but in late 2017 we were contacted by Uniguest, a company that specialized in putting customer-facing personal computers in hotels. They wanted to expand into new markets and saw senior living as a good opportunity. There were some preliminary negotiations in 2017 but the two sides were far apart.

Discussions continued into 2018. Finally on July 11, 2018 we received a letter of intent from Uniguest. They offered us $14 million in cash, plus an earnout of up to $4.5 million additional based on our 2019 profits.

The negotiations were extremely complex. One of the sticking points was liability – who would be on the hook if the deal closed and the buyer discovered afterwards that there was some massive fraud on our part? The buyers insisted that this liability not be limited to the purchase price, but could be, theoretically, unlimited. I knew the company and I was confident that we had no skeletons in the closet and had not perpetrated any fraud. But the other shareholders had no such knowledge or confidence, including Dave Hornig who was the second largest shareholder and was extremely risk averse, to put it mildly. Dave refused to share in the liability, and he said that he would walk away from the deal if it required him to be liable at all. We needed his agreement for the sale to proceed.

To make matters worse, the private equity firm that was funding Uniguest's acquisition of Touchtown also insisted that Ted sign a five year non-compete agreement. Ted reluctantly agreed to this, in order to save the deal.

We were stuck, but finally I resolved this by saying that I would personally accept full liability for anything and everything. In the three years following the acquisition, only two minor matters came up. One was related to some unlicensed graphics that we used in our TV+ smart layout system, and the other was related to some unpaid sales tax. Uniguest collected around $60,000 to compensate them for those two items, but that was paid out of a $1.2 million escrow fund set up for that purpose.

Finally the deal closed on March 4, 2019, a year and a half after the initial meetings with Uniguest. Ted got a nice bonus which he richly deserved.

The Touchtown (now Uniguest) team, with Ted Teele and Jeff Hiscox.

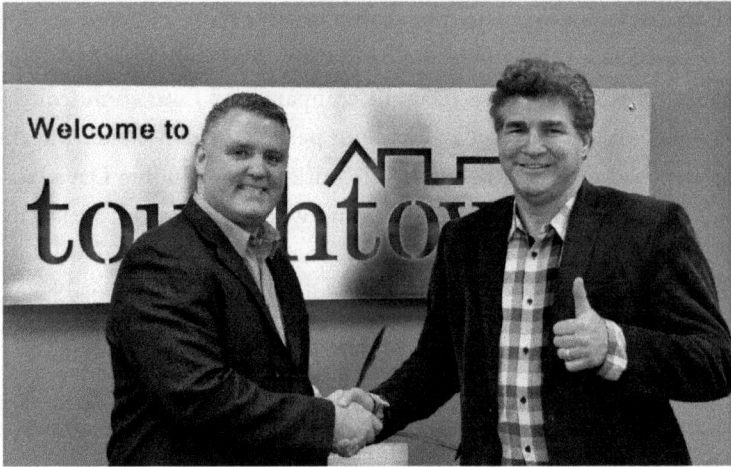

Uniguest CEO Jeff Hiscox with Ted in the Touchtown lobby.

Various other people got bonuses for their work in helping get the deal done. Lots of money went to the lawyers and accountants. The three customers who had received Touchtown stock in return for buying the Safety product received a total of around $600,000. Every full time Touchtown employee had stock options which resulted in cash payments to them at the time of the acquisition. And the remaining funds went to me and the 100 or so other Touchtown shareholders.

Everyone at Touchtown and Uniguest wanted Touchtown to be highly profitable in 2019. Touchtown wanted big profits in order to maximize the earnout that shareholders would receive. And Uniguest wanted big profits because their value was based on a multiple of their total profits. So with support from the parent company, Ted and the team worked furiously all through 2019 to make as much profit as possible. It worked, and the final earnout paid by Uniguest to the former shareholders was much more than anyone had predicted.

An acquisition isn't over on the day the deal closes. Typically there are several years of follow-on work to resolve minor matters that come up. Per advice from our attorney Jim Carlisle, we set up the Touchtown Liquidating Trust to handle the money, the post-acquisition haggles with Uniguest over earnouts and deductions from escrow, the tax issues, and distributing the payouts to shareholders and everyone else. I served as Trustee. Fortunately Uniguest was happy overall with the acquisition, so they were reasonably cooperative. Finally all the problems were solved, the last payments were parceled out, and the Trust was officially closed down in December 2022.

Ted left the company shortly after the acquisition. He was replaced by Mike Rethage, who I'd hired originally several years earlier to help with the Touchtown Safety product. Mike had risen through the ranks to VP of Customer Success. Mike and his team did a wonderful job of growing the company and managing it through the Covid pandemic. They acquired several competitors including our old adversary VCTV, the company that had invented the private channel TV concept and had tried to outmaneuver us sixteen years earlier. The team incrementally expanded the product line. They terminated the lease on the Third Street building and became a virtual company. Revenues and profits both grew nicely, and Uniguest considered the purchase of Touchtown to be a great success.

The acquisition also worked out well for the Touchtown team. Mike Rethage was eventually promoted to Chief Operating Officer of Uniguest, a much larger company that Touchtown was at the time of the sale. Jeff Stonebrook, who ran software development for Touchtown became the Chief Technology Officer of Uniguest. And Christian Kratsas, who ran Touchtown's marketing, was promoted to head of marketing for Uniguest in North America.

For me, it was a mixed experience. It certainly was fun building a company, and the payout at the end was good. On the other hand, 20 years from startup to exit is a really long time, and there were lots of times during that period when we were close to running out of cash and shutting everything down. If I hadn't jumped so quickly into the senior living market, might I have come up with a better idea, one that would have gained more traction and led to an even better end result? Hard to say, of course.

Meanwhile

So I've told the Touchtown saga, from startup in 1999 (age 46) to acquisition in 2019 (age 66). Obviously a lot of other stuff happened during those twenty years. Here are a few stories from that period, in roughly chronological order.

Middle School Robotics

When Kris entered middle school he was interested in building things with Legos. I heard about the FIRST program, where teams of middle school kids built robots and programmed them to solve problems. It sounded fun, so I approached the Winchester Thurston administrators and got permission to start the Winchester Thurston Middle Schools LEGO Robotics program. We did this for three years, 2001 through 2003. The team was called the Hellfish of Doom, a name made up by the kids. One of the kids came from a fundamentalist Christian family and his dad objected to use of the word "hell" in the team title, but the kid ended up wearing the t-shirt anyway. Kris was the lead robot designer, using his excellent mechanical design skills. Another kid, Alex Zhang, was the lead programmer. The group was undisciplined, especially as they got older, but they managed to focus enough to get the job done. They

Me with the Hellfish of Doom. Kris is at left. Alex Zhang center front.

won the Best Robot Design award in the Western Pennsylvania competition in Spring 2002.

Dog Attack

It happened on September 11, 2005, exactly four years after the 9/11 attacks. Our border terrier Mocha was in the house. He saw a couple of big dogs running loose across the street. The front door was open and the screen door was not closed all the way. Mocha charged at the screen door, pushed it open, and ran outside barking wildly. I heard it and ran outside after him. Kathryn and Kris followed.

The two big dogs were owned by a family who lived down the street. One was a Rottweiler and the other was a pit bull mix. Mocha ran after them barking, and the two dogs retreated towards their house but stopped near "Ed's yard" which was a bit of property that we owned just across the street from the neighbor's house. The two owners of the big dogs emerged from their house and came down to Ed's yard. Mocha was still very excited and was barking. One of the big dogs was lurking in some underbrush. Suddenly he ran out and clamped his jaws down on Mocha's neck and back. Without thinking I ran over, tackled the big dog, and rolled him over on his back. He let go of Mocha and fortunately for me, retreated without attacking me. I shouted to Kris to grab the other dog that was standing nearby, which he did.

Mocha was lying on the ground, badly hurt. I picked him up (getting a minor bite in the process) and we took him to the animal hospital, where they treated him. His injuries were not life-threatening, but he was weak for a while and had to wear a wide plastic collar until his injuries healed.

We took the neighbors to court, saying that they had been negligent in constantly letting their dogs run loose through the neighborhood. We hired a local lawyer. They also hired a lawyer, a nice lady who was honestly shocked when we showed her the photos of Mocha's injuries. The judge ruled in our favor and ordered them to reimburse us for Mocha's vet bills.

McAroons

I wanted to get the kids acquainted with starting and running a business. Katelyn showed no interest at all, but Kris seemed open to it, especially when he realized there was money to be made. So around the time he started eighth grade we set up a simple business reselling macaroon cookies. We bought them from the local Giant Eagle supermarket, packed them up, branded them as "McAroons" using some nice artwork that Katelyn created and a simple website, and shipped them to customers.

The business started in early 2004 and lasted for less than a year. We sold to various individuals, and made one large sale to a guy who supplied dessert pastries to several local Starbucks coffee shops.

In September 2004 we went to a little craft-and-food fair south of Pittsburgh. The fair started on a Friday when Kris was in school, so I drove down and set up the 10'x10' booth. It happened to be the day that Hurricane Ivan hit the area. The storm dumped six inches of rain, flooding roads and nearly cancelling the fair. I spent most of the day inside the booth, with the flaps down, listening to the rain. The next day the weather cleared and we sold a good number of macaroons.

Kris liked the idea of a business but really had no interest in macaroons, and to be honest it wasn't a very interesting business. Also, the macaroons tended to dry out and weren't all that tasty by the time they arrived at the customer's doorstep. So I put the business up for sale on eBay, Some guy bought all of our stuff for $300 and I never heard anything about the business again.

I asked Kris what he was interested in. A day later he told me: he wanted to fix iPods. Apparently he'd already figured out how to open them up and make

The McAroons
home page.

simple repairs for his friends at school. So in July 2005 we started an iPod repair service called Kokopelli Music.

Kokopelli Music

We ran this business for three years. On the website people could order repairs for their iPods (we charged $20 labor plus the cost of the parts), then send them in. For a few extra dollars they could get "valet service" where we'd ship them a ready-to-use, postage prepaid box.

Every day a motley assortment of broken iPods in a variety of boxes and padded envelopes would arrive at our house. There were too many to fit in the mailbox, so we bought a big yellow plastic container and put it by the front door for the mail carrier and UPS guy to drop them in. After school Kris cracked the iPods open, fixed them and packed them up. The next day I'd take them to the post office. I became a regular customer at the Verona post office, but things got easier when we bought an automated postage machine, so I just had to drop off the boxes every day or two.

Bad batteries were a common problem with iPods, so we sourced batteries from China. We branded them as Kokopelli Music batteries and sold them to people who wanted to do their own repairs. We offered an unlimited lifetime warranty on the batteries. This worked out well, since most people didn't keep their iPods long, and the batteries rarely failed.

Not many people buy macaroons, but iPods were a huge business, and lots and lots of people had broken ones. So this was potentially a really big business. We had competitors but there was enough business for everyone. Kris was making a lot of money for a high school kid. He used some of it to buy a nice used black BMW.

As the business grew we moved it out of the house, which was fast filling up with broken iPods and boxes of components arriving from China, and moved it into an unused office at the Touchtown facility on Ann Street.

When Kris went away to college I took over the business. I hired a guy to run the day-to-day operations of the business. He left, and I learned shortly afterwards that he'd started a company competing directly with Kokopelli, even going so far as to use the graphics and instruction sheets that were on our website. I hired a couple of other people to replace him, but they weren't as competent as the first guy.

I was busy at Touchtown and didn't really have time to do this, so I started looking around for an exit. Denis Lehotay's grown son, Peter, was working in a job that didn't interest him and was looking for something else to do. He offered to buy the business for a reasonable amount of money, with some part upfront and the rest paid over time.

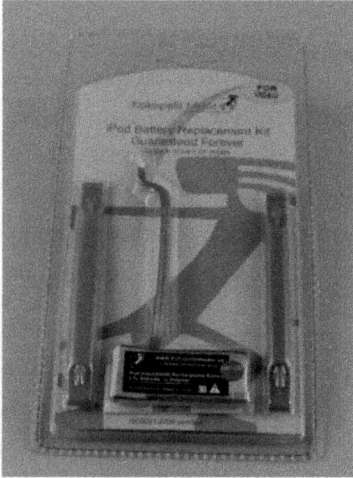

A Kokopelli replacement battery for iPod Video, with installation tools.

The Kokopelli Music home page.

So in September 2008 I sold Peter the business (splitting the proceeds with Kris), and spent some time training him on how to run it. Peter was a bright guy but didn't have the mind of an entrepreneur. He ran the business but he didn't understand how to adapt it to changing market conditions. Over time iPods gave way to iPhones but Peter didn't make the necessary changes to the business. Sale dwindled, and he eventually shut the business down, losing his investment of time and money.

Kristopher Pepper '08 wanted some spending cash but was underage for standard jobs, so he identified a need in the marketplace and turned it into a business. "iPods always seem to be breaking, and everyone is always complaining about them. People send their iPods to me, and I fix them. It turns out it's very profitable." Kris launched an online iPod repair company and, under the auspices of his businessman father and graphic design sister (Kaitlyn Pepper '04), formed and refined Kokopelli Music.

The company provides "the only battery with a lifetime warranty!" Kris gets parts from China and replaces batteries or lets customers self-install; he serves troubled iPod owners across North America via the extensive, techno-styled Web site.

Establishing and maintaining the company has been a constant struggle of perseverance and business tact. "There's a lot of competition. It turned out to be a much larger business area than I thought." Kris explains calmly. "I have to keep spending more on advertising to stay on top of other companies that do exactly the same thing." Kris is humble, but his company offers the best deal. "We excel where it counts," reads the Web site. "[Kokopelli offers] high quality batteries, clear simple directions, professional repair services, and great support if you run into trouble."

Kris's success signifies an auspicious future. "I am thinking about going to school for business administration; this venture has helped me to get a start on that."

Kristopher Pepper '08

Excerpt from an article in the Winter 2007 issue of the Winchester Thurston magazine Thistletalk, "Students Broaden Their Horizons with Unique Learning Adventures."

The Stargate

A trip to the Storm King sculpture center in upstate New York inspired me to create a major sculpture to be placed in our yard. I had been sketching some ideas for a sculpture for a while, but wasn't making much progress. I called my artist friend Joan Lehotay and I told her about my dilemma. She nailed it right away, saying that I needed to first figure out what I wanted to say, then worry about how to say it.

What did I want to say? Well, I'd just read a great little book called *Just Six Numbers: The Deep Forces That Shape the Universe* by the famous British mathematician Martin Rees. The book describes six universal constants that define how our universe works. Change any of these numbers, even by a little bit, and things simply would not work. One of these constants, called E, determines how firmly atomic nuclei bind together. To be more precise, it is the percentage of mass that is converted to energy when two hydrogen atoms fuse to become a single helium atom. That number is 0.00736503, for no reason that anyone has been able to figure out. If E were a bit larger or smaller, the atoms that make up our bodies and everything else would not exist.

This seemed like a good theme for the sculpture. Once I had that, the design came together quickly. I wanted it to be a perfect circle, a stargate, that would represent the mystery of the universe. And engraved on the circle would be the value of E. Just for fun, I wrote it out in binary notation:

0.00000001111000101011

I started building the stargate in Spring 2008. My plan was to make a large horizontal mold shaped as a seven foot diameter circle and balanced on a fulcrum, like a see-saw. Then I would pour concrete into the mold, let it set, then somehow flip it up to vertical and set into the ground. Finally I would pour more concrete to lock it in place.

About a third of the way through the project I realized that I knew something about art and math but not much about concrete, and I hadn't really figured out how to support, much less flip up a structure weighing well over a ton. A friend of mine recommended two of his friends who were professional masons,

Ken Walker and Mark McClafferty. We talked over the project and they agreed to help out, as long as I paid them in cash off the books.

And so, the summer of 2008 became the Summer of Stargate. Ken and Mark came over on weekends and in the evenings to work with me on the project. They knew all about making molds, pouring concrete, erecting scaffolding and sandblasting, and they had access to all the equipment that was needed. After a couple of months it was done.

I made a nice YouTube video youtube.com/watch?v=N7noCF78Klc that shows the project in detail.

After the project was finished, I emailed some photos to Martin Rees, the mathematician who'd written the book that inspired the project. He sent back a nice reply thanking me.

Fifteen years later the stargate is still standing and shows no signs of weathering at all except for a bit of lichen that's starting to appear on the surface, and a couple of nicks near the base where I've hit it with the lawnmower. I've walked through it hundreds of times, but have not yet dematerialized. Maybe next time.

Mom's Final Years

Mom was living in her small house in Huntington Station on Long Island. As she got older she became less and less able to keep up with the activities of daily living, including driving, paying bills, and taking care of the house. Barbara and I talked with her about the idea of selling her house and moving to a retirement community, and to our surprise she was ok with the idea. So she put the house on the market. The real estate market on Long Island was hot at the time, so she got a much better price for the house than she expected. This allowed her to buy in to a continuing care retirement community (CCRC), where one makes a large down payment and then pays a relatively small monthly fee afterwards.

There weren't any good CCRCs near Barbara's area in northwestern New Jersey, but there was a nice one only fifteen minutes from our house in Verona. So in 2009 she moved to Longwood at Oakmont, taking a little garden apartment.

I already knew Longwood well, since they'd been one Touchtown's earliest customers. They were using most of the Touchtown products, including the TV+ in-room television channel, Digital Signs, and Resident Apps.

Two scenes of Longwood residents using Touchtown's products, from the Longwood website.

Mom lived there for several years, with her two dogs April and TJ. She liked to take care of the dogs, and would talk eagerly with any other resident or visitor who had a dog. Although her vision and cognitive skills declined, she continued to drive her Subaru until she started having a series of minor scrapes and fender

Katelyn, Kris and Kathryn visiting Mom at Longwood at Oakmont retirement community, 2014.

benders, including one incident where she started driving on the sidewalk at Longwood thinking it was actually the road. Even after that she still didn't want to give up driving. She only agreed when her doctor told her that he'd report her to the state and have her license taken away. I sold her car for her, to a local mechanic.

As her abilities ebbed, she moved from her garden apartment to a room in the skilled nursing unit. Her dementia progressed and she became increasingly paranoid, convinced that the staff was stealing from her and sneaking into her room when she wasn't there. I got her a security camera for her room but that didn't convince her. She lived in the skilled nursing unit for a few months. As her condition continued to deteriorate she became unable to eat or drink anymore. She had a living will that directed that no extraordinary life support measures should be used, so I spoke with Barbara and we agreed to withdraw the feeding tube equipment. Mom died peacefully in her room on July 14, 2015 at the age of 93.

Yoshi and TJ

Mocha, our first family dog, recovered from the dog attack and lived for seven more years, dying in 2012 at age 17. A year and a half later we got a puppy, a Havanese that we named Yoshi.

In early 2015 Mom was no longer able to care for TJ, her sheltie, so we took him in. TJ had a difficult puppyhood before Mom had gotten him, so he wasn't particularly friendly. He was also getting old and started to become incontinent. On January 22, 2018 I took both dogs out for a walk. As I started walking down the street, a big dog named Blackie, owned by our neighbor "Hawk," got loose, ran up to us and started fighting with TJ. Blackie was bigger and stronger than TJ. He bit TJ several times. TJ yelped, pulled out of his collar, and ran away down the hill behind our house. Yoshi somehow managed to avoid being bitten. I picked up Yoshi. Hawk came up in his car, grabbed Blackie and threw him into the car.

It was cold and there was an inch or two of snow on the ground. I looked everywhere but couldn't find him. I put up notices around the neighborhood and went door to door asking if anyone had seen him. After a week we were starting to give up hope. But a neighbor whose husband was an experienced hunter saw a notice on a "lost

Yoshi and TJ in our kitchen.

dogs" page on Facebook and they came over to help. The husband quickly located TJ, who had apparently been living for a week sheltered under a large fallen log near the bottom of the ravine behind our house. We took TJ back home and cleaned him up, but when we took him to the animal hospital they discovered that the bite in his hip was more serious than it looked and had become infected. Given his advanced age and poor state of health, we agreed to have him put down.

Yoshi.

Kayaking

I really love ocean kayaking. For a while my only kayaking experience was paddling around in little sit-on-tops, in the Caribbean mostly. But sometime around 2005 I wanted to get away for a while, so I signed up for a week-long kayak and camping trip in Mexico. This involved kayaking in the Sea of Cortez along the coast of Baja California. It was a comfortable trip, with Mexican meals cooked by the guides, warm weather, clear water, and plenty of sunshine. One high point of the trip was a close encounter with a school bus-size whale that breached maybe a dozen yards from my boat.

That trip got me hooked on ocean kayaking. Looking for someplace a bit closer, I found an outfitter called Coastal Adventures in Tangiers, Nova Scotia. Easy to get to, just a plane ride to New York and on to Halifax plus an hour in a car. The company was run by an old salt named Scott Cunningham, and his wonderful and patient wife Gayle. Scott was a legend in the Canadian kayaking community, having paddled the entire circumference of Nova Scotia over two years.

I signed up for a three day trip in 2006. I knew this was going to be much more challenging than the Mexico trip. So I trained for it, getting in shape by kayaking two or three times a week in the Allegheny River. It turned out that I didn't need to work all that hard, as the trip was easy, just paddling around the small islands off the coast.

I went back the following summer for a more challenging trip, and again the summer after that. That third trip was the most interesting, as we were hit by a major storm with gale force winds. When the storm hit we hunkered down on a beach on the leeward side of a small island, out of the strongest winds. The rest of the day would have been just sitting around the campsite. I asked one of the trip leaders if she'd go on the water with me for a short paddle. She agreed. We prepared two single boats, paddled around the headland and ran straight into the gale. Waves must have been ten feet high. The rain was coming down almost horizontally. I had on a waterproof paddling jacket and a spray skirt cinched tight around my waist, so I was (mostly) warm and dry even as the water crashed around me.

Daniel Hays' house on Whale Island

The whalebone sink.

It was definitely a peak experience, even more so because I was scheduled for prostate surgery a few weeks later. So it was one of those "If I die, at least I'll have this experience" sort of things.

In 2009 I went again, this time north along the Atlantic coast. One day we found ourselves on a tiny island called Whale Island. We brought the boats onto a beach and walked up to a house, passing large whale bones along the way. The house was open and we explored it, wondering at the clever contraptions we found, like a sink made from a curved whalebone and hinged so you could just lift up the other side and pour out the sink's contents into the drain. It was like something out of a video game.

Looking around, I found a bookshelf with twenty copies of *My Old Man and the Sea*. Later I bought a copy (no, I didn't take one off the shelf). It was a story written by David and Daniel Hays about a father-and-son expedition trip around Cape Horn in a home-made sailboat. It was clear that Daniel was the owner of the house we'd visited. Later, he wrote

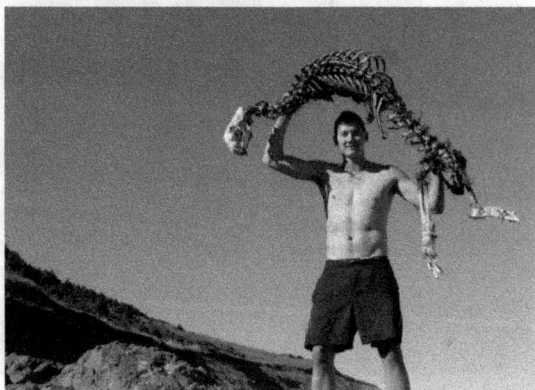

Kris with a seal skeleton

another book, *A Year on Whale Island.*

I went back almost every summer for the next few years. In 2013 I invited Kris to come on a trip to the south coast of Newfoundland, along with my friend and neighbor Ron Kozera. Kris was 27 and adventurous. He was always climbing rocks and exploring. On the other hand, he also helped out with the cooking and made some tasty meals.

Top: paddling in Scotland.

Bottom: in a pub waiting for the rain to stop.

281

I also did a few kayak trips to other places. In 2021 I did two kayak trips in the Pacific Northwest, first with Kris in the San Juan Islands, and a few weeks later paddling up Bute Inlet in Canada. And in 2022 I flew to Scotland for what was supposed to be a week of paddling off the eastern coast. But the weather was so bad that we only did a few day trips, and spent much of our time sitting in our tents or drinking beer in local pubs.

Climbing Mount Whitney

I became friends with Mike Schiller, an outdoorsman and fellow software entrepreneur. He started a nonprofit called Venture Outdoors, where I served as Vice Chair on their first board of directors. Some time later, I ran into Mike in a movie theater. He told me he was planning to climb Mt. Whitney, the highest peak in the lower 48 states. He invited me to participate, and I said yes.

I'd never done any serious mountain climbing before, and I had about six months to prepare. So I did everything I could to get in shape for the climb, including going to the Cathedral of Learning on the Pitt campus and climbing all 36 floors, over and over again, with a backpack full of books. It got to the point where I knew each of the 764 steps personally.

Finally we headed to California for a few days of camping and getting used to the altitude. It was Mike, his climbing buddy Bob ("Banker Bob") Lowery, and three others.

On the day of the ascent, we started before dawn and climbed all day, resting frequently. The region was huge, desolate, and had no trails, just a few rocky cairns built by other climbers. We navigated using topographic maps. By late afternoon we'd gotten to Iceberg Lake, the final stop before the climb to the peak. We set up camp. I lay down in the tent but found that I couldn't catch my breath. We were only at 12,000 feet, much lower than some skiing locations I'd been to. But having just climbed a vertical mile with a heavy pack, I'd developed altitude sickness. So the next day Mike and the others climbed the last 2,000 feet to the summit, while I stayed at camp. We stayed a second night at camp, then descended the following day.

African Drumming

Kathryn showed me a tiny classified ad that she'd seen in the local paper. It was advertising classes in West African drumming. I showed up at the class and was intrigued. The instructor was John Chernoff, a white jazz musician and ethnomusicologist who'd gone to Africa for a short visit and ended up living there for seven years, playing music and immersing himself in Ghanaian culture.

John Chernoff.

He'd written an highly regarded academic work, *African Rhythm and African Sensibility*, and a popular book about the street culture of Ghana called *Hustling Is Not Stealing: Stories of an African Bar Girl.*

I learned to appreciate African percussion. It's every bit as complex as Western classical music, but the complexity is in the rhythms, as opposed to Western music where the complexity lies in the melody and harmony.

When the class was finished I wanted to continue learning, so John invited me to join his weekly drumming classes at his house. I did that for several years, playing djembe and conga as well as learning a bit about bells and other percussion instruments.

Studying with John and his students was great, but I wanted to learn from some "real" African musicians, so I switched to studying with Mama Kadiatou Conte Forte and her students and fellow musicians at the Balafon West African Dance Ensemble. I took lessons and played with them for several more years. The high point of that was when the

Mama Kadiatou Conte.

troupe performed at a City of Pittsburgh outdoor event and they invited me to sit in. To be honest, all I did was play some simple rhythms to help keep the beat, while the Africans did all the difficult stuff. But still, it was an honor to be invited to play with them.

Mama Kadiatou passed away in July 2022.

I discontinued drumming lessons when I developed nerve damage in my hands, as a result of striking a hard goatskin drumhead maybe fifty thousand times in a two-hour session. The Africans didn't seem to have this problem, having drummed since they were toddlers. But my hands weren't used to it. I didn't want to lose all feeling in my hands, so that was the end of my drumming career, other than playing in the occasional drum circle.

Some of the drummers in Mama Kadiatou's troupe.

Prostate Surgery and iDry App

I developed prostate cancer in 2008. I had no symptoms, but a routine checkup revealed an elevated level of PSA in my blood. My doctor recommended I see a prostate specialist for further testing. The specialist did a digital exam, where the word "digital" unfortunately referred not to computers but to the doctor's finger. Yuk. The exam and subsequent biopsy revealed some cancerous areas in the prostate. My PSA levels fluctuated but remained high.

There were three options: do nothing, get radiation treatment, or have the prostate removed surgically. The first two didn't appeal to me. Doing nothing was a risk I wasn't willing to take. Radiation treatment was also uncertain, had some bad possible side effects, and precluded having surgery later. So I quickly decided to have the prostate removed.

The procedure was performed by Dr. Joel Nelson, head of urology at UPMC. It was major surgery and it took several few weeks to recover. The good news was that it was successful, in that the cancer had no spread beyond the prostate "capsule." So I was cured. The bad news was that the surgery also resulted in the loss of one of the two urinary sphincters. That one was the one that I'd learned to use, and it was difficult to learn to use the other one. It's also possible that the surgery had resulted in some nerve damage. Regardless, I ended up with a bad case of urinary incontinence.

Dr. Joel Nelson.

The most common treatment for UI is a sling procedure. It didn't work. A year later I had a second procedure. That didn't work either. Finally, a couple of years after that, I agreed to have a more dramatic procedure where an artificial urinary sphincter was implanted. (I won't go into details, you can google it if you want.) This worked perfectly. The UI was cured.

In the course of all this, I became interested in treatments and strategies for coping with male UI. The recommended non-surgical strategy is to repeatedly perform Kegel exercises to strengthen the remaining sphincter muscle. I came up with the idea of an iPhone app that could be used to track one's progress in overcoming UI. I had some ideas for incorporating some game aspects, and to have it collect data that could be analyzed by researchers.

I talked with Dr. Nelson about it. He was supportive and agreed to be a co-investigator. I wrote up an SBIR grant proposal and sent it off to the National Institutes of Health.

NIH liked the project and in January 2013 they gave us $150,000. I did the design work and outsourced software development to TrueFit, a local software firm. Since I was running Touchtown at the time, I needed some help, so I advertised for a research assistant. The most qualified applicant, by far, was Xiao Hui Wang. She had a Ph.D. in neurobiology and neuroscience, an M.D., and a Masters in information science, and was fluent in Chinese and English. She worked on the project full time for about six months. Her job included such challenging tasks as contacting diaper vendors to get them to send samples, and then dunking the samples in water to measure their absorbency.

Xiao Hui Wang measuring the fluid capacity of an adult diaper.

The app turned out great. We released it in the Apple store as a free download in November 2012. There was a press release and even a YouTube video, see youtube.com/watch?v=PsA-5jYlTB8. It was a cool app. Reviews were positive, including five-star reviews on the app store and this writeup from HealthTechZone which is my favorite:

> "If anything, among the sea of useless apps, iDry is a beacon of purpose."

We had nearly two thousand downloads. I wrote a paper, "Usage results of a mobile app for managing urinary incontinence," that was published in the prestigious Journal of Urology in April 2015. I also presented a poster session at a conference.

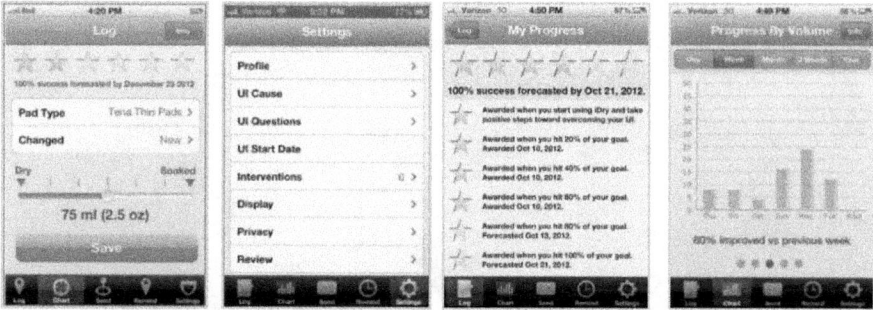

Some iDry screenshots.

As a result of the iDry project, I somehow got a reputation in the urology world as someone who was good at doing tech stuff. This led to a project with Stephen Zderic, a pediatric urologist at Children's Hospital of Philadelphia. Steve wanted to build a better way to record "voiding events" (basically, kids peeing) and train them to control their bladders. I worked on this project for a while, and had some good ideas about how to "gamify" the act of peeing into a toilet. But I was only a collaborator and didn't have overall project responsibility or control. I also, to be honest, made a mistake by using an offshore software development firm to save the client money, when I should have used a more expensive but better local firm. My part of the project was never completed. Later, Steve collaborated with a Philadelphia-based tech company and eventually came up with a product called the Urogenie, described as "a lightweight device that fits on any toilet, empties itself, and auto-uploads the uroflow results into the patient's EMR."

That was the end of my uro-tech adventures.

Table Tennis and ePonger

I started playing table tennis at about age 10. We had a ping pong table in the basement of our Windmill Drive house, and I spent hours playing with friends, or just practicing by flipping up one half the table and hitting the ball against it.

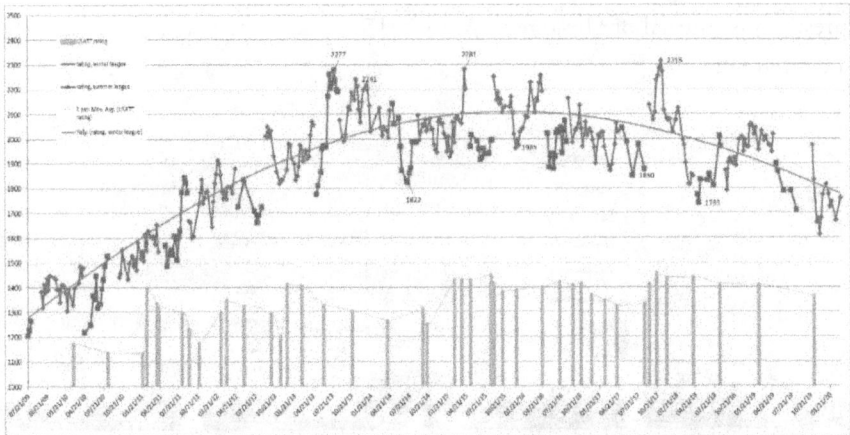

Chart of my weekly ratings at the South Park club, peaking in 2018.

In high school and college I played a lot, winning a couple of tournaments, but then dropped it when I left school and life became more complicated. But at some point around 2008 I started playing again, first in Oakland in an old basement room at Pitt that was originally a squash court, and then at South Park with the South Park Table Tennis Club. The South Park club was, and still is, the oldest continuously operating table tennis club in the U.S. and was the home club of the legendary Seemiller brothers who dominated the sport in the 1970's.

I drove down to South Park almost every Tuesday night. I got reasonably good, peaking at a USATT rating of around 1450. I played in dozens of tournaments and had a collection of trophies and ribbons which I recently tossed out. The South Park club was a melting pot of nationalities and languages, with up to forty players on any given Tuesday night speaking English, Chinese, Hindi, Spanish, and various Eastern European languages.

Although Pittsburgh had a vibrant table tennis culture, but it had been many years since it had hosted any major tournaments. So Chip Coulter and I started the Pittsburgh Regional Table Tennis Association. We organized and ran tournaments twice a year for several years.

The Oakland club needed some software to manage player check-in, recording of weekly scores, and ratings. Mark Krotec, who ran the club, asked me if I could write a spreadsheet program to do it. I started the project but realized quickly that this required more than a simple spreadsheet. So I bought a thick book on Microsoft Basic for Excel, and wrote a sophisticated program that I called ePonger. (Later I learned that this is also a French word meaning "to mop up.") I gave it to the Oakland club. I also did a little bit of marketing of the program, selling to a dozen or so table tennis clubs around the world.

I stopped playing table tennis when I took up pickleball around 2018. I turned the PRTTA over to some other people, but they never ran any more tournaments. And I dropped supporting the ePonger app, although as of 2023 the Oakland club is still using it, over ten years after I wrote it.

Chip Coulter giving instructions to players at the start of an event.

Like a Moth

| Group #: | 1 | | | *Pittsburgh Oakland Table Tennis Club* | | | | Date: | 25-Aug-2015 |
| Games per Match: | 3 | | | *Group 1* | | | | Type: | Mixed |

		Old Rating	1 W L	2 W L	3 W L	4 W L	5 W L	6 W L	7 W L	8 W L	# MATCHES WON/LOST BY FORFEIT W L	Total W L	Change in Rating	New Rating	Won?
1	Alex Meleshenko	1961		1 vs 2 2 1	1 vs 3 2 1	1 vs 4 2 1	1 vs 5 2 1	1 vs 6 1 2	1 vs 7	1 vs 8		7 5	-293	1668	
2	Anish Manocha	1436	2 vs 1 1 2		2 vs 3 3 0	2 vs 4 2 1	2 vs 5 3 0	2 vs 6	2 vs 7	2 vs 8		9 3	78	1514	
3	Aaron Budd	1427	3 vs 1 1 2	3 vs 2 0 3		3 vs 4 1 2	3 vs 5 2 1	3 vs 6	3 vs 7	3 vs 8		4 8	-146	1281	
4	Alan Quackenbush	1000	4 vs 1 1 2	4 vs 2 1 2	4 vs 3 2 1		4 vs 5 2 1	4 vs 6	4 vs 7	4 vs 8		6 6	222	1222	
5	Andrew Davison	993	5 vs 1 2 1	5 vs 2 0 3	5 vs 3 1 2	5 vs 4 1 2		5 vs 6	5 vs 7	5 vs 8		4 8	139	1132	
6			6 vs 1	6 vs 2	6 vs 3	6 vs 4	6 vs 5		6 vs 7	6 vs 8					
7			7 vs 1	7 vs 2	7 vs 3	7 vs 4	7 vs 5	7 vs 6		7 vs 8					
8			8 vs 1	8 vs 2	8 vs 3	8 vs 4	8 vs 5	8 vs 6	8 vs 7						

```
                    1-4    2-4    1-2
                    2-3    1-3    3-4

   5 or 6 Players   1-3    3-5    2-5    1-5    4-5
                    5-6    2-6    1-6    4-6    3-6   ← skip this row for 5 players
                    2-4    1-4    3-4    2-3    1-2

   7 or 8 Players   7-3    4-5    1-3    7-5    2-6    3-4    1-2
                    8-2    1-8    5-8    4-8    7-8    6-8    3-8   ← skip this row for 7 players
                    1-5    2-7    2-4    2-3    1-4    2-5    4-7
                    4-6    3-6    6-7    1-6    3-5    1-7    5-6
```

> Save Group 1 Results

Pittsburgh Oakland Table Tennis Club - Check In

HELP	Start	Print Sign-In Sheet	Set Up Groups	Create New Player	Check in Player As they Arrive While Groups are Playing	Remove Player Leaving Early	Move Player to Different Group	Update settings with played results

Checked In Players: 10 Groups: 2 Games Per Match: 3 Round Number: 1

Powered by ePonger, version 20b

Checked In?	First Name	Last Name	Actual	Modified	Group In Rnd1	Wins in Rnd1	Losses in Rnd1	Win% in Rnd1	Rating After Rnd1	Won Rnd1?	Group In Rnd2	Wins in Rnd2	Losses in Rnd2	Win% in Rnd2	Rating After Rnd2	Rating Chg	Full Name
YES	Alex	Meleshenko	1961	1961	1	7	5	58%	1668							(293)	Alex Meleshenko
YES	Ali	Rezaie	1871	1871	2	8	4	67%	1663	W						(208)	Ali Rezaie
YES	Akbar	Ormes	1495	1196	2	7	5	58%	1446							(49)	Akbar Ormes
YES	Anish	Manocha	1436	1436	1	9	3	75%	1514	W						78	Anish Manocha
YES	Aaron	Budd	1427	1427	1	4	8	33%	1281							(146)	Aaron Budd
YES	Alan	Zajac	1342	1342	2	6	6	50%	1379							37	Alan Zajac
YES	Alexey	Sachivichik	1248	998	2	5	7	42%	1272							24	Alexey Sachivichik
YES	Alan	Quackenbush	1000	1000	1	6	6	50%	1222							222	Alan Quackenbush
YES	Andrew	Davison	993	993	1	4	8	33%	1132							139	Andrew Davison
YES	Alexei	Kolesnikov	938	938	2	4	8	33%	1134							196	Alexei Kolesnikov
NO	Chip	Coulter	2407	2407													Chip Coulter
NO	Marco	Tonellato	2363	2363													Marco Tonellato
NO	Connor	Bockoven	2362	2362													Connor Bockoven
NO	Asaf	Azarsky	2353	2353													Asaf Azarsky
NO	Terrence	Sun	2282	2282													Terrence Sun
NO	Bob	Panhizar	2092	2092													Bob Panhizar
NO	Yash	Kandoor	2086	2086													Yash Kandoor
NO	Anthony	Lewis	2080	2080													Anthony Lewis
NO	Martin	Vomela	2046	2046													Martin Vomela
NO	Simon	Brain	2046	2046													Simon Brain

Check In | G-2 | G-3 | G-4 | G-5 | G-6 | G-7 | G-8 | G-9 | G-10 | G-11 | G-12 | Playoffs 1 | Playoffs 2 | Playoff Results | Results | Sign-In | Sign-In

ePonger screenshots.

Jeff Pepper

Part Three:
Money and Time

Chinese, Tunescribers, Imagin8 Press

2015 – present

Retirement is dangerous, especially for men. I know several guys who sold their businesses and just "retired," whatever that means. They retired *from* their old jobs, but they didn't retire *to* anything in particular. Dad retired when he sold his hardware store, didn't know what to do with himself, and his health and mental acuity both deteriorated rapidly.

For me, idle retirement was simply not an option. It would be intolerably boring to just, oh I don't know, play golf or pickleball or something.

But as things started to wind down at Touchtown I knew that I needed to find some projects that would interest me. Being an entrepreneur, I figured they would be business related. But to make sure I didn't get right back into another financial challenging situation, I had three prerequisites for anything I got into: (1) minimal fixed expenses, (2) no monthly payroll, and (3) very few meetings. It turned out that I found two opportunities that fit this nicely.

And they both came about, one way or another, from my interest in Chinese.

Learning Chinese

My first exposure to the Chinese language was when I was preparing for my first visit to China in 2012. I didn't learn much at all from those few language lessons and was barely able to count from one to ten. But after I returned from the trip, I decided that learning Chinese would be worthwhile. Both of my parents suffered from advanced dementia in their final years, so avoiding or delaying that has always been high on my priority list.

Although there's no way to completely prevent dementia, a healthy diet and regular exercise are both important. But in addition, a major study in 2020 concluded that people who speak two or more languages have, on average, a five year delay in the onset of Alzheimer's disease compared to those who only speak one language. The researchers theorize that this has something to do with distributing mental processes across a larger area of the brain. I could have just brushed up on my Spanish, but learning Chinese seemed like a much bigger challenge. And I'm always up for a challenge.

So I signed up for an adult class at the Pittsburgh Chinese School which met every Sunday at a local high school. I showed up for class the first day, walked into the classroom, and saw Xiao Hui Wang. I knew her of course, because she'd been my research assistant on the iDry project at Touchtown a few years before. Through an amazing coincidence, she was also the instructor for my class! So our roles were reversed: instead of me being her boss, she was now my teacher.

Xiao Hui Wang.

I stayed in the class for around six years. It was a small class, with only one other student, my friend Steve Pirro, sticking with it the entire time. Nancy Pfenning, who many years before had been one of my math instructors at CMU, also stayed in the class for most years. But everyone else came and left, usually giving up because it was just so hard for adults to learn how to speak, read and write Chinese.

Every year the school put on a big Spring Festival event, where each class presented a song, a dance, a skit, or something. Every other class in the school was for kids except for ours, so I wanted us to do something worthy of a bunch of grownups. One year we did a singalong of a Chinese pop song, Ai Wo Bie

The Chinese class preparing for a Spring Festival performance. Nancy Pfenning is 3rd from left, Steve Pirro is at far right next to me.

Zou ("Love me, don't leave"), complete with huge posters of the Chinese characters so the audience could sing along. Another year we did a little skit. The final year we tried a complex choreographed song-and-dance, but we had a bunch of high school kids in the class who refused to learn the music and just sort of stood there on stage. That was the last time I organized the performances.

Table Tennis in China

In June 2015, a couple of years after starting at the Pittsburgh Chinese School I wanted to go to China. This was mostly for the adventure, but I was also wondering if a few weeks of immersion would improve my Chinese language skills, which were still not very good.

I was still playing table tennis regularly at the time, and I discovered that the Zhengding District Table Tennis Training Center (ZDTTC) was accepting visiting players from other countries. As I later discovered, this facility was geared towards training Chinese kids under the age of 14, so I suppose the Chinese felt that the propaganda value of inviting foreigners to train there outweighed any risk of giving away their valuable secrets.

Kids getting their pre-workout instruction at ZDTTC. Note the banner in the background, with lots of group photos and text reading, "The foreign friends at the base."

The training center was in the ancient Zhengding section of Shijiazhuang, south of Beijing. I flew to Beijing, took a two hour bullet train to Shijiazhuang, then took a taxi to the center. The facility had three hot and humid gyms (they had air conditioning but it was never turned on) with maybe a hundred playing tables, a well equipped fitness room, a couple of pool tables, and a cafeteria. There was also a hotel with two wings – a nice one for visitors and a dorm-style wing for the Chinese kids who lived and trained there.

I found that the key to enjoying this trip, and other trips abroad, was to go with a really flexible attitude. Compared to an American hotel the center was crappy, but compared to a camping trip it was great.

The hot and humid ZDTTC gym.

Every day started with a buffet breakfast at 7:30. The morning training session ran from 8:30 till around 11:00, consisting of 15 minutes of jogging and stretching followed by intensive multiball drills. Lunch was at 11:30, then everyone got a long break for walking around the neighborhood, napping, playing pool, studying, working out, or just hanging out. I usually walked down the street to a local restaurant where I could get a big plate of steamed veggie dumplings and a cold beer for $3. The afternoon session ran from 2:30 till 5:00, starting with the same 15 minute warmup but then focusing more on single ball drills. Dinner was at 5:30. Sometimes I ate there, but I could go out and have a fancy (by local standards) dinner for around $10. The rest of the

A typical meal at the ZDTTC cafeteria. This is why I usually went elsewhere to get something to eat.

evening was open. This time was available for practice and pickup games. I played a few pickup games, but most evenings I preferred to walk around the ancient town of Zhengding which was right outside the centers gates.

The neighborhood was an endless source of amazement. Zhengding is an ancient district settled 5,000 years ago. Just around the block was a traditional street market that looked the same as it must have during the Ming Dynasty. And all around the neighborhood were ancient temples and other remnants of the past, some carefully restored and some just crumbling ruins.

My favorite local tourist experience was the Military Amusement Park (no, I'm not kidding, that's really the name). Entrance fee was a couple of dollars. The main building, a museum, was just a random collection of rusting weapons and little green plastic army men in various arrangements. Around the back was a theme-park style ride where a visitor could ride in a rattling open cart that rumbled slowly along a track, while shooting at targets with a real paintball gun. Not something you'd get a chance to do in an American theme park, but just the thing for unwinding after a day of training.

Armed and dangerous at the Military Amusement Park in Zhengding.

Plastic U.S. army men at the Military Amusement Park.

Like a Moth

One weekend I took a couple of buses and toured Cangyan Mountain, an incredible mountainside temple complex where the final scenes in Crouching Tiger Hidden Dragon were filmed.

View of the temple at Cangyan Mountain.

Although the training base was certainly willing to accept short term visitors like me, it was really geared towards longer stays. The Chinese kids were there for years, and most of the foreign players also came to train for a full year. As a result there wasn't much focus on intensive hands-on instruction like you'd see in a one or two day clinic in America. Instead, they learned by practicing the same things day after day with only minimal involvement from coaching staff. I think part of this was a strategy to discover which kids had the most talent and desire and would rise to the top; these kids would then be chosen to move up one rung on the training ladder by transferring to another training base. The rest of the kids were sent home.

Top: with Feng in the ZDTTB gym. Middle: Feng singing karaoke. Bottom: dinner and drinks after playing.

Like a Moth

I was fortunate to arrange private coaching, since the alternative was to just be placed in the general pool of players according to skill level. My coach was Feng, a forty year old athlete and former player on the Chinese national team. He trained me just about every morning. And a couple of times we went out in the evening to play pickup games with a group of his friends. I could never beat Feng of course, since he was a former player on the Chinese national team, but I did manage to win against most of his friends.

Once he invited me to spend the evening in a karaoke bar with him and his friends.

As far as having conversations in Chinese, that simply didn't happen. Chinese is difficult for Americans to understand as it is, and the local Hebei accent made it just about impossible. Despite three years of study, I could not understand an ordinary conversation on the streets of Zhengding. Fortunately, I had SayHi, a realtime translation app for the iPhone. I used it every day to order meals, buy train tickets, talk with taxi drivers, and communicate with Feng who only knew two words of English: "good" and "no."

When the two weeks of table tennis were finished, I returned to Beijing for a week of sightseeing, including hikes on the Great Wall and another memorable visit to a karaoke bar.

That visit was the result of a seemingly random friendship I'd struck up with a Chinese guy while walking around Tiananmen Square. We talked for a while and had a couple of beers. He told me it was his birthday. Later when he said

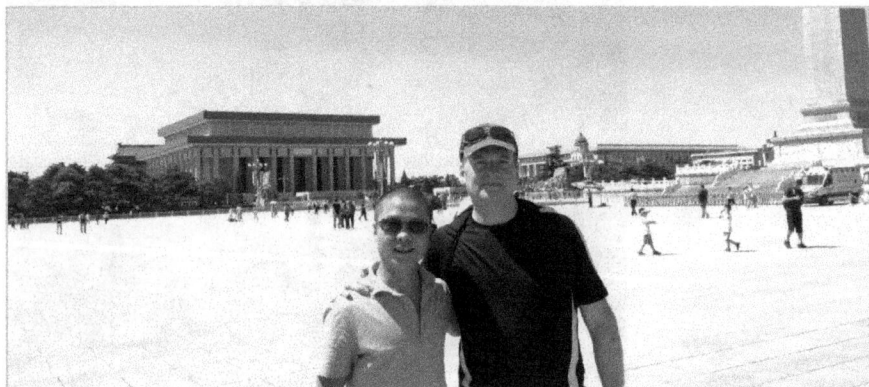

My mysterious friend, in Tiananmen Square, Beijing.

that he liked karaoke and knew a nearby place, I did the gentlemanly thing and offered to treat him to a visit there.

Getting a couple of beers after touring Beijing.

We took a taxi to the karaoke bar and were shown to a private room. I noticed that the people there seemed to know him. We stayed there for a really long time. We ate, we drank, we sang karaoke songs in English and Chinese. Various young women came in to serve drinks and sing along with us, obviously a ploy to get us to drink more and stay longer.

After maybe three hours of this, I was getting tired and said I needed to leave. He convinced me to stay another hour. An hour later I said I really needed to go. The manager came in and handed me the bill. It was around 14,000 RMB, which was over $2,000.

At that point, even through an alcoholic fog, I realized that I'd been scammed. Not that it was an unpleasant scam, as I'd had lots of fun, but it was a scam nonetheless. I'm sure my new friend was all set to receive a cut of the proceeds.

I didn't have anything more than a couple of hundred dollars on me, and I didn't want to try and figure out how to come up with the rest. So I pulled the Ugly American trick. This wasn't too hard, since I was probably six inches taller and fifty pounds heavier than anyone else in the place. I stood up, waved my arms, shouted at the staff (in English), and said that I was leaving and would not pay a single dollar. Fortunately this was not the kind of place where unruly guests were taken to the basement and never seen again. The manager relented and we negotiated a reasonable settlement. I still didn't have enough in my wallet to settle the bill, so a group of them escorted me to the nearest ATM so I could get a few hundred dollars more.

After that, they offered to give me a ride to my hotel. I declined, walked a few blocks down the street, and hailed a taxi on my own.

Tunescribers

While taking classes in the Pittsburgh Chinese School I also became acquainted with China's language and culture, and started listened to Chinese pop music to try and learn the language. I liked one particular song, 雙魚的責任 (Shuangyu De Zeren) by the pop star Bill Bounce. I wanted to learn to play it on the guitar but the chords were tricky.

In an effort to learn the song I looked online for sheet music but couldn't find any. So I tried to find someone who could create the sheet music for me. I found a couple of websites that offered custom-made sheet music. They charged about $40 per minute of music. I then found an individual in Taiwan who happily did the job for only $11 per minute of music.

Hmmm. This gap in prices is what's known as "arbitrage" in the business world, and arbitrage opportunities are always attractive and profitable. Buy low and sell high, as they say. If I could buy transcription for $11 and sell it for $40, that would be a terrific business.

I also noticed that the existing websites were primitive, not much more than digital brochures. If I could also make some major improvements to customers' ordering experience, while undercutting the other sites on price, that would also give me a competitive advantage.

The more I thought about it, the more interested I became in doing this. I didn't know much about music transcription, but I knew how to design a cool website and how build a business.

And so, Tunescribers was born in 2016.

I spent a month or so creating a business plan, writing technical specs and creating a wireframe design for the site. One of the coolest things about the design was that we could ask the customer to give us web address of the song on YouTube. Then we'd make an API call to YouTube to retrieve the song, display it in a window, and let the customer move a couple of little sliders to specify the start time and end time of the portion that they wanted transcribed.

After interviewing a few offshore development firms I selected one in Pakistan. They built the site in about three months. I lined up a half-dozen transcribers from around the world, using freelancer websites. The website went live in January 2017.

Business was slow in the first year, as I really didn't understand much about what customers wanted. I tweaked the website and the advertising, but the first six months of 2017 I had just 26 orders totaling just over $1,000.

Things picked up a bit in the second half of the year as I made more adjustments to the website and the Google Ad campaigns.

Early in 2018, our second year, I received a few emails from customers who had seen samples of sheet music that I'd posted on the website and were interested in buying the whole song. Apparently there was an opportunity to resell our sheet music! In retrospect this made perfect sense: there was no existing sheet music for the songs that people paid us to transcribe, so of course there would be other people who wanted the same sheet music. So I did a bit more design work, and in June 2019 we launched the Songs For Sale portion of the website. Resales grew rapidly, as did our regular custom sales.

Also in our second year, I got to know one member of the transcription team, Sam James who lived in London. He was a talented guy, a professional musician and bandleader who knew way more about music than I did. I hired him as office manager. His skills in dealing with customers and team members proved to be a major factor in the company's growth.

There was one major problem with the Songs For Sale business: I had never gotten around to signing licensing deals with the companies that owned the copyright to the songs that we were reselling. It's not that I didn't want to, it was more that it was really, really difficult to get the big publishers to pay the slightest attention to a tiny website like Tunescribers. I tried to contact the big publishers many times, and even hired a consulting firm to make introductions. No serious response from any of them. From 2018 onward, a lot of my time

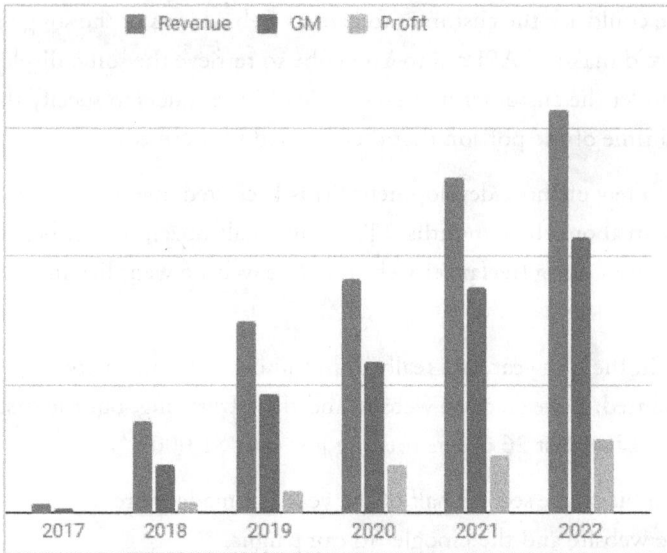

Tunescribers growth in revenue, gross margin and profit, first 6 years.

has been spent trying to figure out how to manage royalty payments: who owns the digital print rights to each song, how much they want as a royalty payment, and how to pay them. We now have digital print licensing deals with a couple of publishers, and are in discussions with several more.

As of this writing in 2023, Tunescribers is modestly profitable. It has a full time office manager in London (Sam James), a weekend office staffer also in London, a software development team in India, several part time consultants handling things like Google Ads, monthly emailings and database work, and a team of 25 very talented transcribers located all around the world.

We also have a lot more competitors than we used to. One competitor has actually copied every major feature of our website, right down to the YouTube API and the sliders and our Terms of Service and Privacy Policy pages. There's not much we can do about this except to try and stay a step or two ahead of them.

Writing Chinese Books

Around the same time that I got interested in the sheet music business, I was still trying to learn Chinese, a seemingly impossible task that I'm still working on. We had a good textbook for use in my class at the Pittsburgh Chinese School, but I wanted to try reading an actual book that was written at my level

304

of reading comprehension. Looking around, I found lots of storybooks for little kids, with stories about kittens, puppies and dragons. There were also books for older kids that focused on adolescent issues – school, homework, friendship, parents, and so on. But for a grownup like me there was almost nothing.

The only book that I found that was both readable and interesting was a little 36 page paperback called *The Herd Boy and the Weaving Maid*, written by Yung Teng Chia-yee and edited by Dr. Mark Peterson. It was based on a famous Chinese folk story about two lovers, a cowherd named Niulang who represented the star Altair, and a weaving maid named Zhinü who represented the star Vega. Their love was forbidden, making them the original star-crossed lovers. The gods banished them to live on opposite sides of the heavenly river, the Milky Way. They were permitted to meet just once a year on a bridge, on the seventh day of the seventh month.

I loved the book, and really liked the way that Peterson had designed it, with Chinese characters on the right-side pages and pinyin phonetic writing on the left-side pages. I contacted him to see if he was interested in publishing more books of this type. We exchanged a few emails but he didn't seem interested in doing any more books.

So I decided to try writing one myself. For source material I used the first three chapters of the classic Chinese novel *The Journey to the West*, using Dr. Joseph Yu's wonderful English translation. The original novel is two thousand pages long. It uses a large vocabulary and complex sentence structures, includes a great deal of poetry, and has hundreds of different characters. I wanted to see if I could tell the story in simple language for readers like myself.

In April 2017 I wrote out the first draft, in English, on a yellow legal paper during a vacation trip that Kathryn and I were taking at Myrtle Beach. I worked on it for a while afterwards, then gave it to Xiao Hui to translate it into Chinese. Then we sat down together at a local Panera and in a couple of sessions we'd hammered out a final version. I followed Peterson's design idea of having each page of pinyin face the corresponding page of Chinese. An English translation and glossary were in the back. I also hired a narrator in China named Junyou Chen to create an audio recording of the book, which I published for free on YouTube. For the front cover illustration I found a freelance artist who created a preliminary version but she disappeared before it was completed. To get the cover finished I used an illustration company in China, NextMars Media, and they completed the artwork.

The title of the book was *Rise of the Monkey King*. To get it published I created a publishing company, Imagin8 Press (in Chinese, 梦梦八 which literally means "dream dream eight"). I created an account on the self-publishing website provided by Amazon KDP. The book was published on Amazon in paperback format in May 2017. In June 2017 we sold our first 21 copies on Amazon. To date we've sold around 5,000 copies of the book.

This was really a lot of fun. As a business, it satisfied the criteria that I'd set for my post-Touchtown projects: it was financially fail-proof and required almost no meetings. So Xiao Hui and I published two more books in the series, *Trouble in Heaven* and *The Immortal Peaches*, releasing them in July and August 2017. Then we wrote three more, finishing up (or so we thought) the series at six books.

 Over time I learned more about publishing and book design. I continued to revise the books, improving the covers and the interiors. Here is the original *Rise of the Monkey King* cover, and the current cover five years and ten revisions later.

Two covers for Rise of the Monkey King. Left, the original cover. Right, the most recent version.

A few months later Yu Jin, the owner of the illustration company NextMars contacted me. He said that he'd created a children's book but never gotten it published. I offered to publish the book for him. So we collaborated on his book, *Dragon Island*, with me substantially rewriting the English but keeping his beautiful artwork and his Chinese text. That was published in December 2017.

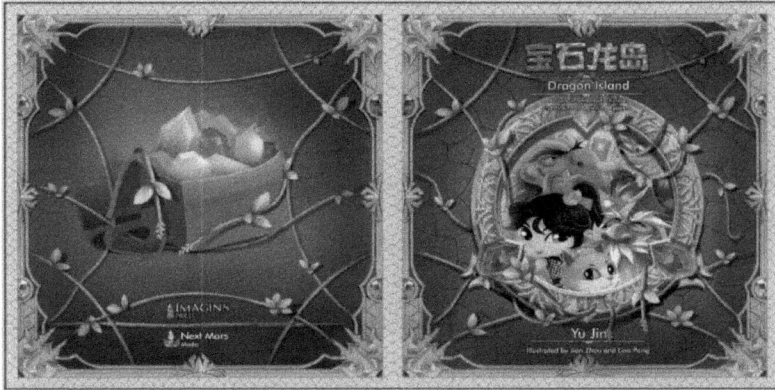

Next, Xiao Hui and I tackled our most ambitious project, a translation and commentary on the *Dao De Jing*, also known in English as the *Tao Te Ching*. I was familiar with this book from a beautifully illustrated version by Gia-Fu Feng and Jane English that I'd read when I was in college. The book had already been translated into English dozens of times, so I thought it would be best to not publish yet another translation, but instead to create a step-by-step translation that showed what the original Chinese words were, how they could be translated word by word into English, and how the deeper meanings of some of the words contributed to the book's powerful meaning.

This project was way more serious, getting into areas of academic scholarship that were unfamiliar. In addition to working with the original text I made heavy use of some online translation tools and several books on Daoism. Xiao Hui corrected and improved my translation, and I had a couple of academics and translation experts review the book before publication.

We published *Dao De Jing: A Step By Step Translation* in April 2018. It's been our best selling title.

DAO DE JING
IN CLEAR ENGLISH
INCLUDING A STEP-BY-STEP TRANSLATION

Translation and Commentary by
Jeff Pepper and Xiao Hui Wang

道德经

"Here's a translation that can speak to a
whole generation of spiritual seekers."
Jan Herman, Georgia State University,
author of Taoism for Dummies

Dao is a bottomless cup that need not be filled.

道冲而用之或不盈。
Dào chōng ér yòng zhī huò bù yíng.

Dao · bottomless cup · so · use · of此 · maybe · not · full.

▶ 冲 (chōng) in ancient Chinese is *a wine cup with no bottom*, resembling an endlessly flowing pipe or tube.

▶ Another possible translation: "Dao: use it like a cup that cannot be emptied." Chapter 9 says more about the virtues of not being full.

Profound and deep, it is the root of ten thousand things.

渊兮，似万物之宗。
Yuān xī, shì wànwù zhī zōng.

Deep · <i> · as if · ten thousand things/creatures · of此 · origin/ancestor.

▶ 渊 (yuān): *deep, profound, an abyss*

It blunts sharpness, loosens tangles.

挫其锐，解其纷。
Cuò qí ruì, jiě qí fēn.

Grind · his/her · sharp, · loosen · his/her · tangles.

Softens brightness, makes us as dust.

和其光，同其尘。
Hé qí guāng, tóng qí chén.

Calm · his/her · brightness, · same · his/her · dust/dirt.

27

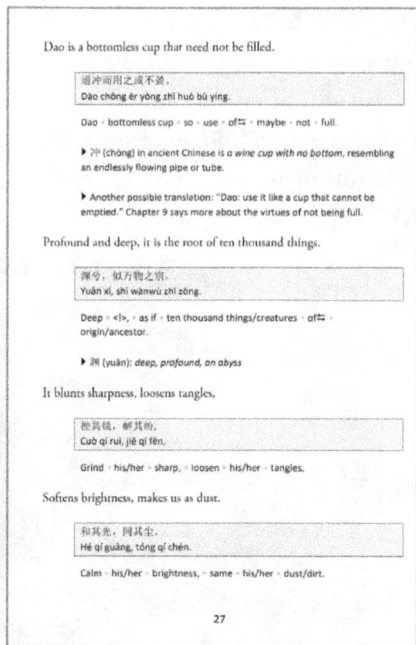

Left: the cover of Dao De Jing in Clear English. Right: a sample page showing the step by step translation and commentary.

I went to China in June 2018 to attend a three-day International Conference on Daoist Studies, but since most of the talks were in Chinese, I ended up skipping most of the talks and just wandering around Beijing. One of the conference speakers was Dr. James Chan. I met him and his assistant Dora over lunch. When the conference was over, they took me on a full-day expedition. We toured lots of ancient temples, and I got detailed explanations from one of the world's most eminent Daoist scholars.

Before heading home, I went on an overnight camping trip on the Great Wall of China. It was a great hike, but the camping left a lot to be desired. I slept, or tried to sleep, in a thin sleeping bag on the hard stone of the Great Wall, with our tour guide snoring loudly a few feet away. tried to sleep, in a thin sleeping

Top: Lunch with some people from the Daoist conference. Dr. Chan is 2nd from right.
Bottom: With Dr. Chan touring Daoist temples in Beijing.

bag on the hard stone of the Great Wall, with our tour guide snoring loudly a few feet away.

Back in America, Xiao Hui and I co-wrote a few more fiction books plus a step-by-step translation of *The Art of War*. I wrote a few books on my own, including a translation of the *Three Character Classic* and a very easy-to-read children's book inspired by Dr. Seuss called *Twenty Three Cats*.

In late 2021 I suggested to Xiao Hui that we should go back and finish the rest of the *Journey to the West* series. She agreed. This was a major commitment of

Two views of the Great Wall of China..

time and effort though, since it would require 31 books to cover the entire story, which in the original Chinese novel ran a hundred chapters and half a million Chinese characters. We set to work, finishing one book per month. The final book in the series, *The Last Trial*, was published in August 2022. Then we converted all 31 of the books into the Traditional Chinese character set, finishing that project in January 2023.

As of the end of 2022, Imagin8 Press has published the *Journey to the West* series as well as 13 other titles in paperback and eBook formats. In total, we've sold almost 30,000 books. This is approximately the number of books in a small public library.

Nonprofit Adventures

I'm most comfortable in organizations that are small, efficient, and focused on getting things done. Tech startups are, in my experience, the best example of this. They have a bare minimum of bureaucratic overhead and are organized around a highly streamlined command structure.

Despite this, I have been involved in several not-for-profit organizations. I am not a big fan of how they're organized, but I really admire what they're trying to accomplish. Here are some of the nonprofit things I've done.

Venture Outdoors, Round 1. This was founded in 2000 by my friend Mike Schiller. Its mission was simple: in Mike's words, to "give people a reason to care" by getting them outdoors. It was originally called the Western Pennsylvania Field Institute. Mike and I were driving to a rock climbing destination when he told me about his plans for WPFI. I made the mistake of giving some free business advice, and he promptly asked me to join the advisory board, which then became an official Board of Directors. I ended up being Vice Chair of the Board, working with Lazar Palnick, the Board Chair. Mike abruptly left the organization shortly afterwards, and Lazar and I and the rest of the board had to hold the organization together and recruit a new executive director. With that mission accomplished, I transitioned off the board, mainly to focus on building Touchtown.

Venture Outdoors, Round 2. Fast forward twenty years. I was having breakfast with Mike and he mentioned that VO was going through another painful transition and could perhaps use some help on the board. Looking into it, I found out that VO had just lost their executive director, their board chair, their finance committee chair, and their treasurer. The organization was in terrible trouble, both financially and organizationally. Fortunately the remaining board members had managed to recruit a terrific new executive director, Valerie Beichner.

I had coffee with Valerie, and she asked me to help her turn things around by joining the board and serving as board chair. I agreed to do it for a year. And that's how I ended up serving as VO's board chair for 2020.

Valerie was like a tornado. She completely transformed VO's organization and mission, while I worked on turning around a dysfunctional board of directors. To make things more interesting, everything shut down in early 2020 because of the COVID pandemic. Somehow despite all this Valerie managed to save VO and get it moving on a new path. I was happy to help, playing the role of hard-nosed turnaround guy. After a year, though, it was "mission accomplished" and I was happy to resign as board chair.

Earth Volunteer Fund. Nonprofit foundations play a critical role in funding worthwhile causes, but they tend to be slow moving and bureaucratic. A major exception is the Gates Foundation, established by Microsoft founder Bill Gates and his wife Melinda. They really showed the world what could be accomplished when a foundation is run like a tech startup, and I really admire what they've done.

When I got the proceeds from the sale of Touchtown, I wanted to apply some of my skills and funds to making the world a better place. I got the idea of starting a nonprofit foundation that would be as efficient as the Gates Foundation, but of course on a far smaller scale. I didn't have enough money to cure world hunger, but I thought maybe I had enough to fund some environmental cleanup in southwestern Pennsylvania. So I started the Earth Volunteer Fund, with a focus on providing small grants to local individuals and organizations who were doing things to restore places to their natural beauty. Our grant application form was just a Google Form on our website, and the total elapsed time from when we received a grant application to when we sent the funds was, on average, just over a day. Funding came from me and from monthly contributions made by Tunescribers.

The EVF ran for about three years. It disbursed grants to 33 recipients, supporting everything from picking up trash to planting trees to restoring streams to their natural state.

There were two reasons why I wrapped up the fund. First, I was really surprised to see how few grant applications the fund received; despite my efforts to put the word out that we were giving away free money, on average we only got around one application every two months. And second, the cost of filing annual tax returns was far more than I expected, and became a significant expense. So in May 2023 I disbursed the remaining funds in the Fund's account and closed it down.

I plan to continue the Fund's mission by just making personal contributions to organizations who are already doing this sort of work.

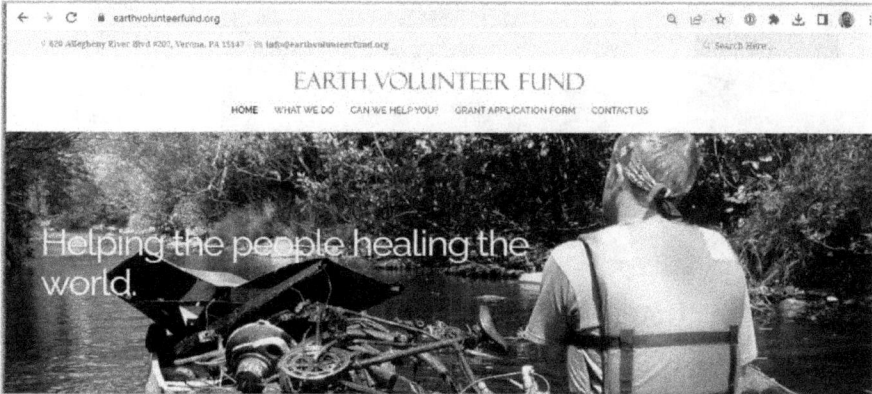

Allegheny Cleanways. This is an organization that does work very similar to what I was funding at EVF, but with a large group of dedicated volunteers, a real board, and multi-year corporate sponsorship. So I offered to join their board of directors. They've accepted me, and I plan to start in June 2023. They'd like me to focus my efforts on helping them develop new revenue opportunities in the for-profit sector.

Verona Improvements

Although we technically live in Penn Hills, our house has a Verona postal address with a 15147 zip code, and I always identified more with Verona than Penn Hills.

Soon after I started playing pickleball, another local player somehow convinced the Borough of Penn Hills to convert an old disused tennis court in Riverbank Park into four pickleball courts with permanent nets. I started playing there because the location of the courts was wonderful with a view of the Allegheny River, and it was very close to our house. But the court surface was bad, unchanged from when the original tennis court was paved several decades earlier. So I organized a fundraising effort to resurface the courts. This became a big and ultimately successful project, resulting in the installation of beautiful new court surfaces, benches, and signage.

Newly resurfaced pickleball courts at Riverbank Park in Verona.

Encouraged by this successful project, I talked with one of the members of Verona Borough's council, Trish Hredzak-Showalter, about installing new welcome signs at the two main entrances to the business district. She was very supportive, as was Karyn Brooks from the local Rotary chapter. So I started that project.

The sign project turned out to be a hugely complicated endeavor, lasting over a year and a half, costing around $15,000, and involving hundreds of emails, phone calls, Zoom calls, online surveys, fundraisers and meetings. I found out that working with local government was nothing like running a tech company. Government committees and councils work on a consensus basis, and anyone with an objection or concern, whether or not it was well-founded, could delay or even cancel a project. Egos had to be soothed, arguments had to be made tactfully, and delays had to be endured. However, the project was eventually completed in September 2022, with the installation of two beautiful new signs on Allegheny River Boulevard.

Jeff Pepper

Left: original welcome sign. Bottom: one of the new signs.

Like a Moth

Looking Back, Looking Forward

Like a Moth

I love stories. And every story needs a good ending.

But that's a problem when it comes to writing one's own memoir. The story that I've been telling has lasted, so far, more than seventy years. But the ending has not been written yet, for which I am grateful.

Writing this book has been an odd experience, because it's forced me to reverse the way I normally look at things. I live looking forward, writing off whatever's already happened in order to focus on what's next. I'm always sketching out future scenarios, schedules, plans, hope and dreams. A new business idea, another travel adventure, a new skill to learn, even little stuff like my next social lunch or meeting … these are the landmarks that, taken together, comprise the landscape of my mind.

But writing a memoir, of course, is just the opposite. It's backwards facing. And over the several months that I've been working on this, I find that my mental landscape has shifted. It's become cluttered with things I've already done instead of things I'm doing or planning to do. Recently I've noticed that when I have a casual conversation with someone, it will trigger memories of events that happened years ago, and I find myself doing that old person thing of comparing what's happening now to what happened "back then."

Honestly, I don't like this at all. The future is always more fun than the past. At some deep level I believe that there are lots of good things waiting for me in the nooks and crannies of my future, and that whatever mistakes I've already made, the shiny and unformed future is my chance to avoid making more of them and to accomplish great things.

And so, while I'm happy that I've written this book, I really hope that I recover soon from the effects of writing it. (There I go, looking to the future again!) I'm not even close to being ready to wrap things up and write the final few pages of my life. I hope there is still plenty of time to do fun and challenging things.

And when the final pages of this book are written, presumably by someone else, don't worry about me. I'll be somewhere, looking forward to whatever is next.

Appendix 1:
Family Stories

Mom, 2014

I recorded a conversation with Mom in 2014, when she was in a nursing facility and suffering from dementia. Here's what she recalled from that time:

> And then the war was over and your father came home, alone, on Grand Central Station, no parades, no nothing. Individual soldiers going home, and that was that. Of course my stepmother arranged the wedding as fast as she could, to get rid of me.

> I was working, but my job ended when the war ended. And then we got this apartment on 96th Street. I remember apartments were very scarce. You usually had to buy them from the previous owner. My folks were doing well, my father's job was doing well, so they loaned us $400 to buy this apartment. Your father went to work for about $50 a week. [Sears] took him back because they had to.

> Of course all along the way, I learned how to cook. I remember the first night that your father was invited for dinner, he was sitting at the table and there was leg of lamb. My stepmother said that I had cooked that, that was to show that I was going to be a good wife, she wanted me out of there. But the maid had cooked it. My stepmother was a good cook but she had a maid and she let the maid do all the work. Meanwhile she played mah jongg and she took her daughter [Neicee] to concerts all over the place, and they had a ball, and Floie and I sorta got along. I read a lot. Floie was a troublemaker at school. She wasn't exactly thrown out, but she joined the Young Communist League for a while. She fought against it, but I sort of ignored it by reading. She was the rebellious one. She did all sorts of things that got her reported at school. But they paid no attention, it was like dusting the furniture. Just feeding, but no attention or interest whatever.

> I moved out of that house when I got married. We had no money, he had a job that paid next to nothing. I had a menial kind of job in a men's underwear company in the Empire State Building. So it was always a struggle with no money, and being as frugal as possible, saving every penny so we could eat or do something. So for my whole life I was saving every penny. That's how I just lived.

Dad, 2000, About Pigeons

Dad's father Harry loved to raise and race pigeons. I have a long interview with Dad that I recorded in 1990. We were driving from New York to Pittsburgh at the time when he moved to the Sherwood Oaks retirement community. Here's what he had to say about his dad's hobby.

What did your dad do for fun?

When he was young he was a plumber, and then for many years he was a private chauffeur. But his only interest outside of the family was his pigeons. He had racing pigeons. And he was very good, he had a terrific reputation around the country with his pigeons. He won many, many prizes. He never made any money at it, and at time it was a penny ante business. I just happened to hear something on one of the talk shows a couple of nights ago, yeah, they had a race. The first prize was twenty five thousand dollars! Incredible. Because when pop had pigeons, when you won a race it might be ten, fifteen dollars.

So how did it work, did they all take their pigeons to some distant location?

No, they belonged to a club, the New York City... a master club for the whole area, a concourse. And several clubs belonged to the concourse. And when they had a race, which was generally every week, you would bring your birds down to the clubhouse and they would band them with a rubber band and a number on the leg of each bird, an identification. And then they would be shipped in these huge crates, as big as this car, down to wherever this race was, Wilmington, Washington. The furthest was Pensacola, Florida, a thousand mile race. And then when everything was set, they would open the doors to all the crates at one time, and thousands of pigeons would be released. And they would circle a bit, and then they would all take off in individual groups. And they would come home. And when they came to their home loft, as we used to call them, we would have traps – they wouldn't hurt the bird, but they had fingers that would come out so the bird couldn't get out. Then we'd have a little cubicle on the inside where you would pick up the bird and take the rubber marker off its leg and put it in a certain type of clock, and turn the crank. And then you

321

would go down to the clubhouse and they would figure out the elapsed time. Let's say the birds were released from say Wilmington Delaware at 6:05 in the morning, and then the clock would show what time the bird arrived at your house, at your loft. And that's how they would determine which bird was the fastest.

They were all released at the same time?

Yes. Now you had to have your loft surveyed before you joined the club, before you participated in any of the races. So let's say we were 201 and 7/10 miles. Now the guy across the street might have been 201 and 5/10 miles. Now of course this was all before computers so they had to do all of this by hand.

Now Pop had a very good reputation. He was acknowledged in the whole metropolitan area as the five hundred mile champion. He used to knock them off one after the other.

Did he have one champion bird?

Oh, we had... we had roughly fifty racing birds that he would continue to race every week or every second or third week. But some were faster than others, and some had more endurance than others. He won the five hundred mile, and several times he won the thousand mile race.

Those birds must have been pretty worn out at the end of a thousand mile race.

Yeah, well of course they didn't do the thousand miles in one lap. One of our best birds that we had, what the heck was his name, I still remember the number, 45567. (laughs) 48867, he did the five hundred miles many times in one day.

We'd be up there, in the coop, the loft, for hours. When the birds were released they'd phone in to club headquarters, say for the five hundred mile race. So starting in mid afternoon, we'd sit up there and wait and wait and wait for the birds. And finally someone'd say, "Here they come!"

Would the whole flock...

No, no, a lot of them dropped out, a lot of them never returned. Of course many of them were shot. Many times a bird would come back with buckshot.

And then we'd use this antiquated clock that we had at that time. And he won the five hundred mile many times. And a couple of times he won the thousand miler. And then there was a nationwide race. It was very, very interesting, because they had birds from all over the country – east, southeast, California, Oregon. And they would all be shipped down to Chattanooga Tennessee. And they'd all, from all over the country, all be released at the same time. Yeah, they would circle for a while to get their bearings. And then this group would take off. Yeah, very very interesting.

How do you raise a champion racing pigeon?

Well, number one, it has to be in his blood. Like a champion dog, or a tracking dog is a better example. They have a... it's inborn. And then it's a question of training, of building up their muscles.

When I was a kid, I used to start off the youngsters, they were generally six to eight months old. I'd take them down to Battery Park in the city, and release them. And then a week or two weeks after that, the next training flight would be in Staten Island, and I'd take them down there. Just our birds... sometimes we'd mix them with other guys from the neighborhood. I would take them down to Tottenville in Staten Island. Then the next training flight I think was Trenton. I didn't go to Trenton. Pop or one of the other fellas would take them down to Trenton. And that was to train their homing instinct.

And then when the birds came home, as I mentioned a little while ago, "Here they come, here they come!" and you'd keep your fingers crossed and hope that one of them was yours. And he'd pull away from the others. Of course by that time they'd thinned out and there was only a handful of other birds instead of hundreds, and three, four, five of them would come over our area. And they'd drop down and go through the box, we'd call it, and into the little trap.

So all the birds from one neighborhood would fly together?

Like a Moth

Sometimes. Sometimes they would, sometimes they wouldn't. This one bird that I mentioned, 48867, he was a loner, he'd always come in by himself. A big bird, he was a monster. He was a great stud. His strain was the Daddy Longlegs strain. Huge birds with an enormous pair of shoulders. And he was some bird, that guy.

And then I have pictures of Pop's favorite, her name was Minnie. She was a wonderful, uh, breeder. So we bred her with this 48867, and we got some great champions out of her.

Owney "The Killer" Madden (1891-1965), he used homing pigeons to carry messages between himself and other New York mobsters.

So did he sell birds too?

(laughs) He was a funny guy. He would very, very seldom sell them. There was one guy, a former gangster, you might have heard of him, Owney Madden. (laughs) He was before your time. He was a gangster with the Irish Mafia. And he wanted this 48867, but Pop would never sell him. So one day Owney, I don't remember if it was a check or a handful of money, he said "Here, Harry, take what you want, I want that bird." Pop wouldn't give it to him. But he gave him a couple of youngsters, and he did very well with them.

Yeah, he would very, very seldom sell a bird.

Now I used to have a couple of... Pop used to have homing pigeons, and I fussed around with fancy breeds, they called an owl – it was still a pigeon, not an owl, with a short beak and a frill and a cap - beautiful, beautiful birds. And then there was a close relative to the owl called a Turban, with a frill and a cap, which is a [???] of feathers on the head. And I also had Rollers, which were very high flying birds that didn't travel far, they'd just circle around the area, but they'd be up so high that you could barely see them. And then the reason they were called Rollers was they were tumblers. They would flip their tail up and go spinning like this. (laughs) Most of the time they could stop. But sometimes they couldn't stop and they'd crash into the roof.

But what started this was Owney Madden and one of his lieutenants, Timmy O'Mara, went to Europe on a pleasure trip. And he brought me back a couple of rollers from England. And I bred them, and I had a lot of fun with them, along with [???] and turbans.

Why would a bird want to do that tumbling?

I don't know, Jeff. They claim, and they've made a lot of progress in analyzing the behavior of birds, at that time they claimed that it was a nervous condition, but I don't know.

See at that time nobody had any idea how birds, particularly homing pigeons, could find their way home. But of course they've made a lot of progress now, and it's all related to magnetic fields, where these birds, all birds, have a compass or a magnetic field built into their brains, and that's how they migrate.

Yeah, and I guess they also have to have very good eyesight, so when they got to your neighborhood they'd be able to pick out your building and recognize the streets...

Well, what we used to do to help them, we used to have decoys, we used to call them chicos. We'd take a bird that couldn't fly, we'd clip his wings so he'd flutter. And when we saw the birds coming over, say about where that sign is, we'd throw one of the chicos up in the air and that would attract them.

Yeah, it was a lot of fun, I enjoyed it. But it used to drive my mother crazy. We never had any money, and Pop would spend what little money we had on pigeon food. See, there was different kinds of food; there was cracked corn and then there was other food that we would feed them when they were nursing the youngsters, and then when they were in training we'd give them another kind of food called racing food, I don't know, I guess it built up their muscles.

Jesus, Jeff, I'm going back sixty, sixty five years.

Dad, 2000, War in the Pacific

Here's what Dad had to say in our 1990 conversation about his time in the Coast Guard:

> Well, I was in boot camp, not boot camp but a staging area in Corolla North Carolina. And then I was assigned to a ship and moved back up here. My ship was built just under the Whitestone Bridge, in the Wheeler Shipyard.
>
> You know, I've been thinking, that while I've always been interested in photography, there are a lot of pictures I should have taken. We ran into a herd of seals in the Pacific. And then when we got down into the warmer waters, there would always be porpoises playing around the bow of the ship. You've probably seen pictures of porpoises jumping across the bow...
>
> *Yeah.*
>
> And every morning we'd find flying fish up on deck. I wish I'd taken pictures of those porpoises and seals... and a other things I should have done, y'know, you get involved, there was a war going on. (laughs)
>
> *So, where did you stop off?*
>
> From New York we were supposed to go down through the canal non-stop, the Panama Canal. But we had trouble with the hydraulic steering on the ship, so we had to put in to... yeah, it went bad off Cape Hatteras. So we had to steer the ship manually. Boy, let me tell you, we had two, sometimes three guys at the wheel because of the strain.
>
> So we put in somewhere, I forget where. And then from there we put in to St. Augustine, no Jacksonville, for repairs. (laughs) That lasted about a day, and it had to be repaired again, so we pulled in to Havana, and in Havana it was fixed pretty well. From Havana we went to Panama, spent a couple of days in Panama, went through the canal, and then up the West Coast, and then we had steering problems again, and we rolled into Manzanillo Mexico, where they did a patchwork job on it. Anyway, it took us up to San Diego, and then they fixed it. San Diego, then the next stop was Pearl Harbor, Honolulu.

This was what, '43?

'44, yeah it was In '44. (laughs) You know, it's funny, it was a little bucket of bolts, what we used to call a pisspot. We pulled out of San Diego and I was up on the bridge, because I was the quartermaster and the assistant navigator. And the guys would come up, hey Pep, where do we pick up the convoy? And I'd ask the captain, "Where do we pick up the convoy?" "What convoy?" "We're not going alone like this, are we?" He said, "You don't think the Japs would waste a torpedo on us, do you?"

Because it was a small ship, only 176 feet long. So we pull out and we're on our way, all by ourselves in this great big, wide Pacific ocean. Yeah, and the only armament we had was a couple of pea-shooters, two twin-fifty caliber machine guns, and then two twenty millimeter cannons, that was our whole armament.

And you're all by yourselves.

All by ourselves. And the skin of our ship was maybe a quarter of an inch thick. Y'see, the ships were originally built for the Merchant Marine, but the Merchant Marine refused to take them to sea because they were such horrible ships. So they tried to pawn them off on the Navy, and the Navy refused them. So they gave them to the Coast Guard.

So we took them out, and the ships used to roll something awful, because they were designed as a type of landing craft with flat bottoms so they could run up on the beach and discharge our cargo or the troops and get the hell out of there as fast as we could.

(laughs) So we pull into Pearl Harbor, and again, I was on the bridge, I was a signalman as well as being the quartermaster. And as soon as we came over the horizon, the lookout tower blinks at me, I had to identify myself with the call letters of the day. I think I was the worst signalman in the service, I was absolutely horrible. So he blinks over to me – I was able to read him all right. So meanwhile we're cruising into Pearl Harbor and this guy's frantically blinking away at me. So the captain comes over and says "What's a matter, Pep?" and I say "I can't read his light, Captain." "Well," he says, "the hell with him, keep going."

(laughs) So I said "What if they blow us out of the goddamned water?" "Aah, don't worry about it." We finally pull in, and the captain heard him on the bullhorn, calling "Identify yourself." And we still couldn't understand it! So finally, we're at the two towers, the two towers at the entrance to the harbor, and the guy gets out with the two semaphore flags. Oh, I was good at that. So he signals to me and I signal back, "FS273, from San Diego, ETA blah blah blah." And then they let us in.

Then much the same thing happened on the little island of Biak – I'm getting ahead of myself. That's off the northwest coast of New Guinea. We pull in there, and the same procedure, I couldn't understand them. (laughs) Oh, boy.

So what was the point of all this? Were you carrying supplies from New York, from San Diego?

Yeah, we carried supplies between the islands. And once we arrived in New Guinea, which was our home port, Finschhafen New Guinea. Then we would go around to all the various islands like Biak or Manus in the Admiralty Islands, or Lae, a couple of other islands. But most of the time we would be carrying bodies, corpses, back to a huge cemetery in

The Coast Guard-manned FS-273 was delivered to the U.S. Army on November 6, 1944 with LT W.P. Clark,Jr., USCGR, as her first commanding officer. She departed New York December 3, 1944 for the Southwest Pacific where she operated during the war. She was decommissioned October 30, 1945, sold and reflagged by a Philippine shipping company, renamed several times, and wrecked in 1978. This photo is actually the identical FS-177. (from http://www.navsource.org/archives/30/07/07273.htm).

Finschhafen. And then we would carry ammunition and other supplies back to the islands.

 The scariest thing was when they were dismantling a base in Darwin, Australia. They loaded us right up to the gunnels, the waterline, with napalm – you know what napalm is? – and detonator caps. And here we were in this little bitty pisspot, loaded with this stuff which could've blown us sky high. So we pull out of Darwin harbor... Now the captain was an old salt, a helluva nice guy, a real rough old salt. The harbor boat signaled over to us, "Do you require a pilot?" I relayed that to the captain, and I won't repeat what he said (laughs) but in better language he told him to go to hell. So I said, "In those exact words, Captain?" He said, "No, send him a negative." So I flipped a negative.

We went, loaded with high explosives, through the Torres Straits, which was very hard to chart because the sands continually shifted. There was a very, very treacherous route. Now in order to go from here to here, you could not go in a straight or anything near a straight line. You would have to go like this. We didn't have any sounding equipment on the ship, so we had to have a couple of guys up on the bow with a – what the hell do you call it – a weighted line. We were able to find our depth that way, everything by hand.

Has this thing [the tape recorder] been going all this time?

Yes.

Oh, for God sakes, you'll have my whole history.

So anyway, through the Torres Straits, next stop was Lae, New Guinea. That was a big base, there was a lot of fighting going on there. And from there back up to Finschhafen to Hollandia which was probably the largest military hospital in the Pacific area outside of Pearl Harbor. As a matter of fact, I found out later that a friend of mine, Lee Carson – you've heard me mention him? – Lee was at the Hollandia hospital and I didn't even know it at that time. And then on to Biak. Now we made a couple of trips to Biak.

Now on this one occasion, we were out on the harbor, and I had duty on the bridge. So anyway, it was right near an airfield. And I remember this very clearly, it's the kind of thing you never forget. One of our planes came in, it was one of the big bombers, a B29 or whatever it was. Anyway, he was coming in, and evidently the tail gunner was dead or had fallen asleep. There was a Japanese bomber right on his tail. And our plane came in for a landing, and the Jap plane right in back of him dropped a load of bombs right on the barracks (unintelligible). What a mess that was.

Dad, 2000, Raising Tropical Fish

Dad also raised tropical fish. Here's what he had to say about that.

I remember you raising tropical fish.

Yeah.

That was after you moved out of the city and out to the Island.

Yeah, well I had them in the city too. As a matter of fact we lived on East 82nd Street, in one of those old railroad flat apartments, I don't know if you know what they are. And when Ralph got married I converted his room into an aquarium, I built a rack out of pipe. I must have had twenty, thirty, forty aquariums in there.

It must have been expensive.

No, not really because fish were cheap at that time. Because we used to buy guppies at that time for a nickel or ten cents apiece. Or buy bettas or Siamese fighting fish, they were expensive, maybe half a buck.

But the fish tanks themselves must have been expensive.

I don't remember them being expensive. See I never bought them with the aerators and the filters, I always had my tanks balanced naturally. And then I worked in a tropical fish store on, I think it was 81st Street. I used to work there once in a while, behind the counter, scooping fish out, I made a few dollars there and he'd give me a few fish.

(pause)

Gee, it's strange Jeff how all of that comes back. God, after so many years!

It's all stored away, you just need one memory to bring it all back.

I was supposed to go on a fish collecting expedition to South America but Mom wouldn't let me go. They were getting a group of collectors together to go to South America, to the Amazon, the Platte [???], and some of the other rivers to collect fish, but Mom wouldn't let me go. I guess she figured that I'd be away for a long time, because that was before we had planes. (laughs)

How were you going to get there?

By boat! But he went down there and met a couple of other fellas, and brought back a lot of these exotic fish. Because at that time tropical fish was just beginning to take hold.

Gee, this is more than I've talked in twenty years, Jeff!

Like a Moth

Appendix 2:
Family History

Pfeffer Family History

The known Pfeffer family tree starts with a rabbi, Raphael Pfeffer, who lived in Lviv in the mid-1800's. Lviv, also called Lwow and Lemberg, was in the Galicia region. This was part of the Austrian Empire at that time, but after the collapse of the empire in 1867 it became part of Poland, later the Soviet Union, and is currently in western Ukraine.

Other than his first name (which appears in his son Morris's burial record), nothing else is known about this rabbi, who was my great great grandfather and the patriarch of the Pfeffer family. But he had at least one child, Morris Pfeffer, my great grandfather, who was born in Lviv in 1857.

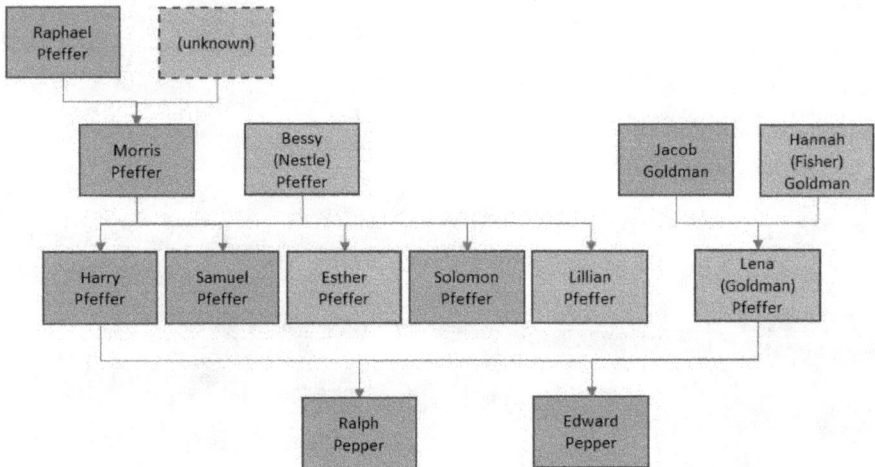

Morris' first marriage was in Lviv. It ended in divorce but produced a daughter named Freida, who was born in 1880 and came to the U.S. in 1900.

Morris then married Bessy M. (Nestle) Pfeffer, who was sixteen years younger than he was. She was born in 1873 also in Lviv. They both spoke German as their native tongue. The two of them emigrated to the US in 1890 when they were age 33 and 17. Morris worked as a tailor and opened a shop on Washington Street in Newark, New Jersey.

Morris (at left) in front of his tailor shop.

*Morris
and
Bessy
Pfeffer.*

1920 census record for Morris and Bessy Pfeffer and their two youngest children, Solomon ("Solly") and Lillian. They lived at 228 Packer St. in Essex, New Jersey.

Morris and Bessy Pfeffer had five children: Harry, Samuel, Esther, Solomon and Lillian.

Harry Pfeffer (July 15, 1888 – 1943), the oldest, was my grandfather. If these dates are correct, Harry's mother Bessy would have been only 15 years old when he was born. I'll talk more about Harry a bit later.

Samuel Pfeffer (1890 – ?), was a violinist who played in the New Jersey Philharmonic. His niece, Claire Rosenberg, described Sam as "good looking like all the Pfeffers, but arrogant." He married Lilly (Reich) Pfeffer and they had two daughters, Cecil and Shirley.

Esther (Pfeffer) Howard (1896 – ?), married and "dropped out of sight and denied her religion" according to Dad. My distant cousin Max Rosenberg, who did a lot of research into our family history, said that she was "legendarily attractive." His cousin Judy Rosenberg said, "Esther was a very beautiful, bright woman and she was a career woman she was a vice president of a girls dress company. Very unusual for a woman of her day." After her divorce she went to work at American Retail and Research Co. as a buyer of children's wear. Later she became a VP at W. T Grant, a large department store, which was quite an accomplishment for a woman at the time.

Solomon "Solly" Pfeffer (1899 – 1997 at age 97) married Ruth (Plaine) Pfeffer (1906 – 2000 at age 94). Sol and Ruth owned a liquor store in East Rutherford NJ. Sol was a Freemason who achieved the 33rd degree, which the Freemasons

Above: Sol Pfeffer in his liquor store. At right: Sol and Ruth.

say is "a supreme honor bestowed only on those who have demonstrated outstanding service to the Brotherhood, as well as professional and personal accomplishments." Ruth was active in the women's suffrage and civil rights movement, and "a real go-getter" according to Max. They were married for 76 years.

Dad took me to visit Sol and Ruth in New Jersey once, I must have been 15 years old. We had lunch at their apartment. The only thing I remember about the visit was the food, which I though was the worst tasting food I'd ever had in my life. Everything was sour, like the borscht soup, and strange, like the beef tongue and sliced beef brains.

Sol and Ruth had one child, Claire. She was a teacher in Bridgeport, Connecticut. She married Lou Rosenberg, a man 15 years older than her. Lou was a butcher and a combat medic in World War II. He became an alcoholic later in life.

Claire and Lou had three children: Stuart (married Pamela Fabrici, had one child, Judge Max Rosenberg), Judith (her partner was Ellen, no children) and David (a butcher, married Amy Warshaw, had two daughters Marci and Lydia).

Lillian "Lilly" (1908 – ?), delivered newspapers. She married a distant cousin named Morris. Claire said that Lilly was "a sweet, generous, good hearted woman, rather childlike. No one would expect her to be the keeper of anything, not even herself." Another person commented that Lilly was "a little touched." Dad's comment about Lillian was:

> "And Lilly, she was nice, and we were fairly close years ago. And she married a second or a third cousin by the name of Morris. Moishe, we used to call him. Boy, he was a character. He was real East Side, what would you call it, a tough guy... He used to deliver newspapers, a really menial job. But a nice guy. But his language was atrocious. (laughs). I remember when he was delivering newspapers... dis guy and dat guy... so's he trows me a hullo and I trows him back a hullo, that's the way he used to talk. He died many years ago and Lilly never remarried. She lives out in Newark. I think she's the only one who still lives in Newark."

Judith Rosenberg said,

> "Lilly was a kind hearted more simple woman who married Uncle Moishe. Uncle Moishe a little scary to kids although he was a nice person he looked kind of rough on the edges. My mother called him the missing link!"

Later in life, after Bessy died in 1949, Morris married for a third time, details unknown. He died at age 70 on September 9, 1928, in Newark.

The oldest of the five children, Harry, was my grandfather. He was a plumber and later a chauffeur and an assistant garage manager. He worked for a Mr. Lusterg at 789 West End Avenue in New York City.

According to Dad he had an excellent tenor voice but had almost no education, "could barely add two and two." However, census records show he completed eight years of school. He came to America either in 1892 at age 4 or in 1895 at age 7, depending on which census report is correct. He lived in the New York area, in the Bronx.

On January 30, 1910 at age 22 he married 19-year old Lena Goldman. Lena was born in Austria in 1890, came to New York at age 3, and worked as a saleslady. They lived at 231 East 84th Street in Manhattan, and later at 442 East 87th Street. They had two children, Ralph born in 1912 and Edward in 1914.

This is from the 1920 U.S. Census:

The Pfeffer household in 1920: Harry (age 32, born in Austria), Lena (29, New York), Ralph (8, New York) and Edward (6, New York).

The Pfeffer family often went to the beach and fished out of Sheep's Head Bay.

Harry loved to raise and race pigeons. I have a long interview with Dad that I recorded in 1990, it's in Appendix 1.

Harry died in 1943. He was up on the roof of their apartment building on East 82nd Street in the Bronx, either installing an antenna for their new TV set or tending to his pigeons, depending on which version of the story one believes. It was raining. He slipped and fell off the roof. He landed on a wrought iron fence and was impaled on one of the fence spikes.

Harry and Lena had two sons, my uncle Ralph Pfeffer and my dad, Edward Pfeffer. According to Ralph's son Larry, "Harry would send my dad out to deal with anyone who might have roughed up your dad. They would also ski down the hills of Central Park on barrel staves and hunt muskrat for their pelts in the swamps near Newark." Harry was a butcher. He had a store called the Golden Rule Market on Briggs Avenue in the Bronx.

Dad on the roof, in the Bronx.

Top: Harry. Lower left: Harry with 3 people, probably an employee (at left) and his clients. Lower right: Dad with parents and an unknown girl.

Ralph became a butcher like his dad. He was born in 1910, married Sylvia. They had two children, Curtis and Larry, and the biggest cat I'd ever seen.

Dad had enlisted in the Army when the US entered World War II, but when his father died he was granted a compassionate discharge, and he went home to care for his mother. Later, though, he enlisted in the Coast Guard.

Left: Dad in his Coast Guard uniform. Right: with his mother Lena Pfeffer.

The Pfeffer brothers Ralph and Ed.

Ralph and Sylvia Pfeffer.

Like a Moth

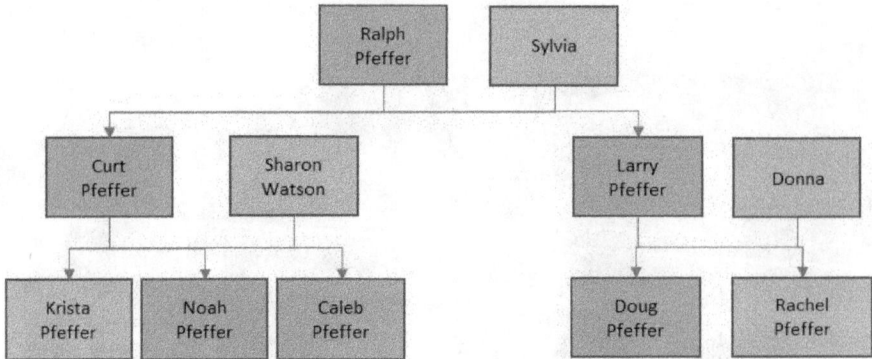

Both of Ralph's children and three of his four grandchildren were (or are) jewelers. The older son, Curtis, had a wild youth. He eventually settled down a bit and moved out to Arizona where he studied traditional jewelry-making from the native Americans there. He opened Aurum Jewelry in Jerome. I visited him once in Arizona, when Kathryn and I were out west for our honeymoon in 1984. We stopped in at the Spirit Room saloon where he spent much of his time, and they directed us to his house outside of town. He wasn't

Curt Pfeffer with his wife Sharon Watson and adopted daughter Krista in Jerome, Arizona, 1984.

home, so we waited and chatted with his wife, Sharon Watson. As Curt drove up, Sharon shouted to him, "Your cousin doesn't look anything like you!" He was tall, lean, sunburned, and had a full dark beard. He looked like he'd just come back from a year of camping in the wilderness.

Curt's adopted daughter Krista now lives in California, and his two sons, Noah and Caleb, both live in Arizona and are jewelers.

Ralph's younger son Larry also became a jeweler. His shop was Country Jewelers in Greenfield MA, and as of 2023 was retired and living with his wife Donna (Gold). Their son Doug is a software engineer, the only Pfeffer who is not a jeweler as far as I know. He lives in Amherst MA. Their daughter Rachel lives in Takoma Park MD, is a jeweler of course, and has two children, born around 2018 and 2021.

Noah Pfeffer   *Caleb Pfeffer*   *Rachel Pfeffer*

Just to finish out the family tree (for now)… my sister Barbara married Bertrand "Randy" Dannenfelser. They have two children, Peter and Keith. Peter married Alissa and had two children, Lilly Grace and Jackson Edward. And I of course married Kathryn and we have two children, Katelyn and Kris.

Like a Moth

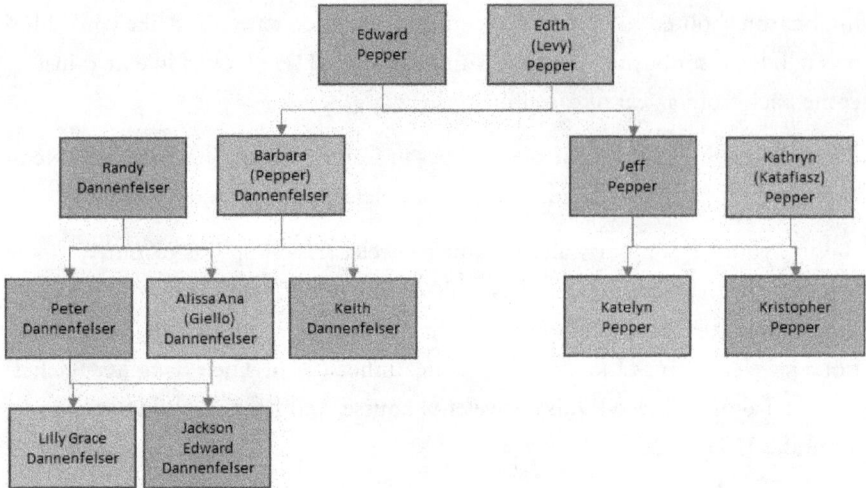

Levy Family History

Mom was from an upper middle class Jewish family in the Upper West Side of Manhattan. But before that, her ancestors came from poverty in Eastern Europe and emigrated to America via Ellis Island.

On her father's side, the family tree starts with Abraham Nathan Gabella and Sara (Rausch) Gabella, who lived in the mid 1800's in Germany. No dates or locations are known. They were my great-great-grandparents.

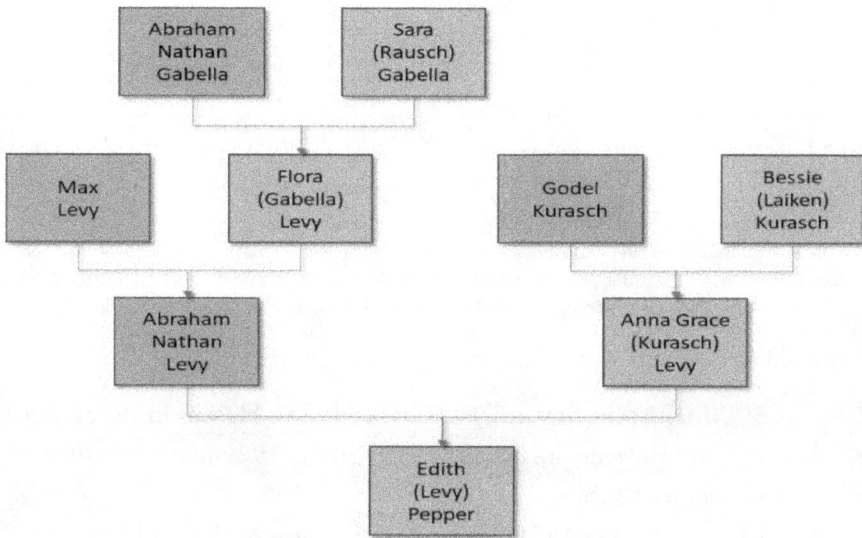

They had a daughter, Flora Gabella who was born in Germany in May 1851, emigrated to New York City in 1865, and died in 1917 at age 66. Her death certificate lists her profession as "housewife." The cause of death was acute nephritis (kidney inflammation) with myocarditis (inflammation of the heart muscle) as a contributing factor.

Flora married Max Levy, who was born somewhere in Russia, date and location unknown. Flora and Max were my great-grandparents.

It's interesting that in 1999 Mom wrote a letter to the Records Management and Archives Service in Missouri to inquire about the birth records of her father Nathan. She stated, "Unfortunately I do not know the names of his parents." It seems incredible that she would not know anything, even the names, of her paternal grandparents, Max Levy and Flora Gabella Levy. She probably never met either of them, since Flora had died five years before Mom was born and Max died (or was otherwise out of the picture) at least twelve years before Mom was born. But still, it's odd that she claimed to not even know their names.

Max and Flora had 12 children, with six surviving into adulthood. Here's the family as listed in the 1900 US Census. Note that Max is not listed, so he likely died before 1900.

The Levy (misspelled Levey) household in the 1900 U.S. census: Flora (age 32) with her five sons Moses (30), Louis (28), Isaac (22), David (20) and Nathan (10), and domestic servant Mary J. Brod (45). They were all born in New York, except Flora who was born in Germany.

From oldest to youngest, the six surviving siblings were:

1. Moses "Moe" Levy (July 1870 – July 22, 1943). He was in the clothing business and allegedly lost all his money in the 1929 market crash. He had a daughter Ruth.
2. Louis Levy (October 1871 – Feb. 17, 1963) was in the clothing business. He married Jean.
3. Isaac Levy (July 1878 – ?), married Gussie and had two "crazy kids" according to Mom, one was a daughter named Henrietta and two sons Adolf and Joey.
4. David Levy (August 1879 – ?), a lawyer who lived in Westchester. His wife was Clara, and they had a daughter Ruth who lived in Manhattan. In his later years he became blind from macular degeneration.
5. Abraham Nathan Levy (Sept. 16, 1888 – June 9, 1957), he was Mom's father and my maternal grandfather. He was born in Kansas City, Missouri, moved to New York, attended NYU Medical School, and supported himself by playing piano in silent movie theaters. Later he became a successful and prosperous physician. He lived at 924 West

End Avenue and later at 875 West End Avenue in New York City, and his office was at 522 West 15th Street near Greenwich Village in lower Manhattan. This office building must have been demolished long ago, as it now seems to be a small park. As kids we always called him Poppop. Mom described him as tall and stout, though I remember him as being pudgy, wrinkled, and a bit stooped over. He had the self-confidence bordering on arrogance that's common to physicians. One

My grandfather, Dr. Abraham Nathan Levy.

story about him is that if he was driving and saw a funeral procession, he would turn on his headlights and join the procession in order to avoid stopping at red lights.

6. Lillian Levy (dates unknown), moved to Florida, and did not marry. She's not listed as living with the family in the 1900 census, so she was either born after 1900 or lived elsewhere.

I'll talk more about A. Nathan Levy, my grandfather. But first, a bit about his brother Louis Levy and his descendants. Louis and Jean Levy had two daughters, Helen (1911 – 2008) and Rita.

Helen married a lawyer named Milton Seasonwein (Jan 20, 1904 – Apr 1, 1940). I remember visiting them once. They lived in a house with a large tree growing right in the middle of the living room and through the roof.

Helen and Milton had two children, a lawyer Roger A. Seasonwein (Sep 25, 1940 - ?) who married Bonnie (Markey) Seasonwein in 1968 and became quite successful with his polling company Roger A. Seasonwein & Associates.

They also had a daughter Bette Jean (Seasonwein) Chandler. She lived in Phoenix Arizona. She died in 1921 at age 78. Mom had once advised me not to contact her because she was part of a cult of some sort. But after doing a bit of research I found out that she was, in fact, a member of the Cross Connections International Fellowship, a Baptist group which might have been evangelical but was almost certainly not a cult. Her obituary listed her as a tax professional

Like a Moth

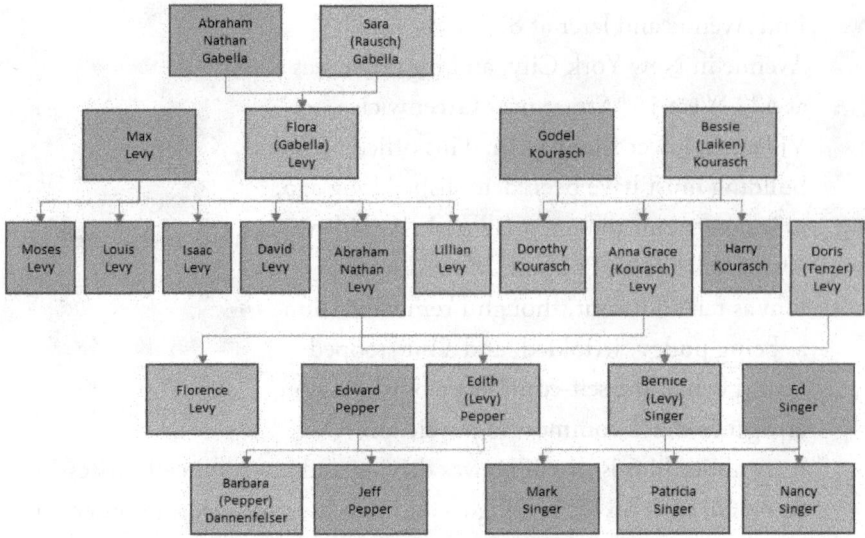

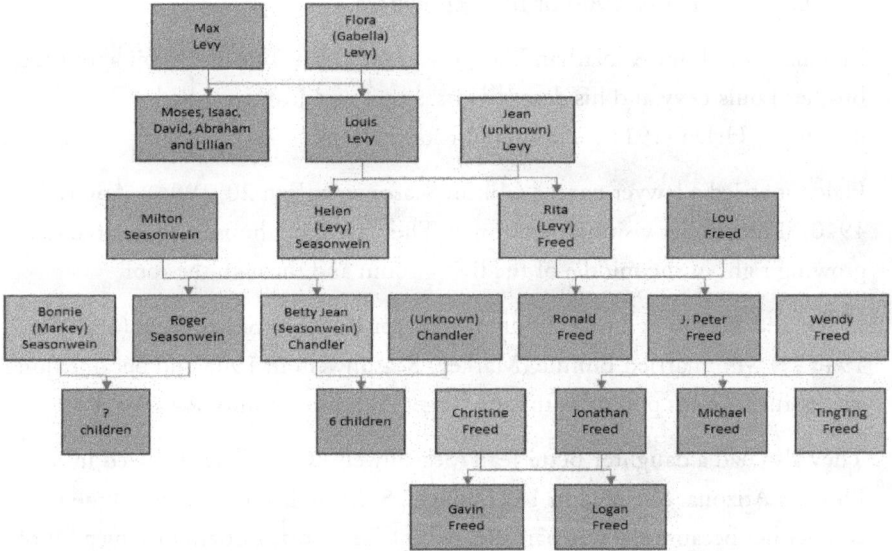

Two views of the Levy family tree. Top: descendants of Abraham Nathan and Sara Levy.
Bottom: detail of the branch showing Max and Flora Levy's descendants.

who also made a trip to Israel late in life. She had six children, eight grandchildren and three great grandchildren.

J. Peter Freed.

Rita married Lou Freed and lived in Allentown PA. One of their sons was J. Peter Freed, an insurance broker who moved to the Pittsburgh area with his wife Wendy Freed. I met them because Peter was one of the five family members who co-owned a burial plot at the Mt. Carmel cemetery on Long Island where Mom wanted to be buried next to her own mother. Peter helped her to track down his brother Ronald Freed who was difficult to locate and uncooperative. Eventually they found out that Ronald had died, and Mom managed to get permission to use the burial plot.

Our family became good friends with the Freed's, seeing them at Thanksgiving and a couple of other times during the year. Peter died in 2022, during the Covid pandemic. The funeral service and burial were sparsely attended because of the pandemic, but many people watched via a Zoom link.

Peter and Wendy had two children. In keeping with the Peter Pan theme, their children are Michael Freed who married Ting Ting and lives in the DC area, and Jonathan Freed who married Christine and has two children Logan and Gavin. At one point Wendy was extremely sick with liver disease, and her son Michael donated half of his liver to her. Both of them fully recovered.

On Mom's mother's side, her grandfather was Godel Kourasch (although he is listed as Gustave Kourasch in the 1900 U.S. census, and my mom recalled his last name as being spelled Kurasch). He was born in April 1861 in the Jewish *shtetl* of Brody, a major Jewish trade center located in Austria at the time but which later became part of Poland and then Ukraine. Interestingly, Brody is only fifty miles northeast of Lviv where Dad's great grandfather was born, but it's unlikely that the two families knew each other. Godel emigrated to the U.S. in 1880 and was a furrier.

Mom's mother was Bessie (Laiken) Kourasch, born in October 1867 in England. In the 1900 census form she is listed as having emigrated to the U.S. in 1887 but that's a year after she married Godel, so it's almost certainly wrong.

LOCATION				NAME	RELATION	PERSONAL DESCRIPTION							
IN CITIES				of each person whose place of abode on June 1, 1900, was in this family.	Relationship of each person to the head of the family.			DATE OF BIRTH					
Street	House Number	Number of dwelling house, in the order of visitation.	Number of family, in the order of visitation.			Color or race.	Sex.	Month	Year	Age at last birthday.	Whether single, married, widowed, or divorced.	Number of years married.	Mother of how many children.	Number of these children living.

102	123	84	877	Kourasch Gustave	Head	W	M	Apr	1861	39	M	14		
				Bessie	Wife	W	F	Oct	1867	32	M	14	3	3
				Dorothy	Daughter	W	F	Mar	1887	13	S			
				Annie	Daughter	W	F	Feb	1889	11	S			
				Harry	Son	W	M	Apr	1895	5	S			
			Melman Dora	Servant	W	F		1883	17	S			

NATIVITY			CITIZENSHIP			OCCUPATION, TRADE, OR PROFESSION	
Place of birth of this Person.	Place of birth of Parents of this person.	Place of birth of Mother of this person.	Year of immigration to the United States.	Number of years in the United States.	Naturalization.	Occupation.	Months not employed.

Austria	Austria	Austria	1880	20	Na	Furrier	0
England	England	England	1887	12			
New York	Austria	England				At School	
New York	Austria	England				At School	
New York	Austria	England					
Austria	Austria	Austria	1897	3		Servant	0

The Kourasch household in 1900, with Godel (spelled "Gustave" here) Kourasch (age 39), wife Bessie (32) and children Dorothy (13), Annie (11), Harry (5), and domestic servant Dora Melman (17).

Bessie and Godel married in 1886. They had three children: Dorothy (born March 1887), Anna Grace (February 1889), and Harry (April 1895). The family lived at 123 102nd Street in New York City. Godel's work as a furrier must have been successful because they had a live-in servant, Dora Melman, an unmarried 17 year old white girl who was born in Austria in 1883 and emigrated to the US at age 14.

Nathan was 25 when he married Anna Grace who was 21. They had two children: my aunt Florence ("Floie") J. Levy born October 10, 1918, and my mother Edith Marjorie Levy born June 24, 1922.

Anna Grace, called Annie as a child, was Mom's mother and my grandmother. She died in 1927 in New York City at age 38. Her occupation on her death

Anna Grace (Kurasch) Levy.

certificate was listed as "housewife" and the cause of death was pulmonary tuberculosis, with chronic myocarditis listed as a contributing factor.

Nathan was 39 when his wife Anna died. Just a few months later he married Doris Tenzer who was just 22. Two years later they had their only child together, Bernice "Neicee." Doris strongly favored her own child over her two stepchildren. Again, my mom was tight-lipped about the details of their home life, but from what little she said, it appeared to be pretty awful.

The 1940 US Census lists six members in the Levy household: Nathan A. (age 51, a medical doctor in private practice), Doris T. (36), Florence J. (21), Edith M. (17), and Bernice E. (10). The sixth was a "negro" servant named Elizabeth Lindsey (age 37). Elizabeth is listed as born in Pennsylvania, married, educated to the 8th grade, and working 70 hours per week, 52 weeks per year, for a total income of $650 in the previous year. That's just $3.75/hour in today's dollars.

Nathan died of a heart attack on June 9, 1957 while driving home after my sister Barbara's 9th birthday party in Huntington. He was 68. Doris never remarried. She died January 6, 1994 at the age of 91. I don't remember anything about her death or the funeral.

The three daughters: Florence, Edith and Bernice.

The Levy household in 1940: Nathan (age 51), Doris (36), Florence (21), Edith (17), Bernice (10), and domestic servant Elizabeth Lindsey (37).

The oldest of the three sisters, Mom's sister Florence, never married and devoted most of her life to earning her Ph.D. in Psychology. She died a few months after her stepmother, on August 22, 1994.

The youngest of the three sisters, Mom's half-sister Neicee, married Ed Singer, a tall, handsome and wealthy heir to a banking fortune. They lived in a large home in Scarsdale in Westchester County. Ed was the classic example of someone who was spoiled by having too much family money and never having to work. He was involved in several business ventures, all of which failed. He never seemed particularly interested in Neicee or the rest of the family including us kids; he barely spoke to us and spent most family gatherings watching sports on television and drinking. Neicee stayed at home and raised three children: Mark Singer, Patricia Singer and Nancy Singer.

My three cousins: Mark, Nancy and Pat Singer.

Neicee and Ed Singer.

Mark Singer.

Mark moved to Boston, married Catherine Perry, and became a financial advisor, branding his company RetireAt55, though he himself did not retire at 55. Patricia moved to Florida, married and had children. Nancy became estranged from the family and is believed to be living in California.

Not surprisingly, Neicee and Ed eventually divorced. Ed moved to California.

From left: me, cousin Pat Singer, Aunt Floie, Aunt Neicee, cousin Nancy Singer, Mom, stepmother Doris Levy.

Neicee began a midlife career as a genetic counselor and became quite accomplished in her field. She worked at several places including Sharsheret, an organization that provides breast cancer information and support to Jewish women. In 1998 she married Sandy Schonberger (born 1937), a real estate agent and expert skier. They were happily married until her death on June 4, 2022 at the age of 93.

As recounted in the main body of the book, my mother Edith Marjorie (Levy) Pepper was born on June 24, 1922 in New York City, the child of Dr. Abraham Nathan Levy and Anna Grace (Kourasch) Levy. She had an older sister Florence J. Levy, and a younger-half-sister Bernice (Levy) Schonberger.

Mom at the Freeds' house at Thanksgiving, with her dog April and Gavin Freed.

She graduated from Brooklyn College and volunteered as a nurse during World War II. Shortly after the end of the war she married my father, Edward Pepper. They had two children: my sister Barbara Lynn on June 9, 1949, and me, Jeffrey Alan on January 13, 1953.

They were married for about 19 years. They separated in the summer of 1966, and were legally divorced shortly afterwards. After the divorce she supported herself as a bookkeeper and office worker, as well as through skillful investing in the stock market. She was an avid dog trainer and member of the Suffolk Obedience Club on Long Island, and she won numerous trophies and titles in obedience and tracking in the U.S., Canada and Bermuda. She continued to compete until her mid-80's.

She was also a skilled designer and creator of stained glass artwork, primarily of dogs but also of butterflies and some abstract art. She sold the stained glass at dog shows as "Dogs of Class in Glass." In addition, she grew and trained bonsai trees and in the late 1970's she visited Japan with the Bonsai Society of New York.

In 2010 she moved to Longwood at Oakmont retirement community in Verona, where she lived until her death on July 14, 2015.

Some photos of Mom, taken at various times in her life.

Dad and Mom.

Dad, me, Mom and Floie, at Mom's house, circa 1988.

Some of Mom's stained glass sculptures at the crafts area of a dog show.

www.ingramcontent.com/pod-product-compliance
Lightning Source LLC
Chambersburg PA
CBHW071404050426
42335CB00063B/967